Topics in Applied Physics Volume 23

Topics in Applied Physics Founded by Helmut K. V. Lotsch

Optical
Data Processing
Applications

Edited by D. Casasent

With Contributions by
N. Abramson N. Balasubramanian D. Casasent
H. J. Caulfield P. S. Considine R. A. Gonsalves
E. N. Leith B. J. Thompson

With 170 Figures

Springer-Verlag Berlin Heidelberg New York 1978

David Casasent, PhD

Department of Electrical Engineering, Carnegie-Mellon University,
Pittsburgh, PA 15213, USA

ISBN 3-540-08453-3 Springer-Verlag Berlin Heidelberg New York
ISBN 0-387-08453-3 Springer-Verlag New York Heidelberg Berlin

Library of Congress Cataloging in Publication Data. Main entry under title: Optical data processing. (Topics in applied physics; v. 23). Includes bibliographies and index. 1. Optical data processing. I. Casasent, David Paul. II. Abramson, Nils H., 1931—. TA1630.064 621.38'0414 77-16676

© by Springer-Verlag Berlin Heidelberg 1978
Printed in Germany

Monophoto typesetting, offset printing and bookbinding: Brühlsche Universitätsdruckerei, Lahn-Giessen
2153/3130-543210

Preface

This book was written to satisfy a variety of needs. First, it is intended to provide an updated summary of the present status of optical data processing: what it has accomplished, what it can accomplish, and how it accomplishes these things. We feel that this presentation of an updated summary is best achieved by treating different applications of optical data processing. A commonality of fundamental tools and operations is used in all cases. These cases are adequately treated in many textbooks and highlighted here in Chapter 1. Since the objective of optical data processing is to apply fundamental techniques to the solution of specific problems, a discussion of specific applications seems appropriate.

This discussion enables the potential user to see the steps required in deciding: if one should use optical processing for a solution to a specific problem; what application areas have been considered, and why; how one uses the fundamental concepts to configure a candidate system solution; how one must modify these basic concepts, refine them and develop new ones to solve specific features of one problem area.

However, this text is also intended for those researchers presently engaged in various aspects of optical processing. By providing an updated review of where various aspects of our field presently stand, we can best direct our future work in the proper direction. By pausing to organize diverse papers and reports and to seek fresh perspectives, we discover what gaps exist in our present understanding, and we can exercise wise choices in deciding which areas to pursue next. Without such a perspective, there is a great danger of overspecialization. By exposing researchers in one area of optical processing to work in other application areas, we often find that techniques and solutions appropriate for one area can be applied to problems in other areas. Quite often, solutions that have been considered for use in one area and found not to be appropriate are quite applicable for use in solving problems in other areas.

For the sake of completeness we include an introductory chapter in which these fundamental concepts and the common concepts of many of the following chapters are highlighted. The specific application areas we select are: crystallography, image enhancement and restoration, synthetic aperture radar, photogrammetry, holographic interferometry and non-destructive testing, biomedical applications and signal processing. A more detailed discussion and review of each of these chapters can be found at the end of Chapter 1.

We thus hope that this text will be of use to those engineers engaged in any form of data processing, to those contemplating the use of optical processing, and to those researchers who are presently involved in one aspect of optical processing. The material is presented in a form which should make it useful for reference, for individual study, and for short courses. If need be, it and Chapter 1 (as well as the rest of the material) can be supplemented by a basic text or by a companion Topics Appl. Phys. volume (Optical Data Processing, Fundamentals, ed. by S. Lee) to provide more detail on the fundamental principles and thus, with the two books, a text for a graduate level course can be assembled.

Pittsburgh, Pennsylvania
November, 1977   *David Casasent*

Contents

Contributors

Abramson, Nils
Department of Production Engineering, Royal Institute of Technology,
S—100 44 Stockholm 70, Sweden

Balasubramanian, N.
Eikonix Corporation, 103 Terrace Hall Avenue,
Burlington, MA 01803, USA

Casasent, David
Department of Electrical Engineering, Carnegie-Mellon University,
Pittsburgh, PA 15213, USA

Caulfield, H., John
Block Engineering Inc., 19 Blackstone Road,
Cambridge, MA 02138, USA

Considine, Philip S.
Eikonix Corporation, 103 Terrace Hall Avenue,
Burlington, MA 01803, USA

Gonsalves, Robert A.
Eikonix Corporation, 103 Terrace Hall Avenue,
Burlington, MA 01803, USA and
Northeastern University, Boston, MA 02100, USA

Leith, Emmett N.
University of Michigan, Department of Engineering and Computer
Engineering, Dept. of Elec. and Comp. Engr.
Ann Arbor, MI 48104, USA

Thompson, Brian J.
University of Rochester, College of Engineering and Applied Science,
Rochester, NY 14627, USA

1. Basic Concepts

D. Casasent and H. J. Caulfield

With 6 Figures

1.1 Introduction

Coherent optics, optical spatial filtering, optical Fourier transformations, lasers, and holography are among the key items which are spawning a revolution in our concepts of optics. Once the lonely domain of lens designers and astronomers, optics has become a vital field affecting all areas of basic research (from quantum theory to medicine) and all areas of applied technology (from nuclear fusion to telephones). This book is a progress report on the underlying field of coherent optical signal and image processing. In this chapter we review the key concepts just mentioned as an aid to understanding subsequent chapters. With this review and the more specialized chapters which follow, the reader will have a self-contained survey of the entire field. Readers already familiar with these basic concepts can proceed immediately to the specialized chapters without fear of missing new concepts.

This brief survey of basic concepts proceeds from the most basic (coherent light) to the most technical (holography and correlation). Numerous books treat one or more of these areas in detail. An annotated bibliography of some of these is appended to this introduction.

1.2 Coherence

"Coherence" is a property of two or more beams of light, and thus is more properly called "mutual coherence". Mutually coherent overlapping beams form a spatial pattern of light which differs from the sum of the patterns of each individual beam. This spatial pattern is called an "interference pattern". When a beam of coherent light encounters a physical aperture, the interference pattern formed by the rays of light emerging from various parts of the aperture is called a "diffraction pattern". In the usual interferometer (any device used to generate an interference pattern) a beam of light from a single source is divided into two parts, an optical path length difference is introduced between the two beams, and the two beams are recombined to form an interference pattern. Analysis of this system is easy. If the two paths from the source point merge at a given point, the interference is constructive and this region of the output plane is bright. When the path difference is a half wavelength plus or minus an integral (including zero)

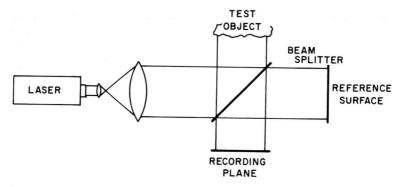

Fig. 1.1. Schematic diagrams of an interferometer

number of wavelengths, the interference is destructive and the region of the output plane is dark.

Unfortunately, there are two inevitable errors in such a simple analysis. Because fully monochromatic light is impossible for many reasons, a path difference cannot be precisely one wavelength (or any other multiple of one wavelength other than zero) for all wavelengths present. The need for partially monochromatic light is called the "temporal coherence" requirement for interference. Indeed, the path difference can become so large that constructive interference occurs for one wavelength at the same point where destructive interference occurs for another wavelength. This allowable path length mismatch is called the "temporal coherence length". Beams mismatched by this length or greater lengths produce very low contrast interference patterns.

Because mathematical point sources are also excludable in principle, rays reach any point in the interference pattern from all points within the source "point". As a result, perfect path matching is impossible. The requirement for point-like sources is often called the "spatial coherence" requirement for interference. If rays travel directly from the source to the interference plane by the shortest route (called the "optical axis") the spatial coherence problem is not troublesome. If the angle between rays leaving the point-like source becomes large enough, the paths cannot be balanced at any point. This maximum angle subtended at the physical aperture of the system determines a distance called the "spatial coherence length". Thus to achieve good coherence (temporal and spatial), a source must be as small and as monochromatic as possible.

1.3 Lasers

Before the advent of the laser, we could achieve good coherence only by spectral filtering (to make the usual "thermal" sources as monochromatic as possible) and spatial filtering (to make the source as small as possible). Unfortunately these filtering operations result in considerable light loss. Thus a strong, coherent light source was a contradiction in terms. That situation changed with the availability of lasers which automatically produced highly monochromatic light capable of being focused to a very small point. Thus the laser is the key source for coherent optics because it can be very bright and very "coherent" simultaneously.

"Laser" is an acronym for *Light Amplification by Stimulated Emission of Radiation*. For our purposes, the key feature is that the laser radiation is an amplified version of a very few stimulating photons which initiated the process by being present in the laser and traveling in the right direction with the right wavelength by naturally occurring spontaneous emission. The laser can only amplify photons if their wavelengths and directions of travel fit within certain narrow bands. Thus the amplified photons are precisely those we would like to select out by spectral and spatial filtering to achieve good coherence. Therefore we can say that for ordinary thermal light sources coherence filtering must be external to the source and hence very lossy, whereas for a laser the filter is built into the source and causes no loss.

1.4 The Optical Fourier Transform

The use of lenses with coherent light leads quite naturally to the concept of the optical Fourier transform. It is well known that the light amplitude distribution in the back focal plane of a spherical lens is the two-dimensional complex Fourier transform of the amplitude transmittance in the lenses front focal plane. This property is the hallmark of a coherent optical system and is used constantly in all applications throughout this volume. This operation of a coherent optical processor is considered in more detail in Chapter 2 in which other conditions and alternate placements of the input and transform lens are discussed.

Since the mathematical concept of the Fourier transformation is the basis for many sciences and data processing applications, we discuss its highlights briefly in this introduction. The supporting theory can require considerable mathematical sophistication; however, the basic concepts are quite simple. Let us consider the one-dimensional case for simplicity. If $f(x_1)$ is a suitable input function (a concept we will not expound on because we will seldom if ever encounter an unsuitable function), its Fourier transform is:

$$F(u) = \int_{-\infty}^{\infty} f(x_1) \exp(-j2\pi x_1 u) dx_1 \tag{1.1}$$

where $j = \sqrt{-1}$, $x_1 u$ is dimensionless, and u has units of reciprocal length. We refer to the coordinate u of the Fourier transform plane as a "spatial frequency" with typical units of line pairs/mm = lp/mm. The spatial frequency variable u can be related to the actual distance coordinate x_2 of the transform plane by

Table 1.1. Several simple Fourier transform pairs and their physical significance

Input functions $f(x)$	Fourier transform $F(u)$	Comment
$\delta(x)$	1	A point in x goes to a constant in u
l	$\delta(u)$	Converse of above
$ag(x)$	$aG(u)$	Multiplication by a constant
$g(ax)$	$\dfrac{1}{\lvert a\rvert}G(u/a)$	Scaling law
$g(x-a)$	$e^{-2\pi jau}G(u)$	Shift law
$\text{rect}\left(\dfrac{x}{a}\right)$	$\text{sinc}(au)=\dfrac{\sin\pi au}{\pi au}$	$\text{rect}\left(\dfrac{x}{a}\right)=\begin{cases}1 & \text{for }\lvert x/a\rvert\leq 1/2\\0 & \text{otherwise}\end{cases}$
$xf(x)$	$\partial F(u)/\partial u$	Differentiation
$f(x)g(x)$	$F(u)*G(u)\equiv\displaystyle\int_{-\infty}^{\infty}F(\eta)G(\eta-u)d\eta$	Convolution

$x_2 = f_1 \lambda u$ where f_1 is the focal length of the transform lens and λ is the wavelength of the laser light used.

The inverse Fourier transform operation is also easily proven to produce:

$$f(x)=\int_{-\infty}^{\infty}F(u)\exp(2\pi jxu)du . \qquad (1.2)$$

We follow conventional notation in representing spatial functions by lower case variables and their Fourier transforms by the corresponding upper case variable. If we consider these basic equations more closely, we note that each point u in the Fourier transform plane receives a contribution from every point x in the input plane and vice versa. Several typical Fourier transform pairs are listed in Table 1.1 and are easily obtained by substitution into (1.1). The physical meaning of these simple transform pairs sheds considerable light on the process involved. The first transform pair states that a point x in the input plane produces a uniform response in the transform plane or that a point in x transforms into a plane wave in Fourier space. The last transform pair states that multiplication in input space is equivalent to convolution in transform space and vice versa. We will revisit this last transform pair in more detail in discussing optical pattern recognition.

For now let us attempt to gain further insight into this key Fourier transform operation performed by an optical processor. Refer to Fig. 1.2. We denote the input plane as P_1 and the transform plane as P_2 with coordinates (x_1, y_1) and (x_2, y_2) respectively. We place an input transparency with amplitude transmittance $f(x_1, y_1)$ in the front focal plane of the Fourier transform lens L_1 and

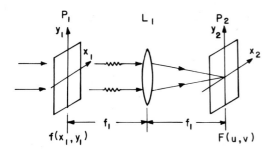

Fig. 1.2. Schematic representation of an optical Fourier transform system

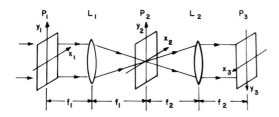

Fig. 1.3. Schematic representation of an optical image processing and spatial filtering system

illuminate it with a uniform amplitude and uniphase beam of coherent light. We assume an input beam of unit amplitude and describe the complex transmittance of plane P_1 by

$$f(x_1, y_1) = A(x_1, y_1) \exp[-j\phi(x_1, y_1)] \qquad (1.3)$$

where $A(x_1, y_1)$ is a positive definite quantity representing the amplitude and $\phi(x_1, y_1)$ represents the phase of the input function. (For physical definiteness, we can identify A with the electric or magnetic vector of the electromagnetic wave describing the traveling light beam.) The phase is a mutual quantity like the coherence it is designed to represent. This means that no physical change would occur if an arbitrary fixed phase were added to all the phases in our calculations.

In two dimensions, the pattern in plane P_2 of Fig. 1.3 is

$$F(u, v) = F(x_2/\lambda f_1, y_2/\lambda f_1) = \int\!\!\int_{-\infty}^{\infty} f(x_1, y_1) \exp[-j2\pi(x_1 u + y_1 v)] dx_1 dy_1 \quad (1.4)$$

by analog with (1.1), where

u, v = spatial frequency coordinates of plane P_2,
$x_2 = u\lambda f_1$, $y_2 = v\lambda f_1$ = physical distance coordinates of plane P_2,
λ = wavelength of the light used, and
f_1 = focal length of the transform lens L_1.

To visualize this relationship, recall from Table 1.1 and basic geometrical optics that a lens focuses or converts an input plane wave to a point at plane P_2. For an input point source at $(x_1, y_1) = (a, b)$, (1.4) becomes

$$\delta(x_1 - a, y_1 - b) \leftrightarrow \exp[-j2\pi(au + bv)] = \exp[(-j2\pi/\lambda)(ax_2/f_1 + by_2/f_1)],$$

$$(1.5)$$

where $\leftrightarrow$ denotes a Fourier transform pair. From this case, we see that the direction cosines a/f_1 and b/f_1 of the wave that results from an input point source at $(x_1, y_1) = (a, b)$ are proportional to the location of the point source in plane P_1. We will return to this point in Section 1.8 in describing optical pattern recognition.

1.5 Image Processing and Spatial Filtering

If we place a second transform lens L_2 behind the transform plane P_2 as in Fig. 1.3, the pattern in the output plane P_3 is the double Fourier transform of the input $f(x_1, y_1)$ pattern or $f(x_3, y_3)$, where the coordinates of P_3 and P_1 are related by $x_3 - (f_2/f_1)x_1$ and $y_3 - (f_2/f_1)y_1$. As shown in Fig. 1.3, the coordinate axes of the output plane P_3 are reversed. The output image is thus a left-right and up-down inverted image of the input with the magnification factor being the ratio of the focal lengths of lenses L_2 and L_1. This is exactly the same process that occurs in a slide projector camera.

We are now on the verge of optical image processing. Let us recall that the input light is coherent and that the pattern formed at P_2 is the Fourier transform $F(u, v)$ of $f(x_1, y_1)$. If at P_2 we place an opaque spot on axis, we block the "dc" portion of the input pattern, so only light from the higher spatial frequency components of the input image is transmitted. This produces a high-pass filtered version of $f(x_1, y_1)$ at P_3. With a linear graded filter at P_2 whose transmittance increases with radial distance from the center, we produce the differentiated version of $f(x_1, y_1)$ at P_3 (see Table 1.1). By placing opaque spots at specific locations in P_2, we can remove various frequency components present in the input pattern. These are some of the simpler spatial filtering methods used in image enhancement and image processing.

Far more sophisticated versions of image processing exist (see Chap. 3). If the transmittance of P_2 in Fig. 1.3 is $M(u, v)$ (where M is the Fourier transform of m), the light distribution leaving plane P_2 is $F(u, v) M(u, v)$ and at plane P_2 we find the Fourier transform of this product of two transforms or the convolution $f(x, y) * m(x, y)$ rather than simply $f(x, y)$ (see Table 1.1). By proper choice of $M(u, v)$, we can remove various distortions such as a blur or linear smear present in the input function $f(x_1, y_1)$ thus performing image enhancement or restoration. The proper choice of the filter function $M(u, v)$ for most interesting cases usually requires a complex function M.

1.6 Holography

To see how such a complex function can be represented spatially, we now discuss holography, the fascinating invention of *Dennis Gabor* by which the whole (Greek "holos") amplitude and phase of a wavefront $F(u, v)$ can be recorded. This is most remarkable because all detectors are intensity sensitive and record only $|F(u, v)|^2$ thereby losing the phase information $\phi(x, y)$ present in $F(u, v)$ $= |F(u, v)| \exp [j\phi(u, v)]$.

To record the phase as well as the amplitude of an input wavefront, we do not seek to record the spatially varying phase directly. Rather, we cause the entire wavefront to have a known and easily regenerated phase pattern so that the loss of phase information becomes unimportant. We achieve this by adding to $F(u, v)$ a reference wavefront $R(u, v)$ chosen so that $|R(u, v)|^2$ is greater than $|F(u, v)|^2$ at every point (u, v) (see Fig. 1.4).

The pattern recorded at P_2 is

$$|F_H(u, v)|^2 = |R(u, v) + F(u, v)|^2 = |R(u, v)|^2 + |F(u, v)|^2$$
$$+ R^*(u, v)F(u, v) + R(u, v)F^*(u, v), \tag{1.6}$$

where * denotes complex conjugation and the subscript "H" denotes the hologram of $F(u, v)$. As shown by (1.6), the phase of $F_H(u, v)$ is the phase of $R(u, v)$. If we illuminate a photographic record at plane P_2 (whose amplitude transmittance is described by $|F_H(u, v)|^2$) with a copy $R(u, v)$ of the reference beam, the light distribution leaving the plate is

$$R(u, v)|F_H(u, v)|^2 = [|R(u, v)|^2 + |F(u, v)|^2]R(u, v)$$
$$+ |R(u, v)|^2 F(u, v) + R(u, v)R(u, v)F^*(u, v). \tag{1.7}$$

If the reference and object beams are not coaxial, each of the three terms in (1.7) will travel in a different direction upon leaving the plate at plane P_1. The first term in (1.7) is simply the reference wavefront as it would appear if transmitted through a double exposure photograph of $|R(u, v)|^2$ and $|F(u, v)|^2$. The second term in (1.7) is the desired complex transmission function $F(u, v)$ as it would appear if transmitted through a photograph of $|R(u, v)|^2$. It is easy to make $|R(u, v)|^2$ essentially constant simply by making R a planewave. This is the usual

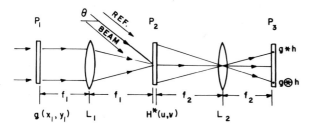

Fig. 1.4. Schematic representation of an optical frequency plane correlator using a matched spatial filter for pattern recognition

choice. This second term corresponds to light which emerges from the plate on one side of the reference beam, whereas the third term in (1.7) corresponds to light which emerges from the other side. These are referred to as the primary and conjugate object wavefronts. What we have described is a classical Fourier transform hologram. With other kinds of recording geometries other kinds of holograms result. Many of these are discussed in Chapter 7 and elsewhere. By reversing the reference beam (ray for ray) in replay we obtain $R^*(u, v)$. Illuminating the hologram $F_H(u, v)$ with $R^*(u, v)$ produces the terms

$$R^*(u, v)|H(u, v)|^2 = [|R(u, v)|^2 + |F(u, v)|^2]R^*(u, v)$$
$$+ |R(u, v)|^2 F^*(u, v) + R^*(u, v)R^*(u, v)F(u, v). \tag{1.8}$$

Clearly the second term in (1.8) represents a direction-reversed object beam. Thus we can propagate the object beam away from the hologram and either toward or away from the original object position.

Holography is best known for its use in recording and displaying three-dimensional scenes (Chap. 7). Other uses include data and image storage, metrology and nondestructive testing (Chap. 6), imaging outside the visible domain, e.g.: acoustic, electron, X-ray, infrared, or microwave holography (Chap. 7), spectroscopy, multiple image generation, seeing through distorting phase media, specialized optical elements, and pattern recognition (Chap. 3, 6, 8).

1.7 Matched Spatial Filtering

Holographic recording techniques have other uses besides production of the well-known three-dimensional images we have all seen. As noted in Section 1.4, holographic techniques are useful in the synthesis of complex image enhancement and restoration filters $M^*(u, v)$. Similar holographic recording techniques are also used to produce the matched spatial filters used in optical pattern recognition. We consider this case next. Refer to the schematic diagram of Fig. 1.4 which is quite similar to that of Fig. 1.3.

This procedure whereby the matched spatial filter is synthesized at P_2 is analogous to the holographic synthesis procedure described in Section 1.5. However, this time we will be quite precise in the formulation.

We consider the use of this system of Fig. 1.4 to correlate an input function $g(x_1, y_1)$ with a reference function $h(x_1, y_1)$. The function $h(x_1, y_1)$, whose matched spatial filter we desire to form at plane P_2, is placed at plane P_1. The amplitude distribution $U_2(x_2, y_2)$ at plane P_2 is the Fourier transform of $g(x_1, y_1)$:

$$U_2(x_2, y_2) = (1/\lambda f_1)G(u, v) = (1/\lambda f_1)G(x_2/\lambda f_1, y_2/\lambda f_1), \tag{1.9}$$

where the coordinates of planes P_1, P_2, and P_3 are (x_1, y_1), (x_2, y_2) and (x_3, y_3), respectively, where f_1 and f_2 are the focal lengths of lenses L_1 and L_2 and where the constant term $(1/\lambda f_1)$ in front of (1.9) arises when the optical Fourier transform process is analyzed in detail.

A plane-wave reference beam of uniform amplitude r_0 incident on plane P_2 at an angle θ to the optical axis is described by the amplitude distribution

$$U_r(x_2, y_2) = r_0 \exp(-j2\pi\alpha y_2), \tag{1.10}$$

where $\alpha = (\sin\theta)/\lambda$ is the spatial frequency produced by the planewave at an angle θ.

At plane P_2, we record the interference of the reference beam (1.10) and the transform (1.9) of the input pattern. Since coherent light is used, the pattern recorded on a detector such as film at plane P_2 is the modulus squared of the sum of the amplitudes of U_2 and U_R. The total intensity distribution at plane P_2 is then

$$\begin{aligned}
I(x_2, y_2) &= |U_2 + U_r|^2 \\
&= |r_0 \exp(-j2\pi\alpha y_2) + (1/\lambda f_1)H(x_2/\lambda f_1, y_2/\lambda f_1)|^2 \\
&= r_0^2 + (1/\lambda^2 f_1^2)|H(x_2/\lambda f_1, y_2/\lambda f_1)|^2 \\
&\quad + (r_0/\lambda f_1)H(x_2/\lambda f_1, y_2/\lambda f_1)\exp(j2\pi\alpha y_2) \\
&\quad + (r_0/\lambda f_1)H^*(x_2/\lambda f_1, y_2/\lambda f_1)\exp(-j2\pi\alpha y_2).
\end{aligned} \tag{1.11}$$

In practice, H is a complex function with amplitude A and phase ϕ described by

$$H(x_2/\lambda f_1, y_2/\lambda f_1) = A(x_2/\lambda f_1, y_2/\lambda f_1)\exp[-j\phi(x_2/\lambda f_1, y_2/\lambda f_1)]. \tag{1.12}$$

Equation (1.11) can then be rewritten as

$$\begin{aligned}
H(x_2/\lambda f_1, y_2/\lambda f_1) &= r_0^2 + (1/\lambda^2 f_1^2)A^2(x_2/\lambda f_1, y_2/\lambda f_1) \\
&\quad + (2r_0/\lambda f_1)A(x_2/\lambda f_1, y_2/\lambda f_1) \\
&\quad \cdot \cos[2\pi\alpha y_2 - \psi(x_2/\lambda f_1, y_2/\lambda f_1)].
\end{aligned} \tag{1.13}$$

From (1.13), we clearly see that the amplitude and phase are recorded as a modulation of the high spatial frequency carrier at α produced by the tilted reference wave in Fig. 1.4. The film on which the pattern described by (1.13) is recorded is then developed to produce a transmittance $t(x_2, y_2)$ assumed to be exactly equal to (1.13) (see Chap. 3 for a discussion of film transmittance vs exposure curves). For simplicity, we omit the argument of H and assume both lenses to be of focal length $f = f_1 = f_2$. We can then write

$$\begin{aligned}
t(x_2, y_2) &= r_0^2 + (1/\lambda f)^2|H|^2 + (r_0/\lambda f)\cdot H \exp(j2\pi\alpha y_2) \\
&\quad + (r_0/\lambda f)H^* \exp(-j2\pi\alpha y_2).
\end{aligned} \tag{1.14}$$

The fourth term in (1.14) is the desired term of interest proportional to H^*. This term can be separated from the others by proper choice of the angle θ in Fig. 1.4.

The filter described by (1.14) is placed at plane P_2, the reference beam is blocked, and $g(x_1, y_1)$ is placed at the input plane P_1. The light distribution incident on plane P_2 is

$$(1/\lambda f)G(x_2/\lambda f, y_2/\lambda f). \tag{1.15}$$

The amplitude distribution U'_2 of the light pattern emerging from plane P_2 is the product of the input light distribution in (1.15) and the transmittance of plane P_2 given by (1.14) or

$$\begin{aligned}
U' &= t(x_2, y_2)(1/\lambda f)G(x_2/\lambda f, y_2/\lambda f) \\
&= r_0^2 G/\lambda f + (1/\lambda f)^2 |H|^2 G \\
&\quad + (r_0/\lambda^2 f^2) + HG \exp(j2\pi\alpha y_2) \\
&\quad + (r_0/\lambda^2 f^2)H^*G \exp(-j2\pi\alpha y_2).
\end{aligned} \tag{1.16}$$

This plane P_2 is the front focal plane of lens L_2 in Fig. 1.4. The pattern in plane P_3 of Fig. 1.4 is now the Fourier transform of (1.16) multiplied by $(1/\lambda f_2)$. Recalling the reflected coordinates of plane P_3 shown in Fig. 1.3, we obtain for the amplitude distribution in the output plane P_3:

$$\begin{aligned}
U_3(x_3, y_3) &\propto r_0^2 g(x_3, y_3) + \frac{1}{\lambda^2 f^2} [h(x_3, y_3) * h^*(-x_3, -y_3)] \\
&\quad + \frac{r_0}{\lambda f} [h(x_3, y_3) * g(x_3, y_3) * g(x_3, y_3) * \delta(x_3, y_3 + \alpha\lambda f)] \\
&\quad + \frac{r_0}{\lambda f} [h^*(-x_3, -y_3) * g(x_3, y_3) * \delta(x_3, y_3 - \alpha\lambda f)].
\end{aligned} \tag{1.17}$$

The first and second terms in (1.17) are centered at the origin of P_3. The bracketed portion of the third term is

$$\begin{aligned}
&h(x_3, y_3) * g(x_3, y_3) * \delta(x_3, y_3 + \alpha\lambda f) \\
&= \int\int_{-\infty}^{\infty} h(x_3 - \xi, y_3 + \alpha\lambda f - \eta)g(\xi, \eta)d\xi d\eta.
\end{aligned} \tag{1.18}$$

This is the *convolution* of h and g centered at $(0, -\alpha\lambda f)$ in the (x_3, y_3) plane. The bracketed portion of the last term in (1.17) is the term of interest. It is the *cross-correlation* of h and g centered at $(0, \alpha\lambda f)$ in the (x_3, y_3) plane as shown below:

$$\begin{aligned}
&h^*(-x_3, -y_3) * g(x_3, y_3) * \delta(x_3, y_3 - \alpha\lambda f) \\
&= h(x_3, y_3) \circledast g(x_3, y_3) * \delta(x_3, y_3 - \alpha\lambda f) \\
&= \int\int_{-\infty}^{\infty} g(\xi, \eta)h^*(\xi - x_3, \eta - y_3 + \alpha\lambda f)d\xi d\eta.
\end{aligned} \tag{1.19}$$

1.8 Optical Pattern Recognition

This anatomy of an optical pattern recognition system is shown in Fig. 1.4. In plane P_3, we find the correlation $g \circledast h$ which we desire for optical pattern recognition and the convolution $g*h$ used in image restoration and enhancement. The key to complex matched spatial filtering is to record the interference of a plane wave reference beam and the transform of h, just as we did in holography. A simple optical interpretation of the matched spatial filter process is shown in Fig. 1.5. The uniphase wavefronts are shown in Fig. 1.5 to aid in visualizing the process. The input plane P_1 containing the signal $s(x_1, y_1)$ is illuminated with a plane wave. The phase fronts of the wave imaging from plane P_1 and incident on plane P_2 are now curved and distorted. The phase transmittance of the matched filter $S^*(U, v)$ at plane P_2 must be the conjugate "match" to the phase of the transform of $s(x_1, y_1)$. All phase variations present in the wavefront incident on plane P_2 are thus removed by the filter leaving a plane wave emerging from P_2. Lens L_2 then focuses this planewave to a point in plane P_3 as shown in Fig. 1.5.

If the input is not $s(x_1, y_1)$, the wavefront curvature will not be exactly cancelled by the filter, and the distribution in plane P_3 will be a spot of less intensity or no spot at all. If the input $s(x_1, y_1)$ is centered at the origin of plane P_1, the bright spot of light in the output plane will be centered at the origin of plane P_3 as shown in Fig. 1.5. If the input $s(x_1, y_1)$ is shifted or displaced up or down (or left or right) from the center of plane P_1, the uniphase wavefront emerging from plane P_2 will lie at an angle to the optical axis as noted earlier. The Fourier transform will still occur on axis at plane P_2, but will have a constant phase slope across it. The uniphase wavefront emerging from plane P_2 will thus form an angle with the optical axis. Lens L_3 simply focuses this plane wavefront to a spot in plane P_3. As $s(x_1, y_1)$ is displaced up or down (or left or right) from the center of plane P_1, the location of the bright output peak of light in plane P_3 shifts down or up (or right or left) respectively.

Thus the coordinates of the bright output peak of light in plane P_3 are proportional to the coordinates of the signal $s(x_1, y_1)$ in the input plane (with a magnification factor f_2/f_1), and the intensity of this peak of light in plane P_3 is proportional to the degree to which the input and filter functions are matched. Since the system is linear, superposition holds and the above arguments are valid for multiple signals $s_n(x_1, y_1)$ at different locations in plane P_1. Multiple output

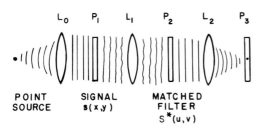

Lo P₁ L₁ P₂ L₂ P₃

POINT
SOURCE

SIGNAL
s(x,y)

MATCHED
FILTER
s*(u,v)

Fig. 1.5. Schematic representation of the optical pattern recognition process

peaks of light occur in plane P_3 with the position and intensity of each providing a measure of the degree to which each input signal is matched to the filter function. Multiple filters each encoded on a different carrier (a different angle θ in Fig. 1.4) are also possible. From this brief scenario, the high speed and parallel processing features of an optical processor should be apparent.

Let us now refer to Fig. 1.4 and discuss one final aspect of this system: the choice of the reference beam angle θ. As shown by (1.17), the correlation $g \circledast h$ is centered at $(x_3, y_3) = (0, \alpha\lambda f)$ in plane P_3. The physical area of this correlation plane is $W_h + W_g$ on a side, where W_h and W_g are the physical widths of the functions h and g (we assume for simplicity that the width and height of the functions are equal and equal focal lengths for L_1 and L_2). The position of the correlation peak within this $(W_g + W_h)^2$ region of plane P_3 tells the location of h in g. The term in (1.17) that appears on axis has an area in plane P_3 of $(2W_h + W_g)^2$. To allow adequate separation of the desired correlation term from these on-axis terms, we select the center-to-center separation $\alpha\lambda f$ of the off-axis terms to be larger than $(1/2)(2W_h + W_g + W_g)$ or for $W_g = W_h = W$, we select the angle θ to satisfy

$$\sin\theta \geq 5W/2f. \tag{1.20}$$

Many examples of this and alternate optical pattern recognition schemes are given in Chapters 3, 5, and 8.

1.9 Joint Transform Correlator

The matched spatial filtering system of Fig. 1.4 is known as a "frequency plane correlator". Many alternate correlator topologies exist; one that occurs quite often in succeeding chapters is the joint transform correlator, which is discussed below for background purposes and as an example of an alternate system architecture. The schematic representation of this joint transform correlator is shown in Fig. 1.6. Here the input functions g and h to be correlated are placed side-by-side in the input plane. The amplitude transmittance of plane P_1 in one dimension for simplicity is then

$$U_1(x_1) = g(x_1 - b) + h(x_1 + b), \tag{1.21}$$

where the center-to-center separation of the two functions is $2b$ and the physical extent of each is assumed to be b. Lens L_1 forms the Fourier transform of

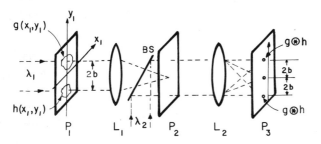

Fig. 1.6. Schematic representation of an optical joint transform correlator for pattern recognition

$U_1(x_1, y_1)$ at plane P_2. Assuming transmittance to be proportional to the input light intensity, we can write the subsequent transmittance of P_2, after exposure by $|U_2|^2$ and development, as

$$t(x_2, y_2) = |U_2(x_2, y_2)|^2$$

$$= |G(u, v)\exp(-j2\pi ub) + H(u, v)\exp(j2\pi ub)|^2$$

$$= |G|^2 + |H|^2 + GH^* \exp(-j4\pi ub) + G^*H \exp(j4\pi ub). \qquad (1.22)$$

This distribution is recorded at plane P_2 and the write light beam blocked. Plane P_2 is then illuminated with a normal planewave (using beam splitter BS) and the Fourier transform of $t(x_2, y_2)$ formed at plane P_3 by lens L_2. At plane P_3, the light amplitude distribution is the transform of (1.22) or

$$U(x_3, y_3) = g \circledast g - h \circledast h - g \circledast h * \delta(x_3 - 2b) + h \circledast g * \delta(x_3 + 2b). \qquad (1.23)$$

From (1.23), we see that output plane P_3 contains the desired correlation of g and h centered at $x_3 = \pm 2b$ (equal focal lengths are assumed for L_1 and L_2 for simplicity).

1.10 Scope of This Text

For those readers who require a brief refresher or a brief summary of the fundamental concepts that recur throughout the applications discussed in the following chapters, we have included the previous review.

Chapter 2 provides considerable detail and refinement on the optical Fourier transform synthesis process. Numerous examples of the optical Fourier transform of crystallographic image patterns are included. It is interesting that the use of optical analog techniques in X-ray diffraction developed independent of the work in optical data processing. However, many important conceptual ideas developed from the X-ray analog work. Although optical analysis methods are not widely used in the solution of crystal structures, we find that these methods have been an important input to the fundamental understanding of the field. These areas of crystallography and the optical Fourier transform are merged for the first time in this chapter. As the reader will see, the results provide insight into the optical Fourier transform and a novel use of optical computing techniques. This also represents an important first chapter which provides an introduction to coherent optics, the optical Fourier transform, depth of focus, resolution considerations, the array theorem, amplitude and phase, partial coherence and convolution.

Chapter 3 addresses the areas of image enhancement and restoration. This chapter provides the detailed fundamental concepts of optimum filtering including correlation and convolution and the use of photographic film. The conditions for optimum filtering are derived for five cases: the amplitude-only filter, the phase-only filter, the amplitude and binary phase filter, the amplitude and simple (wedge, step, etc.) phase filter, and the unconstrained filter. This provides a complete analysis of noise and optimum filtering. Coherent, non-coherent, and partially coherent systems are included. Filter fabrication schemes, applications, examples and the engineering aspects of this application area are emphasized here and throughout all of the chapters.

In Chapter 4, one of the major practical achievements of optical computing—its use in synthetic aperture radar systems—is discussed. This was the application area that initiated most of the work in coherent optical processing in the 1960s. For the first time this work and the historical development of the optical systems used for this application are placed in perspective. The basic system is described from both a correlation approach and a holographic approach. Again, considerable attention is given to the practical engineering aspects of the problem, and issues such as the coherence required and the effects of aircraft motion are discussed. A comparison of optical and digital solutions to this application area, once solely the domain of the optical computer, is also included.

Chapter 5 provides a comprehensive summary of the use of optical processing in photogrammetry. The mapping process itself involves data acquisition by remote sensing, data processing, data storage and display. This area involves and touches nearly all facets of optical data processing and provides a stopping place at which to put the many aspects of optical processing into perspective. The present treatment emphasizes data processing and the extraction of aspect data. This is photogrammetry. It involves conversion of an aerial image into a topographic map from which pertinent terrain data can be extracted. Interferometric, image plane correlation, and frequency plane correlation methods are all used and the way by which they provide the desired data discussed. Through a comparison of the systems described in this chapter with those of other chapters (such as 3, 6, 7 and 8), one can see how the basic optical processor architectures are modified and adapted for use in specific applications.

In Chapter 6, interferometry is treated in detail and its use in non-destructive testing and metrology emphasized. This application is of considerable importance in industry, quality control, product testing, etc. Although the basic method used is holographic interferometry, the intended application requires the use of new analysis methods and new measurement and synthesis techniques. These are emphasized herein. Holographic non-destructive testing involves double-exposure holographic interferometry and is used in the study of deformations and vibrations of an object and their dimensions. The basic principle is to apply a force to an object between two successive exposures of the object. The resultant fringe pattern reveals the object's deformations and defects. The analysis and evaluation of the resultant fringe pattern represents a formidable problem to a non-expert in the field. By moire analogy, the concept of wavefronts of observation is introduced; and by numerous examples the analysis of the resultant fringe patterns is made clear in this chapter. Practical engineering methods for the planning, making and calculations involved are provided and recent developments such as "sandwich holography" are included.

In Chapter 7, biomedical applications of optical processing are considered. Various three-dimensional biomedical imaging methods and applications of optical processing are discussed. Remarks are included on future research directions and comments advanced on the key points that determine why and where optical processing in biomedical applications will prevail. The many three-dimensional imaging concepts are clarified in this chapter. These include: holography (in which the full 3-D information is recorded); 2-D projections in which one dimension is collapsed to provide an accurate 2-D image ambiguous in the third dimension (as in X-ray projection and shadow projection); 2-D or 3-D imaging from 1-D projections (as in transaxial tomography) or 2-D projections (as in pseudo parallax images and cylindrical multiplexed holograms); profiling in which one of the three coordinates is ignored and methods by which the z dimension of an image is encoded as depth, contours, etc. Tomography, transaxial imaging, acoustic holography, and other biomedical data processing methods are all discussed. The importance of numerical aperture and depth of focus are clearly and vividly shown. This presentation thus provides an in-depth look at many holographic systems and their uses in biomedical and other applications.

Chapter 8 considers the signal processing applications of optical data processing. This runs the full gamut of many application areas. A folded spectrum optical spectrum analyzer by which frequency resolution such as 33 Hz in a 100 MHz bandwidth input signal is possible is described and applications of it presented, such as RF signal processing, signal demodulation, EEG signal processing, non-destructive testing and extraction of a signal in noise. This type of optical signal processor vividly demonstrates the parallel processing and high space bandwidth features of an optical processor and how one system can be used in a variety of diverse applications. A brief discussion of real-time spatial light modulators and real-time optical transducers is also included. Applications of non-coherent optical processing in speech recognition and coded waveform correlation are also included. The signal processing area emphasized is radar signal processing. Here lies the domain in which the high-speed, parallel processing, and high space bandwidth features of an optical processor are desperately needed. System configurations and examples of optically processed phased array, pulsed Doppler, FM stepped, and multi-channel coded radar signals are provided. A multi-channel 1-D matched filter correlator is described, a new method for correlating long coded waveforms, and a novel space variant optical processor for Doppler signal processing using the optical Mellin transform are included among others.

1.11 Summary

We hope that the capsule remarks included on the Fourier transform, holography, interferometry, and correlation will serve as an adequate reference base for the succeeding chapters. The application areas selected are the major ones in which optical data processing has made and promises to make significant contributions.

Bibliography

The texts listed below are selected to offer the interested reader a way to gain a deeper insight and more detailed information on the subjects treated in this chapter. This list makes no attempt at completeness. These are simply the books we routinely recommend as the best for their particular purposes.

A. Optical Background

1.1 F.A.Jenkins, H.E.White: *Fundamentals of Optics* (McGraw-Hill, New York 1957)
1.2 M.Born, E.Wolf: *Principles of Optics* (MacMillan, New York 1964)
      The former is more readable; the latter, more comprehensive.

B. Fourier Transforms and Optics

1.1 J.W.Goodman: *Introduction to Fourier Optics* (McGraw-Hill, New York 1968)
1.2 R.N.Bracewell: *The Fourier Transform and Its Applications* (McGraw-Hill, New York 1965)
1.3 A.Papoulis: *The Fourier Integral and Its Applications* (McGraw-Hill, New York 1962)
1.4 H.Lipson: *Optical Transformations* (Academic Press, New York 1972)

C. Holography

1.1 W.T.Cathey: *Optical Information Theory and Holography* (Wiley-Interscience, New York 1974)
1.2 H.M.Smith: *Principles of Holography*, 2nd ed. (Wiley-Interscience, New York 1975)
1.3 R.J.Collier, C.B.Burckhardt, L.H.Lin: *Optical Holography* (Academic Press, New York 1971)
1.4 H.J.Caulfield, S.Lu: *The Applications of Holography* (Wiley-Interscience, New York 1970)
1.5 W.E.Kock: *Lasers and Holography* (Doubleday, Garden City, New York 1969)

D. Statistical Optics, Communication Theory, and Information Study

1.1 F.T.S.Yu: *Optics and Information Theory* (Wiley-Interscience, New York 1976)
1.2 D.Gabor: "Light and Information", in *Progress in Optics*, ed. by E.Wolf, Vol. 1 (North-Holland, Amsterdam 1961)
1.3 E.L.O'Neill: *Introduction to Statistical Optics* (Addison-Wesley, Reading, Mass. 1963)

E. Coherence, Interference, Diffraction

1.1 G.B.Parrent, B.J.Thompson: *Physical Optics Notebook* (Society of Photo-Optical Instrumentation Engineers, Bellingham, Washington 1969)
1.2 A.R.Shulman: *Optical Data Processing* (Wiley-Interscience, New York 1970)

The former is a classic and is still available from S.P.I.E. at the address given above, zip code 98225.

2. Optical Transforms and Coherent Processing Systems —With Insights From Crystallography

B. J. Thompson

With 19 Figures

2.1 Historical Background

Optical diffraction has proved to be a very valuable tool in a variety of fields for measurement of small objects and distances, for testing and evaluation of components, and as the primary mechanism in image processing. The use of diffraction is quite old; early workers recognized that when an object is small (say a few microns), it is difficult to image and measure its size accurately without extremely high magnification and without very high quality optics. The Fraunhofer diffraction pattern associated with such a small object can be large, and the object size can be measured accurately from its diffraction pattern; the small object is measured with a ruler! One of the first examples of this method was the so-called Young's eriometer [2.1]. While often described in its application to the measurement of blood cells, this device was actually invented for measuring the mean diameter of wool samples; the wool fibers were combed to cause them to become aligned before the measurement was made. The mean diameter was determined by measuring the appropriate width of the resulting diffraction pattern. Work still continues today on more sophisticated versions of this basic device [2.2, 3]; work also continues on the measurements of a wide variety of particulate parameters [2.4] and measurements of small distances [2.5].

   The Foucault knife edge test is one of the earliest testing methods for optical components. The focused light is removed and the component is viewed with the light diffracted by blemishes on the component's surface. These flaws then stand out as bright "images" in an otherwise dark field. In a real sense this is closely related to the optical processing methods that are being discussed in this and other chapters in this volume. Schlieren systems (the credit for the invention of these systems is usually given to *Topler* [2.6]) are another class of device that uses a weak diffraction process. The *Abbe* theory of vision in a microscope [2.7] and in particular the experimental illustrations of this theory by *Porter* [2.8] are again important forerunners of today's optical processing systems. In 1927, *Michelson* [2.9] illustrated how an image may be formed by reconstructing a recorded diffraction pattern after adding the important phase information; admittedly the experiment was carried out with a simple slit object but nevertheless is related to the optical synthesis experiments conducted in more recent times.

Perhaps the most famous historical optical processing systems are those used in microscopy, particularly the phase contrast microscope [2.10].

Optical processing took on a new lease of life in the 1950s after the introduction of communication theory ideas into optics and the particularly stimulating work of *Maréchal* and *Croce* [2.11]. The emphasis of this work, and much effort since, has been on the processing of images with particular reference to aberration balancing or image deblurring. Another application in the area of the processing of an image is to recognize certain features present in that image—this is the pattern recognition area.

The topics mentioned above, as well as others, are covered in other chapters of this volume. In this particular chapter we will be concerned with some of the basic properties of optical transforms and some applications in crystallography. It is an interesting historical fact that the use of optical analog techniques to X-ray diffraction developed essentially independently of the work in optical processing. It is interesting, however, that many important conceptual ideas developed out of the X-ray analog work. Optical methods in X-ray crystallography have not been widely used in solving crystal structures but have had a very important impact on the fundamental understanding of the field. These methods have also a great deal of relevance to those involved in diffraction techniques in general and optical processing in particular. Naturally there is a considerable literature on optical analog techniques to X-ray diffraction, and this literature is important reading for those involved in that particular field. It is also an extremely important body of literature to those involved in optical diffraction and image processing. It is because of this fact that I have the timerity to discuss this subject even though there are better qualified experts in the field than I. The most important literature on optical methods in X-ray diffraction can be found in a series of books that review the field [2.12–15].

2.2 System Description and Design

The classical Fraunhofer diffraction pattern that is so well known in optics is mathematically the Fourier transform of the object distribution producing the diffraction pattern. The Fraunhofer pattern is, of course, characteristic of the object that produced it. Optically the Fourier transform can be formed under an approximation called the far field condition and, more importantly in this discussion, in an exact way by the use of a lens. This second condition is usually called the Fraunhofer condition and is the one of interest here.

For the purposes of the present discussion, we will consider the optical system shown in Fig. 2.1a. (For simplicity, it will be considered in a one-dimensional situation, although it goes over quite readily to the two-dimensional case.) A source on axis illuminates the object or input plane a distance S from the source. The object distribution is $g(\xi)$ and is located a general distance z_1 in front of the lens which is located in the α plane. The output plane is a general distance

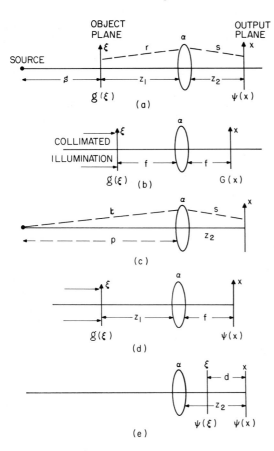

Fig. 2.1. Systems for producing a Fraunhofer diffraction pattern, which is the Fourier transform of the input complex amplitude

z_2 on the other side of the lens and contains an amplitude distribution $\psi(x)$. The distance from the source to the lens is p, the variable distance from the object plane to the lens is r, and that from the lens to the output plane is s. We will examine this system under a variety of particular conditions.

2.2.1 Source at Infinity

a) Object at Front Focal Plane. The usual case that is considered in optical Fraunhofer diffraction is when the source is located at infinity (i.e., by use of an auxiliary collimating lens) and the distance z_1 is equal to the focal length of the lens f (Fig. 2.1b). The output plane is such that $z_2 = f$. Ignoring the effect of the finite lens aperture, the distribution in the x plane is then the exact Fourier transform of the input distribution $g(\xi)$, i.e.,

$$G(x) = D \int_{-\infty}^{\infty} g(\xi) \exp(-jkx\xi/f) d\xi, \tag{2.1}$$

where $k = 2\pi/\lambda$, D is a constant, and the transform size is scaled by the factor $1/\lambda f$. That is, the longer the focal length the greater the extent of the transform, and the longer the wavelength the greater the extent of the transform. Equation (2.1) is readily derived from the usual Kirchhoff diffraction formula; thus, assuming collimated (plane wave) illumination of the object, the distribution in the x-plane $\psi(x)$ is given by

$$\psi(x) = A \int\limits_{-\infty}^{\infty} \int\limits_{-\infty}^{\infty} g(\xi) \exp(jkr/r) \exp(-jk\alpha^2/2f) \exp(jks/s) d\xi d\alpha ; \qquad (2.2)$$

the terms $\exp(jkr/r)$ and $\exp(jks/s)$ are the appropriate spherical waves and the term $\exp(-jk\alpha^2/2f)$ is the phase term introduced by the lens. A is a new constant that includes D. The effects of r and s varying have a major effect in the exponential terms but only a small effect in the denominator; hence r and s in the denominator are taken outside the integral and replaced with the constants z_1 and z_2. This is equivalent to a small angle approximation, and under that same approximation we can write

$$r = z_1 + \frac{(\alpha - \xi)^2}{2z_1}, \qquad s = z_2 + \frac{(x - \alpha)^2}{2z_2}. \qquad (2.3)$$

When (2.3) is substituted into (2.2) we obtain

$$\psi(x) = A \exp(jk(z_1 + z_2)/z_1 z_2) \int\limits_{-\infty}^{\infty} \int\limits_{-\infty}^{\infty} g(\xi)$$
$$\cdot \exp\{\tfrac{1}{2}jk[(\alpha - \xi)^2/z_1 - \alpha^2/f + (x - \alpha)^2/z_2]\} d\xi d\alpha. \qquad (2.4)$$

Under the important condition that $z_1 = z_2 = f$ (Fig. 2.1b), (2.4) becomes

$$\psi(x) = A \exp(2jk/f) \int\limits_{-\infty}^{\infty} \int\limits_{-\infty}^{\infty} g(\xi) \exp\{jk[\alpha^2 + \xi^2 + x^2 - 2\alpha(x + \xi)]/2f\} d\xi d\alpha.$$

If the square is now completed on $[\alpha - (x + \xi)]^2$ and the α integration performed, then

$$\psi(x) = G(x) = A \exp(2jk/f) \int\limits_{-\infty}^{\infty} g(\xi) \exp(-jkx\xi/f) d\xi. \qquad (2.5)$$

Equation (2.5) is the result stated earlier in (2.1). It will be noted that the Fourier transform is located in the plane which contains the image of the source point and further that it is centered at the location of that source image.

    The analysis above incorrectly ignores the effect of the finite lens aperture. However, the literature usually proceeds in this way since it is the transform condition that is of interest. The most straightforward way to include the effect of the lens aperture is to recognize that the source does not image as a point onto the Fourier plane. What is the image distribution of that point source in the Fourier plane? This is readily achieved by again considering the normal propagation problem. Figure 2.1c shows the necessary parameters for the system; the distance along the axis from the source to the lens is $S + z_1 = p$ and t is the general distance from the source point to a point in the lens aperture. The lens aperture function will be written as $l(\alpha)$ which in general includes all the lens effects other than the idealized quadratic phase term $\exp(-jk\alpha^2/2f)$. Thus we may write

$$\psi(x) = A \int_{-\infty}^{\infty} \exp(jkt/t)l(\alpha)\exp(-jk\alpha^2/2f)\exp(jks/s)d\alpha. \tag{2.6}$$

Under the small angle approximation, (2.6) reduces to

$$\psi(x) = A \exp[jk(p+z_2)/pz_2] \int_{-\infty}^{\infty} l(\alpha)\exp(\tfrac{1}{2}jk\alpha^2)\left(\frac{1}{p} + \frac{1}{z_2} - \frac{1}{f}\right)$$
$$\cdot \exp(jkx^2/2z_2)\exp(-jk\alpha x/z_2)d\alpha. \tag{2.7}$$

Since the source is imaged onto the x plane, then

$$\left(\frac{1}{p} + \frac{1}{z_2} - \frac{1}{f}\right) = 0$$

and

$$\psi(x) = C \exp(jkx^2/2z_2) \int_{-\infty}^{\infty} l(\alpha)\exp(-jk\alpha x/z_2)d\alpha$$
$$\cdot L(x)C \exp(jkx^2/2z_2), \tag{2.8}$$

where $L(x)$ is the Fourier transform of $l(\alpha)$. Thus we have the well-known and expected result that the image of the point object is the classical amplitude impulse response which is, of course, the Fourier transform of the aperture function. There is, however, the quadratic term in the output plane coordinate present. The scale of the amplitude impulse response depends upon λ and z_2. In the specific case under consideration, $z_2 = f$ and hence (2.8) becomes

$$\psi(x) = C \exp(jkx^2/2f) \int_{-\infty}^{\infty} l(\alpha)\exp(-jk\alpha x/f)d\alpha, \tag{2.9}$$

and the scaling is the same as that for the transform of the input function.

The results expressed by (2.5) and (2.9) can be combined. Clearly the Fourier transform of the input function is convolved with the amplitude impulse response function of the lens. Thus we may write the total complex amplitude in the x plane as $\Psi(x)$ given by

$$\Psi(x) = G(x) * \psi(x), \tag{2.10}$$

where the asterisk denotes a convolution, $G(x)$ is the Fourier transform of $g(\xi)$ and $\psi(x)$ is defined by (2.9) and is the Fourier transform $L(x)$ of $l(\alpha)$ times the quadratic phase term. Even this analysis does not contain the complete answer. An important consideration is the stationarity of the optical system producing the transform. This question has recently been examined [2.16] but will not be considered further here.

b) **Arbitrary Position of Object (i.e., $z_1 \neq f$).** Under this condition and with a similar analysis to that given above, the complex amplitude in the output plane, which is still the rear focal plane of the lens (Fig. 2.1d), is given by

$$\psi(x) = C \exp[jkx^2(f-z)/2f^2] \int_{-\infty}^{\infty} g(\xi)\exp(-jkx\xi/f)d\xi. \qquad (2.11)$$

The Fourier transform is still in the same location with the same scale but it is multiplied by the quadratic phase term in x^2. In the limit when the input function is in the aperture of the lens, then the quadratic phase term reduces to $\exp(jkx^2/2f)$. Naturally the final distribution in the output plane involves a convolution with the impulse response function and will be similar to (2.10).

   If the input object is moved to the other side of the lens and is at a general distance d from the output plane (Fig. 2.1e), then

$$\psi(x) = C \exp(jkx^2/2d) \int_{-\infty}^{\infty} g(\xi)\exp(-jkx\xi/d)d\xi. \qquad (2.12)$$

Notice again the presence of the quadratic phase term and the fact that the transform is now scaled according to d. Thus the size of the transform can be changed continuously over some restricted range by moving the input object along the axis. The transform remains located in the real focal plane of the lens. In all these examples the transform is always located at the image of the source point.

   If it is only the intensity of the transform that is of interest, then these additional phase factors that have been discussed are of no importance since they are removed when the intensity is formed.

2.2.2 Arbitrary Position of Source

a) **Object at Front Focal Plane.** The output plane of interest now is the plane containing the image of the source and hence z_2 is the image distance of the source image from the lens. The distribution in the output plane is

$$\psi(x) = G(x) = C \int_{-\infty}^{\infty} g(\xi)\exp(-jkx\xi/f)d\xi. \qquad (2.13)$$

Equation (2.13) represents an interesting result that was pointed out recently by *Warren* [2.17]; the transform is exact and the scale of the transform is independent of the source to image distance and hence of the source position. However, the location of that transform is dependent on the source position. The total amplitude distribution in the output plane is now a convolution similar to (2.10) but the impulse response width is larger since it does scale with the lens to output plane distance.

b) Arbitrary Position of Object. It will now be no surprise that when the input object is moved away from the front focal plane, an additional phase factor is again included in the expression.

$$\psi(x) = C \exp\{jkx^2(f-z_1)/2[z_2(f-z_1)+fz_1]\}$$

$$\cdot \int_{-\infty}^{\infty} g(\xi) \exp\{-jkx\xi f/[z_2(f-z_1)+fz_1]\} d\xi . \tag{2.14}$$

The scale now changes as the object position is changed. When the object is in the aperture of the lens, $z_1 = 0$, the quadratic phase term reduces to $\exp[jkx^2/2z_2]$ and the transform of $g(\xi)$ scales with the distance z_2.

Finally, when the object is on the other side of the lens, (2.12) still holds, but, of course, the physical location of the transform plane is not the same as the condition for which (2.12) was developed.

A summary of these various situations is contained in Table 2.1, which is self-explanatory. Naturally similar expressions could be written for virtual source position, i.e., converging illumination of the object rather than the collimated or diverging illumination discussed above.

Table 2.1

Source position	Object position (relative to lens)	Output plane	Phase term	Scale proportional to
∞	f in front	f behind	—	f
∞	z_1	f behind	$\dfrac{x^2(-z_1)}{2f^2}$	f
∞	0	f behind	$x^2/2f$	f
∞	behind lens distance d from output plane	f behind	$x^2/2d$	d
p	f in front	$z_2 = \left(\dfrac{p-f}{pf}\right)^{-1}$	—	f
p	z_1	$z_2 = \left(\dfrac{p-f}{pf}\right)^{-1}$	$\dfrac{x^2(f-z_1)}{2[z_2(f-z_1)+fz_1]}$	$\dfrac{z_2(f-z_1)+fz_1}{f}$
p	0	$z_2 = \left(\dfrac{p-f}{pf}\right)^{-1}$	$x^2/2z_2$	z_2

2.3 Properties of Transforms

Many of the properties of Fourier transforms are, of course, well known. The task in this section is to recall many of those properties and see how important and visible they are in optically produced Fourier transforms.

2.3.1 Scale

The scaling theorem is of considerable importance and is a well-understood property of diffraction—that is, in diffraction there is a reciprocal relationship between the object and its diffraction pattern. The smaller the object the bigger the diffraction pattern, and the larger the object the smaller the diffraction pattern. Since the diffraction pattern is the Fourier transform of the diffracting object, this reciprocity is clearly a property of the Fourier transform. This is easily seen in the following way: Let the Fourier transform of a function $g(\xi)$ be $G(x/\lambda f)$. Then if the input function is $g(a\xi)$, the transform is $G(x/a\lambda f)$. This property is illustrated in Fig. 2.2; the lower row shows the input function which is a circular aperture and of increasing radius. The intensity distribution in the diffraction patterns of these aperture functions are shown in the upper row; these photographs are of the Fourier transform squared. The reciprocal relationship is evident.

2.3.2 Shape

A direct follow-on from the discussion of the scale effects are the properties that relate to shape. Simply, when we are dealing with a two-dimensional input and

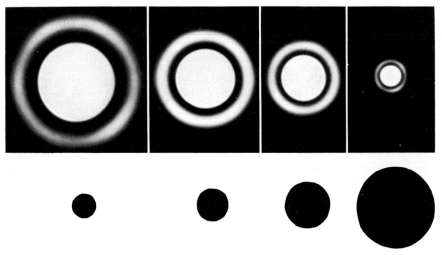

Fig. 2.2. Diffraction by a circular aperture—effect of scale. The upper set of four photographs of the diffraction patterns is produced by the lower row of circular apertures

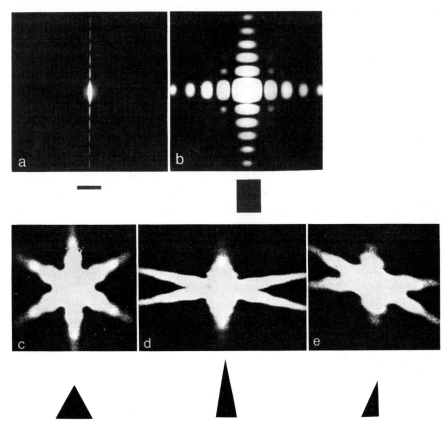

Fig. 2.3a–e. Diffraction by a rectangular aperture of different height to width ratios: (a) and (b). Diffraction by various triangular apertures: (c) equilateral; (d) isosceles; (e) right-angled. In each case the photograph of the diffraction pattern is shown above the corresponding aperture

hence a two-dimensional output (a two-dimensional Fourier transform), the relative scale of the object in various directions relates reciprocally to properties in the transform. This is illustrated in Fig. 2.3. Figures 2.3a and b compare the intensity distributions in the diffraction patterns associated with rectangular apertures of the same width but different heights. The relative scale of the height and width is clearly apparent in the resulting diffraction pattern. The functional form of the two distributions is, of course, the same; it is just the scale of the distribution function in the horizontal direction that changes. Because of the symmetry of the aperture function the diffraction pattern is also highly symmetrical about the horizontal and perpendicular axes, and the phase associated with the pattern is simple. Only two values of phase are present $(0, \pi)$ and the phase changes each time the intensity goes through a zero value. Hence the central region is of uniform phase as is each separate region of intensity.

A second example is shown in Figs. 2.3c–e, which show the intensity distributions in the diffraction patterns of a series of triangular aperture functions of different shape. Figure 2.3c is an equilateral triangle; the resulting pattern relates to that symmetry with an "arm" in the pattern running perpendicular to each side and the pattern is symmetric about the vertical and horizontal axes. The phase distribution is not now simple; the phase function is constantly varying over the field and the phase contours all pass through the points of zero intensity. Figure 2.3d shows the result for an isosceles triangle and Fig. 2.3e for a right-angled triangle.

2.3.3 Shift

The so-called shift theorem turns out to have enormous value in the optical systems described above. The question to be asked here is what is the effect of a lateral shift in the position of the input object. We are therefore interested in the Fourier transform of a shifted function $g(\xi - a)$. The transform is $\exp(-kax/f)G(x/\lambda f)$. The original transform $G(x/\lambda f)$ is multiplied by a linear phase term. This means that as the input is moved laterally, the resulting transform remains centered on the optical axis of the system; this is of considerable advantage in optical diffraction and processing systems since a detector array placed in the transform plane can be maintained in a fixed location independent of the lateral position of the object. The same is true if a filter is placed in the transform plane. The linear phase term is only apparent if the resulting transform is used, say, to record a Fourier transform hologram or, in fact, in any situation where the transform has a second beam added to it; then the linear phase term will result in a set of cosine fringes. This point is illustrated in Fig. 2.4. Figure 2.4a shows a plot of a cross-section of the well-known diffraction pattern of a circular aperture of radius b, $|2J_1(kbx/f)/(kbx/f)|^2$ and Fig. 2.4b the same aperture and the pattern recorded in the same location but with a plane wave added; the circular aperture is centered on the optical axis. The intensity distribution associated with this plot is $|1 + 2J_1(kbx/f)/(kbx/f)|^2$. Finally, Fig. 2.4c is the resultant intensity profile when the circular aperture is shifted laterally; the profile is essentially that associated with Fig. 2.4b but with an additional cosine modulation. The intensity profile is

$$|1 + \exp(-kax/f)2J_1(kbx/f)/(kbx/f)|^2 ,$$

where a is the lateral shift of the circular aperture and is set here at $a = 5b$.

2.3.4 Convolutions and Products

A very useful relationship in Fourier transform theory, and a result that manifests itself over and over again in optical diffraction, is the Fourier transform of a product or the Fourier transform of a convolution. Consider that we have two functions $g_1(\xi)$ and $g_2(\xi)$ which have transforms $G_1(x/\lambda f)$ and

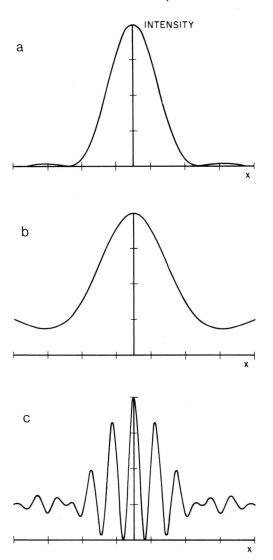

Fig. 2.4a–c. An illustration of the linear phase term in the transform when the diffracting object is subject to a lateral shift: (a) properties of the diffraction pattern of a circular aperture, (b) resulting intensity distributions when a uniform constant is added to (a), (c) resulting intensity distribution when the circular aperture is shifted laterally

$G_2(x/\lambda f)$, respectively; then we may inquire what is the Fourier transform of the product $g_1(\xi)g_2(\xi)$. The transform of this product is the convolution of the individual transforms and, of course, the inverse is also true that the Fourier transform of a convolution is the product of the individual transforms. This relationship is readily shown in the following way. We start with the statement of the Fourier transform of a product, i.e.,

$$G(x) = \int_{-\infty}^{\infty} g_1(\xi)g_2(\xi)\exp(-jkx\xi/f)d\xi. \tag{2.15}$$

Equation (2.15) may be rewritten

$$G(x) = \int_{-\infty}^{\infty} \left[\int_{-\infty}^{\infty} G_1(x'/\lambda f)\exp(jkx'\xi/f)dx' \right]$$
$$\cdot g_2(\xi)\exp(jkx\xi/f)d\xi, \tag{2.16}$$

where $g_1(\xi)$ has been written as a Fourier transform with some new variable x' in the x coordinate. The order of integration can be changed to give

$$G(x) = \int_{-\infty}^{\infty} G_1(x'/\lambda f)$$
$$\cdot \left\{ \int_{-\infty}^{\infty} g_2(\xi)\exp[-jk\xi(x-x')/f]d\xi \right\}dx'. \tag{2.17}$$

The inner integral can now be carried out to give the required result that

$$G(x) = \int_{-\infty}^{\infty} G_1(x'/\lambda f)G_2[(x-x')/\lambda f]dx', \tag{2.18}$$

which is the convolution integral. We will see several illustrations of this result in later sections of this chapter.

2.3.5 The Array Theorem

A result that relates to the analysis of the last section is the array theorem that came into use in optics from the field of antenna theory and practice. If the input function to our optical system consists of a repetitive arrangement of a particular aperture function, then the total input function can be considered to be made up of two functions. The first of these is a function that represents the set of positions at which the particular aperture is located; these positions can be represented as a set of δ-functions, and it is this set of δ-functions that is often termed the array function, $h(\xi) = \sum_{n=1}^{N} \delta(\xi - \xi_n)$. The second function describes the particular aperture function $b(\xi)$. The total input function is then the convolution of these two functions; thus

$$g(\xi) = \int_{-\infty}^{\infty} b(\xi')h(\xi - \xi')d\xi'. \tag{2.19}$$

Fig. 2.5. The intensity distribution associated with the optically produced Fourier transform of a pair of circular holes

The Fourier transform of $g(\xi)$ is then the product of the individual transforms of the two functions in the convolution integral. A very simple example of this result can be seen if we consider the Fourier transform of two circular apertures. The array function consists of two δ-functions separated by the appropriate distance d. The Fourier transform of the array consisting of two δ-functions is a cosine function $\cos(kdx/f)$ and the result is hence

$$G(x, y) = \left[2J_1 \left(\frac{kbr}{f} \right) \middle/ \frac{kbr}{f} \right] \cdot \cos \frac{kdr}{f}, \tag{2.19a}$$

$$I(x, y) = G(x, y)G^*(x, y) = \left| 2J_1 \left(\frac{kbr}{f} \right) \middle/ \frac{kbr}{f} \right|^2 \cos^2 \frac{kdx}{f}, \tag{2.19b}$$

where r is the radial coordinate and $r^2 = x^2 + y^2$.

This well-known result is illustrated in Fig. 2.5 which is a photograph of the result expressed in (2.19b).

A more interesting example is to consider the input function displayed in Fig. 2.6 which consists of a two-dimensional array of small circular holes. This input can be considered as a convolution of an array function representing the positions of the circular holes and the function representing the circular holes. In fact, it is advantageous to consider the array function itself as a product of an infinite array and a rectangular function which truncates that array. The advantage of this consideration of the array function is that the transform of the array function is another array of δ-functions that is reciprocally related to the array in input space (Figs. 2.6d and g). The rectangular function (Fig. 2.6b) that limits the array in input space has the well-known transform shown in Fig. 2.6e, which, since it is an intensity display, equals the transform squared and has the form $\text{sinc}^2(kax/f)\,\text{sinc}^2(kcy/f)$. The remaining function, the circular aperture, has its transform as $2J_1(kbr/f)/(kbr/f)$ when r is the radial coordinate $(x^2 + y^2)^{1/2}$. The intensity associated with the transform is shown for completeness in Fig. 2.6f. The complete input function is then written as a product and a convolution,

$$g(\xi, \eta) = b(\xi, \eta) * [h(\xi, \eta)\,\text{Rect}(\xi|a;\eta|c)], \tag{2.20}$$

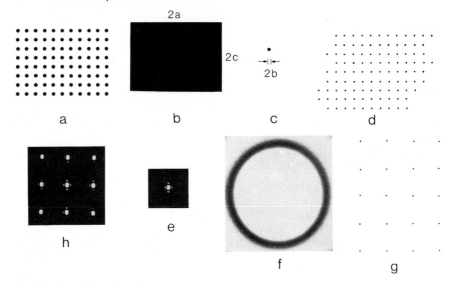

Fig. 2.6a–h. An illustration of the array theorem: (a) the object that can be separated into the three functions shown in (b), (c), and (d). The diffraction patterns associated with (b), (c), and (d) are shown in (e), (f), and (g), and the total pattern is (h)

where $h(\xi, \eta)$ is the infinite array function, the asterisk denotes a convolution, and Rect$(\xi|a; \eta|c)$ is the two-dimensional rectangular function of half-width a and half-height c. The total transform of the total input function consists of a convolution and a product, i.e., the convolution of (2.20) results in a product and the product term gives a convolution

$$G(x, y) = B(x, y)\,[H(x, y) * \text{Sinc}(x, y)]. \tag{2.21}$$

The result is displayed in Fig. 2.6h; the intensity is, of course, displayed here and only the portion within the central maximum of the diffraction pattern of the small circular hole is shown. This function is the envelope function. The array function clearly produces a reciprocal array, and the transform of the large rectangular function that limited the array is now located at each array point in the transform. This example turns out to be an excellent illustration of the convolution and product theorem discussed in the last section.

2.4 System Parameters

In the previous two sections we have discussed the basic system for producing the two-dimensional Fourier transform by optical means, and we also reviewed and illustrated some of the basic properties of optical transforms. There are some other system parameters that are worth discussing which include depth of focus of the Fourier plane, resolution in the Fourier plane, and coherence requirements of the system. As will be seen, some of these parameters are interrelated.

2.4.1 Depth of Focus

When optical systems are used for producing the two-dimensional Fourier transform, the question of being able to locate the correct plane is not only critical but is also non-trivial. This particular problem faced workers in optical analogues to X-ray diffraction in the 1950 s, and after a number of attempts a useful solution was obtained [2.18]. The method relies on the properties of the

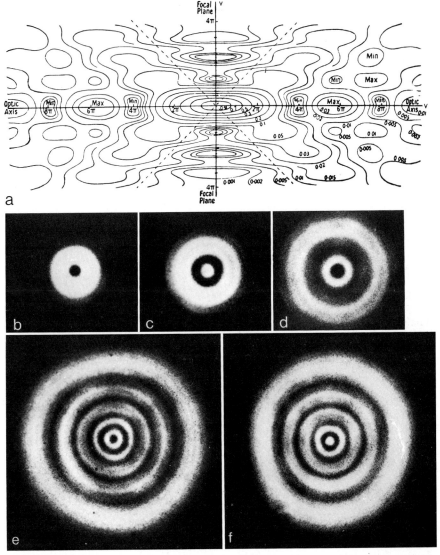

Fig. 2.7a–f. The intensity distribution near the focus of a spherical wave: (a) isophote (line of equal intensity) diagram; (b) photograph of the intensity distribution at $u = 4\pi$; (c) $u = 6\pi$; (d) $u = 8\pi$; (e) $u = 20\pi$; (f) $u = 18\pi$ (after *Taylor* and *Thompson* [2.20])

three-dimensional distribution of intensity in the focal region of a converging spherical wave and specifically of that spherical wave propagating from the lens in Fig. 2.1. This distribution had been examined theoretically by several workers (see, e.g., [2.19]) and also studied experimentally [2.20]. Figure 2.7a shows an isophote (contour of equal intensity) plot of a section through the three-dimensional intensity distribution in the focal region. The coordinates here are the dimensionless coordinates $u = (ka^2/f^2)\Delta f$ and $v = kar/f$; a is the aperture radius and Δf is the shift from the focus. The complete distribution would be found by rotation about the u axis. The distribution in the v plane is the normal pattern associated with the Fourier transform of the circular aperture; the lines at 45° represent the geometrical projection of the aperture. In planes other than the focal plane the intensity distributions are those associated with classical Fresnel diffraction.

Photographs of the intensity distributions in several planes are shown in Figs. 2.7b–f. Figure 2.7b is the distribution at $u = 4\pi$, the first zero on axis; Fig. 2.7c, $u = 6\pi$, the next maximum on axis; Fig. 2.7d, $u = 8\pi$, the next axial zero. The zeroes on axis occur at multiples of 4π and the intensity distribution in the plane containing the fifth axial zero is shown in Fig. 2.7e; the maximum at $u = 18\pi$ is shown in Fig. 2.7f.

For a good lens of large f number, the distribution is symmetric on either side of the focal plane. It will be readily observed that the central region has a relatively long tubular structure and the isophotes run parallel to the u-axis; this results in some depth of focus of the transform of the circular aperture but at the same time means that it is difficult visually to select the exact transform plane. By contrast the positions of zero intensity on the axis at $u = 4\pi$, 8π, etc., are more accurately located. If a pair of zeroes is located one on either side of the focal

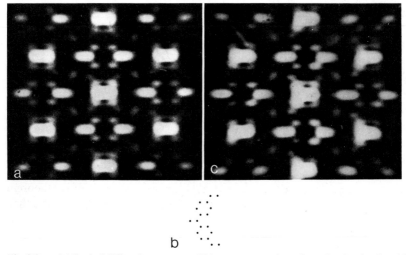

Fig. 2.8a–c. (a) Optical diffraction pattern of (b), a representation of a molecule of p-di-anisly nitric oxide, and (c) slightly out-of-focus pattern (after *Taylor* and *Thompson* [2.19])

plane (say the third or fourth on either side) then the focal plane can be accurately located as the plane midway between these two zeroes. The usefulness of this method is illustrated in Fig. 2.8a, which shows the intensity distribution in the diffraction pattern of the arrangement of holes shown in Fig. 2.8b, which is a representation of the projection of a single molecule of di-p-anisyl nitric oxide; for comparison, Fig. 2.8c shows a result for a slightly out-of-focus distribution. Before this particular technique was developed, results of the sort shown in Fig. 2.8c were not untypical—in this instance the error is obvious because of the slight asymmetry of the resulting pattern.

2.4.2 Resolution

When the optical system shown in Fig. 2.1b is used to produce the Fourier transform, it is important to consider the resulting resolution. This really consists of two questions: a) What is the highest spatial frequency present in the transform? b) What is the resolution between adjacent components? Both of these factors depend in rather different but related ways to the f-number of the lens. Let us consider first the highest spatial frequency present in the transform; this is determined by the width of the impulse response function of the lens in the input plane. Any spatial frequency whose fundamental spacing is smaller than the impulse response will not be transmitted by the lens. (It will be noted that there is no such restriction if the input function is placed in the aperture of the lens). The resolution of adjacent frequency components is determined by the width of the impulse response function in the transform plane, as indicated by (2.10). It must be recalled, however, that in this particular case the lens itself might not be the limiting factor; instead, the determining factor might be the aperture which limits the input object. This is clear from the discussion of Section 2.3.4 and specifically from (2.21) and Fig. 2.6h.

2.4.3 Coherence Effects

It has been assumed in previous discussions that the illumination of the input object was ideally coherent, of uniform phase and constant amplitude. However, it often occurs that the illumination is not fully coherent and this itself affects the resolution of adjacent frequency components. The coherence requirements of such an optical system have been reviewed in some detail in a recent article [2.21], and it will be possible only to review the salient features here.

We will consider first that the illumination is provided by a small incoherent source. The degree of coherence is predicted by the van Cittert-Zernike theorem and thus if the incoherent source is a circular source of uniform intensity, then the degree of coherence is given by

$$\gamma(\xi_1, \xi_2) = 2J_1 \left[\frac{ka(\xi_1 - \xi_2)}{z} \right] \Big/ \left[\frac{ka(\xi_1 - \xi_2)}{z} \right] \tag{2.22}$$

which is, of course, radially symmetric, and z is the distance propagated from the source to the plane of interest $z \gg a$; a is the radius of the source. If a collimating lens is used to provide collimated illumination of the object, then z is the focal length of that collimating lens. The field illuminating the input object is partially coherent but has a quite uniform intensity. Conversely, if the small source is coherent, then the illuminating field is coherent. The amplitude, though, of that field is not constant but is, in fact, the diffraction pattern associated with that small source; assuming that the phase is constant it will be $2J_1(ka\xi/z)/(ka\xi/z)$, $z \gg a^2/\lambda$. The trade-off here is quite clear; it is between a fully coherent illumination with slight amplitude taper, or uniform intensity of illumination with a slight decrease in the coherence.

When the illumination is only partially coherent, the effects can be evaluated in two ways and, depending on the particular problem, each method may have its advantages. For a uniform incoherent circular source it will be necessary to make sure that the input function is smaller than the coherence interval of the illumination [i.e., the half-width of the function of (2.22)]. Even then, of course, the contrast of the fringes produced by the interference between outer parts of the input function will be less than unity. This means that the lower frequencies will not be properly represented. If the above condition is not met, then it may be that the opposite outer portions of the object will not be coherent with respect to each other and hence those frequencies will not be represented in the diffraction pattern. Thus the effects can be evaluated and sometimes used to achieve a particular purpose. Figure 2.9 shows how the spatial coherence can be tailored to meet a specific requirement. Figure 2.9a shows an input function that is a representation of the projection of many molecules of hexamethylbenzene ([2.22, 23]). The illumination is arranged so that the light is sensibly coherent over the individual "molecule" but incoherent from one molecule to the next. The resulting diffraction pattern is then that associated with a single molecule

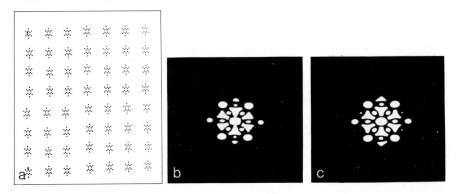

Fig. 2.9a–c. An illustration of coherence control: (a) is the input function consisting of an array of many molecules of hexamethylbenzene; resulting diffraction pattern (b) when the illumination is coherent over an individual molecule but incoherent from one molecule to the next; (c) diffraction pattern by one molecule alone (after *Thompson* [2.22])

with no interference term produced by the array function. This result is shown in Fig. 2.9b and compared with Fig. 2.9c, which is the diffraction pattern produced by one molecule on its own. Naturally Fig. 2.9b is very much brighter than the pattern of Fig. 2.9c; but, of course, this does not show in the photograph.

The second way to look at the effect of the finite size of the source function is to recall that the transform plane is located in the image plane of the source. Thus if the source is incoherent, the resulting diffraction pattern in intensity is a convolution of the source function with the intensity distribution in the diffraction pattern formed by a point source located at the center of the real source. This can be illustrated rather well by considering an input object that is a large rectangular array of circular dots (Fig. 2.10a). The illumination of this object is provided by a uniform circular incoherent source whose size is chosen so that the object is not illuminated coherently over its whole extent. The resulting intensity distribution in the diffraction pattern is seen in Fig. 2.10b. By application of the array theorem we expect to see the reciprocal array (the transform of the object array) and we do; diffraction by the small circular dots provides the envelope function. The function located at each point in the reciprocal array is, however, an image of the source function. It can be noted that effectively the diffraction pattern associated with the function that limits the input array is much smaller than the image of the source. If the source function is coherent, the illumination is coherent and the resultant complex amplitude distribution is a convolution of the complex amplitude distribution of the image

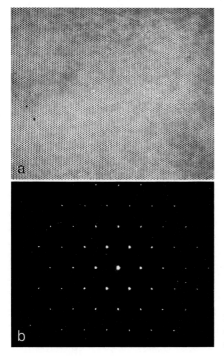

Fig. 2.10a and b. Diffraction pattern with a finite sized incoherent source of a regular array of small opaque dots

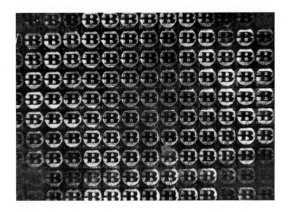

Fig. 2.11. Replication of a source function by a diffraction method (see, e.g., [2.23])

of the source with the Fourier transform of the input object for a point source located at the center of the actual source.

This concept has been used for multiple imaging since the source function can be any distribution function [2.21, 24]. Figure 2.11 illustrates this result; the source function is actually a letter B. The light from the source is used to illuminate a two-dimensional rectangular array periodic function; the light is sufficiently coherent to produce the necessary diffraction and the Fourier plane consists of an array of the source function. In this example, the source was incoherent; that is, the original letter B, the effective source for the system, was illuminated incoherently. Naturally the B could have been illuminated coherently with a similar result. Coherently illuminating the function to be replicated leads to an important modification of the method. The function to be replicated is now the input function to the standard diffraction system. The Fourier transform is then sampled appropriately and a second lens used to carry out an inverse transform thus produces an image of the input replicated in a manner determined by the sampling function in the Fourier plane [2.25]. The system just described is, of course, an optical processing system. A considerable versatility can be added to the system by using a hologram as the periodic element that does the sampling in the Fourier plane [2.26–29].

The latter part of the above discussion is somewhat of an aside at this point. We can return to the main theme of this section to discuss further this effect of finite source size on the diffraction pattern. Naturally this discussion relates to the earlier consideration of resolution of adjacent spatial frequencies. Clearly the source size may be the limiting factor if too large a source is used. In a good design the limiting function will be the aperture of the input function.

In these discussions we have assumed that the light is temporally coherent. The actual coherence length that is necessary is determined by the maximum path difference involved in the interference process that produces the resultant diffraction pattern. In effect there is yet another convolution to perform and that is with the function that represents the spectral profile of the incident illumination.

2.5 Transforms of Interest in Crystallography

When optical analogue methods are used in X-ray crystallography, some liberties have to be taken. For example, the individual atoms are represented as circular holes; real atoms do not have sharp edges. Different atoms scatter the X-rays differently according to their atomic weights and this can partially be represented by different sizes of holes or better still, by the same size of hole with different transmissions. This difference in transmission is often accomplished by the use of fine gauze placed across the hole. The resulting diffraction by a single hole has already been illustrated in Fig. 2.2. When representations of molecules and unit cells are studied, the region of interest in the diffraction pattern is usually contained within the central maximum of the diffraction pattern of a single hole. For an illustration here, we will use a hypothetical molecule that consists of six atoms in the arrangement shown in Fig. 2.12 [2.12]. The intensity distribution associated with the diffraction pattern of this hypothetical molecule is shown in Fig. 2.12a. The phase associated with the transform of this molecule is not readily apparent since it is continuously varying. Figure 2.12b shows the phase contours at 10° intervals that are associated with this complex amplitude distribution of the hypothetical molecule [2.12]. If two such molecules are located about a center of symmetry, the resulting intensity distribution in the diffraction pattern is that illustrated in Fig. 2.12c. When two pairs of such arrangements are used, a clear fringing function is added (Fig. 2.12d). A representation of the X-ray diffraction data from an actual crystal can be simulated by adding more and more pairs of molecules in a symmetric array (Figs. 2.12e and 2.12f). In Fig. 2.12f the diffracting mask is illustrated on a reduced scale; however, the diffraction pattern is, of course, on the same scale as the other photographs in this series. The diffraction pattern of Fig. 2.12f would bear a very close resemblance to the X-ray diffraction data put onto a weighted reciprocal lattice. These results can be interpreted directly from a knowledge of the array theorem discussed earlier.

A particularly important structure is the arrangement of six atoms that form the so-called benzene ring (the six atoms lie on a circle for a plane molecule). Such ring structures (not necessarily benzene) occur in many organic materials and their transforms are readily identified even when not planar and are often used as the basis for the first attempt at structure determination. Figure 2.13 shows the optical transform of a plane benzene ring. It will be immediately noticed that the six atoms in this ring are at the corners of a regular hexagon; characteristic maxima are seen in the transform that also lie on a regular hexagon. This hexagonal arrangement of maxima is related to the hexagonal arrangement of atoms in the ring, and a reciprocal relationship manifests itself in this case by a simple rotation of the hexagon through 90°.

We may now refer to earlier figures. In Fig. 2.9b, the optical transform of a representation of a molecule of hexamethylbenzene was shown. The characteristic benzene ring structure is again readily visible as is the outer ring structure in the molecule which produces the inner hexagon of spots in the transform. The reciprocal relationship is even more noticeable now since the benzene ring in the molecule is not planar but is slightly elongated vertically. In the transform the

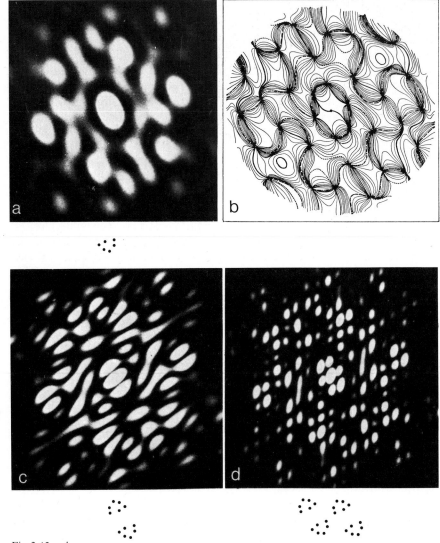

Fig. 2.12 a–d

Fig. 2.12a–f. Optical analog to diffraction by a hypothetical substance; (a) diffraction pattern of a single molecule; (b) calculated phase associated with (a). Each line is a phase contour and the intervals are 10°, 0°——, 90°– – –, 180°– – –, 270°– – –; (c) pattern associated with two molecules related by a center of symmetry; (d) two pairs of molecules; (e) four pairs of molecules; (f) many pairs of molecules (after *Lipson* and *Taylor* [2.12])

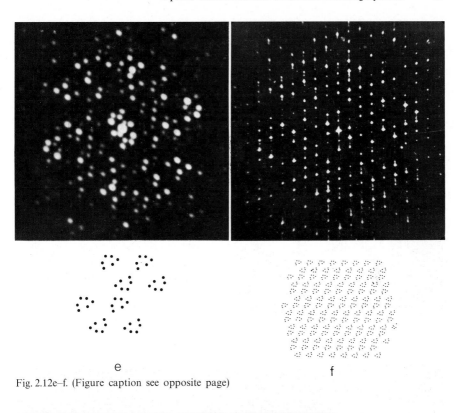

e   f

Fig. 2.12e–f. (Figure caption see opposite page)

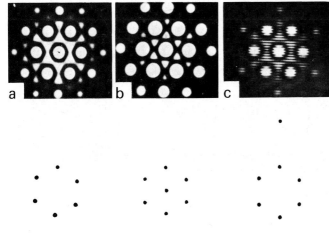

Fig. 2.13a–c. (a) Diffraction patterns of a planar molecule of benzene; (b) the pattern of the same molecule with an additional hole at the center; (c) the pattern of the same molecule with the addition of a pair of widely spaced holes (after *Taylor* and *Lipson* [2.13])

hexagonal array of peaks is elongated in the horizontal direction. Finally, Fig. 2.8 illustrates the transform of di-p-anisyl nitric oxide which again contains the characteristic ring structure. Space is limited here but the reader is referred to the recent volume by *Harburn* et al. [2.15] which contains a beautiful and instructive set of optical transforms that start from simple arrangements of atoms to relatively complicated structures such as the circular and spiral lattices associated with fibrous minerals like chrysotile and to partially ordered structures. An earlier volume [2.13] also contains an excellent set of illustrative plates.

2.5.1 Amplitude and Phase of Transforms

When a transform is produced optically and recorded, only the amplitude information is retained. In general, transforms are, of course, complex and to obtain the complete transform the phase must also be determined. It is worth noting that if the diffracting object has a center of symmetry, the transform is a real function and hence the only values of phase allowed are 0 and π. Furthermore, the phase changes when the intensity goes through its zero values; lines of zeroes of intensity are continuous functions in the transform. A simple example was shown in Fig. 2.2; the transform of a circular aperture changes phase in each ring. A similar result is apparent in the photographs of the diffraction patterns of the rectangular apertures of Figs. 2.3a and b. In structures which contain a heavy atom which dominates the scattering, the phase may be essentially constant, i.e., the interesting part of the transform is real and positive. In more complicated centrosymmetric structures the same results are still true. Here we may choose the benzene transform as an example; the phase can be followed from peak to peak through the photograph (Fig. 2.13a) with the phase changing as we pass through the zero intensity points. Figure 2.12c shows another example of an input function with a center of symmetry, and, again, the simple phase relationship exists. It does, of course, get more difficult to keep track of the phase changes as the pattern gets more complicated.

By comparison, when the input function does not have a center of symmetry, there are only point zeroes of intensity and the phase is continuously variable throughout the pattern. An excellent example of this result is seen in the transforms of the triangular apertures of Fig. 2.3. A more specific example is contained in Figs. 2.12a and b; since the input function does not have a center of symmetry, the phase part of the transform is not interpretable from Fig. 2.12a. Figure 2.12b indicates the contour lines of equal phase; the phase contours all passed through the points of zero intensity. The contour lines were drawn at $10°$ intervals with the contour lines for $0°$, $90°$, $180°$, and $270°$ indicated by separate symbols given in the figure caption.

Some interesting techniques have been developed for so-called sign determination of the transforms. In today's scientific environment one might immediately suggest making a hologram of the transform, i.e., a Fourier transform hologram. Before holography was a well-known technique, a method was developed which could be considered as a hologram although it was not considered in that context (see, e.g., [2.13]). In fact, it was an important part of the idea to produce a transform such that the phase could be directly inferred from the intensity pattern. The idea consisted of adding an additional hole at the center of the mask representing the molecule of interest. The contribution in the transform plane from the extra hole is to add a constant across the transform of the molecule. Since the constant is added coherently, its contribution must be added in amplitude and phase to the existing Fourier transform; thus the intensity of the original optical transform will be modified. A comparison of the optical transforms with and without the extra hole provides a method of determining the sign of the phase of the peaks in the original intensity distribution.

Figures 2.13a and b are such a pair of patterns; Fig. 2.13a is the transform of a plane benzene ring and Fig. 2.13b the same benzene ring with an additional hole at the center. Since in this simple example there are only two values of phase to be concerned with, it is necessary only to determine whether a given region of intensity has increased or decreased. If the intensity is increased, then that region is in phase with the additional contribution; on the other hand, if the intensity is decreased, then that region is out-of-phase with the additional contribution. Naturally, if the molecule consists of a large number of holes, the contribution from the additional one at the center is too small; hence the transmission of the holes associated with the atoms in the molecule must be reduced in comparison with the additional hole. In present-day terminology, the intensity distribution resulting from the addition of the extra hole is a Fourier transform hologram of the "molecule", but, of course, is not used as a hologram in this example.

A second related method is illustrated in Fig. 2.13c. In this technique a pair of extra holes are added well separated from the arrangement of holes representing the molecule. A set of fringes is then coherently added to the transform, and the relative location of those fringes allows the relative phase to be estimated. The simple example in Fig. 2.13c is again the planar benzene ring; the two values of phase are easily determined by following each fringe horizontally through the photograph.

2.5.2 Real and Imaginary Parts of Transforms

Since the Fourier transform is complex, an equally valid pair of functions that can be displayed is the real and imaginary part of the transform. This has been well illustrated in the literature (see, e.g., [2.13]). An example of the production of the real part of a transform is illustrated in an earlier figure. The optical transform in Fig. 2.12c is actually the real part of the Fourier transform associated with Fig. 2.12a. This was produced by taking the input distribution and putting the same distribution down again reflected through a center of symmetry that is outside the function. The imaginary part of this same transform can also be displayed by taking the diffracting mask of Fig. 2.12c and changing the phase of one of the molecules with respect to the other. While the result is quite interesting, it has not attracted much attention and hence is not being applied to specific problems.

2.5.3 Systems Used for Producing Optical Transforms

Diffraction pattern analysis has proved to be extremely useful over the years in a wide variety of fields; this usefulness continues today. Researchers in optical analogues to X-ray diffraction have developed their own special instrumentation which deserves some comments, since many of the design features are of considerable general value. The basic idea of using optical diffraction as an analogy to X-ray diffraction was first suggested by *Bragg* (1939) and an apparatus was put together by Crowe at the Cavendish Laboratory. *Bragg*'s idea was, at this point in time, to produce by diffraction an "image" of the molecule. (This Fourier synthesis technique will be discussed in more detail later.) *Bragg* realized, of course, that he now had a powerful optical analog computer available to him. The relationship between the optical transform and the Fourier transform was first pointed out for use in crystallography by *Ewald* [2.31] and by *Knott* [2.32]. The optical diffractometer was perfected by *Lipson* and his coworkers at the University of Manchester during the period 1951–60.

The fundamental system is shown in Fig. 2.14a. The primary light source, S_0, is a high pressure mercury arc source that had one of its hot spots imaged onto a small pinhole at S_1 by the condenser lens L_0. A filter is used to select one of the

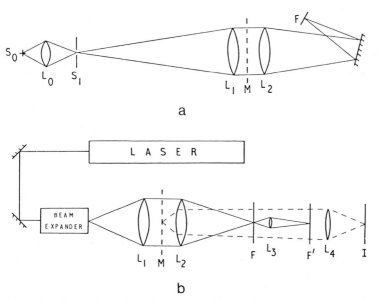

Fig. 2.14a and b. (a) The optical diffractometer; (b) the optical diffractometer with a laser light source (after *Harburn* et al. [2.15])

spectral lines in the output of the mercury arc, e.g., the yellow line at 579 nm or the green line at 546 nm. The pinhole at S_1 acts as the effective incoherent source for the system and is usually from 5 to 200 microns in diameter. This source is placed in the rear focal plane of lens L_1 which is a long focal length lens (~ 1.5 m). Thus, collimated illumination is used to illuminate the diffracting mask M placed in the intermediate plane between the lenses, each of which has an aperture of approximately 6 inches in diameter. The second lens L_2, of essentially the same focal length as lens L_1, produces the required optical transform in plane F. A mirror at 45° is a useful part of the system since it allows the optical transform to be produced in such a plane that it is convenient for the operator to be able to insert the mask and view the transform through a microscope at the same time. Considerable work has been carried out to optimize this system. The coherence conditions have been carefully studied and reported upon [2.21, 33] and an excellent alignment procedure developed [2.33]. In addition, useful focusing methods have been developed as discussed in an earlier section [2.18]. These systems were developed before the design of special-purpose Fourier transform lenses—and hence existing components—were used. Doublets designed for telescope objectives proved to be a useful choice. Figure 2.14a is illustrated here horizontally, whereas the actual device was usually used in a vertical arrangement.

It must be remembered that these systems were developed before the laser was invented. Now that the laser is readily available, the system has been redesigned by *Taylor* and his colleagues at the University College, Cardiff, and their system is shown in Fig. 2.14b [2.34]. Light from a 50 mW He–Ne laser is expanded to fill the lens aperture L_1. The Fourier transform of the mask M is produced by lens L_2 at F and can be magnified before recording using lens L_3. Lens L_4 is used to form an image of the input function so that it can be viewed while in position. More importantly, the system may be used for optical processing by placing the filter at either F or F'; the processed image then appears at I.

2.6 Optical Fourier Synthesis

Optical diffraction methods have proved to be quite important in X-ray crystallography, particularly for producing the diffraction patterns of suggested arrangements of atoms in a particular structure. A large number of ideas can be tried out in a very short space of time, and real insight into the problem can be obtained. Many devices have been designed for this purpose, the most well known ones being those discussed in the previous section. As indicated earlier, *Bragg*'s original technique was for producing images; however, he rapidly extended the idea to the simplest diffraction method that is variously called a multiple pinhole camera or fly's eye camera. The arrangement of atoms of interest is put down on a very small scale and then many such units repeated.

This multiple diffracting mask is then illuminated and the required diffraction pattern produced by propagation.

It is important to return to *Bragg*'s original idea of Fourier synthesis—synthesizing an image of the molecule from the appropriate set of fringe patterns. This method has been refined considerably but has not received any extensive use. Nevertheless it is extremely interesting and is currently under closer scrutiny using holographic techniques [2.35]. Hence it will not be appropriate to go into extensive detail here; an excellent review paper is available in the literature [2.36].

2.6.1 Amplitude and Phase Control

If the X-ray diffraction information is to be used to produce an image optically, the appropriate diffracting mask must be fabricated. Data from an actual crystalline material is highly localized in that it consists of a series of discrete spots of various amplitudes and phases. For example, Fig. 2.12f shows the optical diffraction pattern of a two-dimensional array of groups of molecules associated with a hypothetical structure. The X-ray diffraction data would be essentially this same information. Naturally, once the radiation is detected, the phase information is lost.

For the moment let us consider that all the spots are in phase. If a mask is now made with an array of holes in the same positions as the spots in the diffraction pattern and the holes are made of various sizes in proportion to the amplitude of the diffraction spots, then the mask can be illuminated coherently and the resulting Fourier transform is an image of the original molecules making up that projection of the crystal. We will consider an example of this particular situation in the next section (Sect. 2.6.2). There is a problem with representing the amplitude of the diffracted X-ray spots by varying sizes of holes since the diffraction patterns of the holes do not overlap; the central maximum associated with the diffraction pattern of the larger holes is much smaller than that associated with the smaller hole. Annular apertures for the holes have been suggested to partially overcome the problem.

Continuous amplitude control can be accomplished by using holes of the same size covered with small mica half-wave plates that are placed between crossed polarizers. The mica plate is then rotated to the appropriate angle to produce the required amplitude.

A third method is to use holes of all the same size and vary their transmission by means of fine gauze placed over each hole. Gauze of standard transmission can be produced by etching techniques and then used appropriately.

To attack the problem of Fourier synthesis in a more general way requires that the phase of the light passing through the holes also be controlled. Structures that produce X-ray diffraction patterns that are real and positive are rare; however, structures that produce X-ray diffraction patterns that are real are less rare. We have seen examples of such centrosymmetric structures earlier.

The relative phases of the various peaks now have values only of either 0 or π. *Bragg* suggested a method to achieve this phase control in 1942 [2.37] using half-wave mica plates. The hole requiring the π phase shifts have the mica plates oriented at right angles to those covering the 0 phase holes. Tilted mica plates have also been suggested to achieve a similar result. The mica plates used in plane polarized light described earlier for amplitude control can also produce phases of 0 and π.

For the most general case it is necessary to produce all values of phase. A versatile method for this purpose has been described [2.38]. Half-wave plates of mica are again used but this time in a beam of circularly polarized light; as the orientation of the half-wave plate is changed, the phase can be varied continuously from 0 to 2π.

2.6.2 Examples of Fourier Synthesis

Perhaps the earliest general example of Fourier synthesis was the experiment conducted by *Michelson* and reported on in his book in 1927 [2.9]. This experiment consisted of recording the intensity distribution in the Fraunhofer diffraction pattern of a slit and then making a phase element to add the necessary π phase shift to the alternate peaks of the diffraction pattern. The phase function was used together with the recorded diffraction pattern so that they could be illuminated coherently to produce the transform. This transform is an image of the slit.

Bragg's original illustration of optical Fourier synthesis was carried out using diopside, $CaMg(SiO_3)_2$. The atoms of calcium and magnesium overlap in the (010) projection, thus simulating the effect of a heavy atom and dominating the diffracted X-ray pattern. Thus there is no phase needed for the synthesis; relative amplitudes were obtained by varying the hole size. A more sophisticated result was obtained [2.39] for the molecule of nickel phthalocyanine. Again phases are all constant because of the presence of the heavy atom, nickel. Figure 2.15a shows the representation of the X-ray diffraction data (weighted reciprocal-lattice section) with the hole size controlling the amplitude. The image resulting from forming the optical transform of Fig. 2.15a is shown in Fig. 2.15b and is a fairly good representation of the phthalocyanine molecule shown for comparison in Fig. 2.15c.

An excellent example for a centrosymmetric structure is the optical synthesis of hexamethylbenzene [2.40]. The amplitude and phase of the holes in the mask were adjusted by the use of half-wave plates of mica in plane-polarized light. In practice, in this example the mica plates were rotated to examine all the possible combinations of phase. Figure 2.16a shows the result when the correct value of the phases had been obtained.

Finally, Fig. 2.16b illustrates the result obtained [2.41] for the non-centrosymmetric projection of sodium nitrite. In this example the required amplitudes were obtained by the use of gauze, and half-wave mica plates in circularly polarized light provided the relative phases.

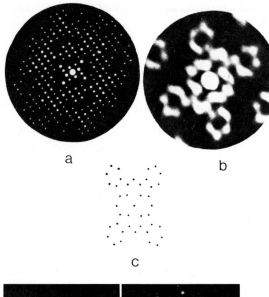

a   b

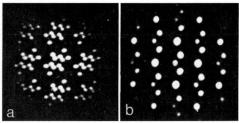

c

Fig. 2.15a–c. Optical Fourier synthesis of nickel phthalocyanine: (a) diffracting mask representing X-ray data; (b) image of molecule formed from (a); (c) arrangement of atoms in this projection of the molecule (after *Harburn* [2.36])

Fig. 2.16a and b. (a) Optical Fourier synthesis of the centrosymmetric molecule of hexamethylbenzene [2.40]; (b) optical Fourier synthesis of the non-centrosymmetric molecule of sodium nitrite $NaNO_2$ (after *Harburn* and *Taylor* [2.41])

a   b

   All these methods result in projections of the structure rather than a three-dimensional reconstruction. At a recent meeting, *Stroke* [2.42] reported briefly on some new results that apparently do produce three-dimensional information. A series of projections in the Fourier domain are recorded as holograms which are in turn used to produce a reconstructed real space structure. The details of this work are still in press [2.35] so no further details can be presented here.

2.7 Optical Processing Systems

The properties of optical processing systems are essentially determined by the initial diffraction process. The Fourier transform of the input function is then modified by the use of a filter which changes the relative amplitudes and/or phases of the Fourier transform. The resulting complex amplitude distribution is then retransformed to produce an image. The requirements of the second Fourier transform system are identical to those of the system which produced the original transform. The ratio of the focal length of the two transform lenses determines the magnification of the image. Discussions of this overall system are contained elsewhere in this volume, as are details of the types of filter and their fabrication. For the purposes of this chapter we will restrict our attention to applications that relate to the area of optical analogs to X-ray diffraction.

2.7.1 Optical Processing Methods in Crystallography

The optical systems used for optical analogs to X-ray diffraction were described in an earlier section and are illustrated in Fig. 2.14. The system, shown in Fig. 2.14a was modified by placing a lens after the Fourier plane so that an image of the diffracting object could be formed [2.14]. Optical processing was then performed by modifying the Fourier transform. The initial work was to illustrate many of the concepts of resolving power and to demonstrate the principle of the Abbe theory of vision in a microscope. In subsequent work the idea was extended so that the specific components that contribute to the diffraction pattern of a mask representing a molecule could be studied [2.44].

An instructive example that is worth illustrating here is the effect of series termination errors in the calculation of the electron density contour map of the molecular arrangement from the diffraction data. This is illustrated by using the [110] projection of the molecule of bishydroxydurylmethane, a structure determined by *Chaudhuri* and *Hargreaves* [2.45]. The diffracting object for the optical experiment was a representation of the [110] projection consisting of 28 molecules on a scale of 1 cm = 0.1 nm and as in earlier discussions, the atoms are represented by circular holes 0.5 mm in diameter. Figure 2.17 shows the mask of these 28 molecules. The Fourier transform of this distribution is produced and then truncated with a series of circular aperture functions. As is well known, when a spectrum (or Fourier series) is limited, spurious effects can result in the image produced from that limited spectrum.

Figure 2.18 illustrates the effect of truncating the Fourier transform and forming an image from the remaining information [2.13, 21, 46]. Figure 2.18Ia shows resulting optical transform produced by the mask of Fig. 2.17; the portion shown is limited to that contained within the central maximum of the diffraction

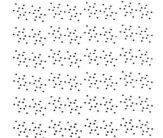

Fig. 2.17. Arrangement of holes representing 28 molecules of the [110] projection of bishydrozydurylmethane

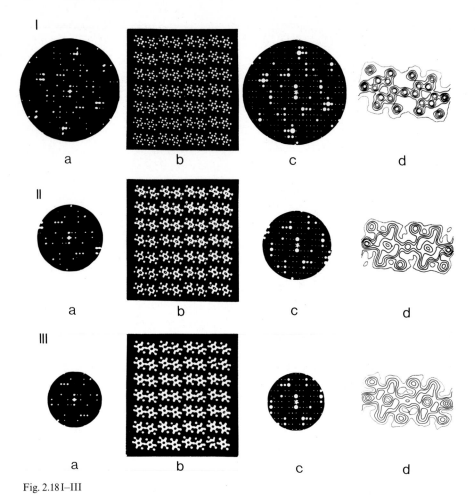

Fig. 2.18 I–III

Fig. 2.18a–d. Illustration of series termination errors. In each section of the figures I–VI (a) is a photograph of the portion of the transform used to produce the image seen in (b); (c) is that portion of the weighted reciprocal lattice information used to calculate the electron density map (d)

of an individual hole. When the amount of the transform is limited in this way, the image is still quite acceptable but the edges of the individual holes are not sharp (Fig. 2.18Ib). For comparison, Fig. 2.18Ic represents the equivalent portion of the X-ray diffraction data put in the form of a weighted reciprocal lattice with the size of the spot indicating the intensity of the diffracted X-rays at that point. Figure 2.18Ic should be compared to Fig. 2.18Ia, and they are seen to be very similar. The X-ray data shown in Fig. 2.18Ic is used to calculate an electron density map of the molecule and the result is shown in Fig. 2.18Id. Naturally the phase information associated with the X-ray intensities must be

IV

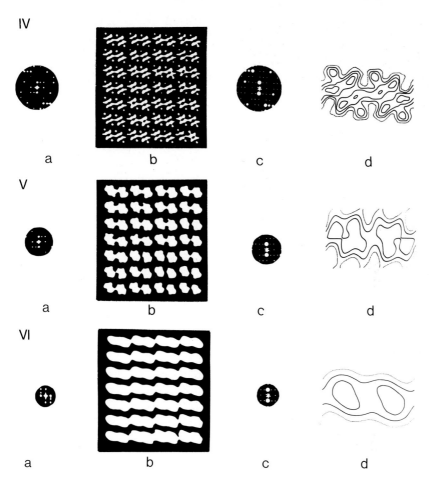

    a   b   c   d

Fig. 2.18IV–VI. (Figure caption see opposite page)

used for this calculation and the values used were those determined by *Chaudhuri* and *Hargreaves* [2.45]. (This particular calculation was carried out by *Morley* [2.47] for the purposes of illustration). By comparison, the phase information associated with the optical process is retained in the complex amplitudes of the diffraction pattern and is propagated onto the image plane. In the subsequent sections of this same figure, (a) is the amount of the optical transform used to produce the image shown in (b) and the equivalent calculation is shown in (d) for the same amount of X-ray data. Spurious effects are apparent as the resolution of the image is decreased and the atomic positions become less well defined. It will be noticed that the spurious information is usually associated with negative peaks in the electron density map. Some related optical results with this same molecule are presented by *Harburn* et al. [2.15].

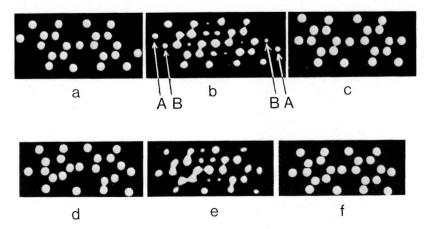

Fig. 2.19a–f. Optical processing by filtering with a function representing the X-ray intensities: (a) a mask representing a molecule of bishydroxydurylmethane with two atoms misplaced; (b) image of mask (a) produced after filtering; (c) revised position of atoms from (b); (d) a mask representing a molecule of bishydroxydurylmethane with all atoms slightly misplaced; (e) image of mask (d) after filtering; (f) revised position of atoms from (e)

A further interesting illustration of optical processing uses the same molecule of bishydroxydurylmethane [2.13, 23, 45]. A diffracting mask was made with two of the atoms displaced from their true positions (Fig. 2.19a). The Fourier transform of this mask is filtered with a function representing the weighted reciprocal lattice. This filter was produced by etching the distribution seen in Fig. 2.18c in copper foil using a photoresist technique. Thus the amplitudes of the transform are somewhat controlled by the filter and the phases are those produced by the diffraction pattern of the input mask. Naturally the peaks in the transform can only be reduced by the filter function; they cannot be increased. Admittedly this is a simple experiment, but it does produce interesting results. The image of the atoms which were incorrectly positioned shows much lower intensities (A), and a strong peak occurs at the correct location of that particular atom (B) (Fig. 2.19b). A new arrangement of the atomic positions can thus be prepared which is a better approximation than the original (Fig. 2.19c). A second example uses a mask with all the atoms slightly misplaced (Fig. 2.19d); the processed image is shown in Fig. 2.19c, and the corrected arrangement of atoms is illustrated in Fig. 2.19f.

2.8 Conclusions

This particular chapter is probably somewhat unusual because its purpose is a little different than some of the other contributions. We are not looking at how optical methods are being used to solve problems in a particular field even though there is a continued activity in the area of optical analogs to X-ray diffraction. The thesis has really been that there have been interesting pieces of work carried out by researchers actively engaged in optical analog techniques that can provide considerable insight to those working in the various aspects of diffraction and optical processing. I trust that this proves to be true.

References

2.1 R.W.Ditchburn: *Light* (Academic Press, New York 1976) p. 190
2.2 J.T.Thomasson, T.J.Middelton, N.Jensen: SPIE Proc. Coherent Optics in Mapping **45**, 257 (1974)
2.3 G.G.Lendaris, G.L.Stanley: Proc. IEEE **58**, 198 (1970)
2.4 A.L.Wertheimer, W.L.Wilcock: Appl. Opt. **15**, 1616 (1976)
2.5 N.George, H.L.Kasdan: International Optical Computing Conference, Digest of paper, IEEE **120** (1976)
2.6 A.Topler: Pogg. Ann. Phys. Chem. **127**, 556 (1866)
2.7 E.Abbe: Arch. Mikrosk. Anat. **9**, 413 (1873)
2.8 A.B.Porter: Phil. Mag. **11**, 154 (1906)
2.9 A.A.Michelson: *Studies in Optics* (Univ. of Chicago Press, Chicago, Illinois 1927) p. 60
2.10 F.Zernike: Z. Tech. Phys. **16**, 454 (1935)
2.11 A.Maréchal, P.Croce: Compt. Rend. **237**, 706 (1953)
2.12 H.Lipson, C.A.Taylor: *Fourier Transforms and X-Ray Diffraction* (G. Bell and Sons Ltd., London 1958)
2.13 C.A.Taylor, H.Lipson: *Optical Transforms, Their Preparation and Application to X-Ray Diffraction* (G. Bell and Sons Ltd., London 1964)
2.14 H.S.Lipson (ed.): *Optical Transforms* (Academic Press, London 1972)
2.15 G.Harburn, C.A.Taylor, T.R.Welberry: *Atlas of Optical Transforms* (Cornell University Press, Ithaca, New York 1975)
2.16 M.E.Krisl: In preparation (1977)
2.17 D.Warren, M.S.: Thesis (University of Rochester 1977)
2.18 C.A.Taylor, B.J.Thompson: J. Sci. Instrum. **35**, 294 (1958)
2.19 M.Born, E.Wolf: *Principles of Optics* (Pergamon Press, New York 1969)
2.20 C.A.Taylor, B.J.Thompson: J. Opt. Soc. Am. **48**, 844 (1958)
2.21 B.J.Thompson: *Optical Transforms*, ed. by H. Lipson (Academic Press, New York 1972) Chapts. 2 and 8, pp. 27—68, 267—295
2.22 B.J.Thompson: J. Opt. Soc. Am. **56**, 1167 (1966)
2.23 B.J.Thompson: *Optical Information Processing*, ed. by Yu E. Nesterikhin, G.W.Stroke, and W.E.Koch (Plenum Press, New York 1976) p. 313
2.24 G.B.Parrent, B.J.Thompson: J. Soc. Photo-Opt. Instr. Eng. **5**, 74 (1966)
2.25 S.Lowenthal, A.Wertz, M.Rembault: C. R. Acad. Sci. **267**, 120 (1968)
2.26 G.Groh: Appl. Opt. **7**, 1643 (1968)
2.27 G.Groh: Appl. Opt. **8**, 967 (1969)
2.28 R.P.Grosso, S.J.Kishner, R.M.Vesper: *Applications of Lasers to Photography and Information Handling*, ed. by R. Murray (SPSE, Washington, DC 1968) p. 131
2.29 S.Lu: Proc. IEEE **56**, 116 (1968)
2.30 W.L.Bragg: Nature **143**, 678 (1939)
2.31 P.P.Ewald: Proc. Phys. Soc. **52**, 167 (1940)
2.32 G.Knott: Proc. Phys. Soc. **52**, 227 (1940)
2.33 C.A.Taylor, B.J.Thompson: J. Sci. Instrum. **34**, 439 (1957)
2.34 G.Harburn, J.K.Ranniko: J.Phys. E: Sci. Instrum. **5**, 757 (1972)

2.35 G.W.Stroke, M.Halioua: Trans. Amer. Cryst. Assoc. **12**, 27—41 (1976)
2.36 G.Harburn: *Optical Transforms*, ed. by H.S.Lipson (Academic Press, New York 1972) Chap. 6, p. 189
2.37 W.L.Bragg: Nature **149**, 470 (1942)
2.38 G.Harburn, C.A.Taylor: Proc. R. Soc. **204**, 339 (1961)
2.39 B.D.Dunkerley, H.Lipson: Nature **176**, 81 (1955)
2.40 A.W.Hanson, H.Lipson: Acta Cryst. **5**, 362 (1952)
2.41 G.Harburn, C.A.Taylor: Nature **194**, 764 (1962)
2.42 G.W.Stroke: International Optical Computing Conference, Capri, Italy, August 31– September 2. Digest of Papers, IEEE, p. 4
2.43 A.W.Hanson, H.Lipson: Acta Cryst. **5**, 362 (1952)
2.44 H.Lipson, B.J.Thompson: Bull. Nat. Inst. Sci. India **14**, p. 80 (1959)
2.45 B.Chaudhuri, A.Hargreaves: Acta Cryst. **9**, 793 (1956)
2.46 B.J.Thompson: Ph. D. Thesis (University of Manchester 1959)
2.47 K.Morley: Private communication (1958)

3. Optical Image Enhancement and Image Restoration

P. S. Considine and R. A. Gonsalves

With 27 Figures

Overview

Supported by a firm mathematical basis and by a potential for very large information processing capacity, optical processing remains a subject receiving justified impetus. On this basis we have organized this chapter to review the fundamental considerations supporting optical processing and have surveyed the technology to demonstrate techniques and examples with the objective to help define valid applications areas. As in any technology the question of best method must be defined with options for optical, digital, or hybrid methods [3.1]. Imaging operations are inherently optical. Some processing operations can be performed either by optical or digital means. In other cases only digital methods provide the accuracy and flexibility required in image processing. Our goal is to provide a kernal to aid others in continuing their investigations of optical processing in order to help determine its role in image processing technology.

3.1 Preliminary Information

Two mathematical operations that can be performed in an optical processor are multiplication and Fourier transformation. These provide the basis for spatial filtering of a given scene or the cross-correlation of two scenes [3.2].

The main justification for optical image processing is the joint and simultaneous capability of imaging and information processing. A well-corrected optical system can resolve $100 \, \text{cy} \, \text{mm}^{-1}$ input information over a flat field of more than $2 \, \text{cm}^2$ and readily maintain a resolved amplitude of 6 bits. With six bits/sample and two samples/cycle this yields a (conservative) throughput of $4.8 \cdot 10^7$ bits for instantaneous implementation of Fourier transformation, multiplication with an appropriate filter and inverse Fourier transformation. The relevance of this data throughput is great if the data input-output capability does not limit the process. The optical capability for data throughput far exceeds capabilities of present digital processors.

Optical processing of imagery is one applications area where this large space-bandwidth capability is required. Image processing is performed with many optical system designs, including partially coherent or coherent systems. Both complex and real optical filtering operations can be performed. Imaging with concommitant image processing can be realized by classical Gaussian imaging optics or by holographic recording and reconstruction techniques [3.3].

In the following sections we give a simple model for the observed image, present optimal techniques for filtering and detection, give the theory of operation of optical processors, examine typical design principles, and present some applications and examples.

3.2 Simple Model for the Observed Image

Objects and images are observed to have both spatial and temporal variations. For example, an elementary object which is small and harmonic can be represented by

$$f(x, t) = \delta(x) \cos(\omega t + \theta). \tag{3.1}$$

Here the delta function indicates a point object in the plane. (We use one-dimensional objects and images for simplicity of notation and without loss of generality, except as noted). The temporal variation indicates that the object has only one color of wavelength λ,

$$\lambda = 2\pi c/\omega, \tag{3.2}$$

where c is the velocity of light.

Any complete treatment of an imaging system must consider this interaction of space and time. However, if the object is small, if its temporal bandwidth is small (a monochromatic object), and if the temporal variations are independent from point to point on the object, the problem is greatly simplified. The observables will be the intensities of the object and image, averaged over a time interval which is long compared with the temporal variations. If we call these $i(x)$ and $o(x)$ for input and output, respectively, of the optical system, in the absence of noise they will be approximately related by

$$o(x) = \int_{-\infty}^{\infty} i(\sigma)p(x - \sigma)d\sigma, \tag{3.3}$$

where $p(x)$ is the point spread function of the optical system. In shorthand notation for the convolution integral, we write

$$o(x) = i(x) * p(x). \tag{3.4}$$

With the convolution theorem we can write the equivalent expression in the spatial frequency domain,

$$O(f) = I(f)P(f), \tag{3.5}$$

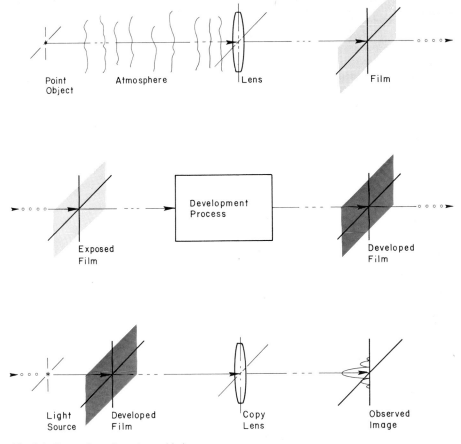

Fig. 3.1. Generation of an observable image

where $P(f)$ is the optical transfer function. (Capital letters will be used throughout this text to denote the Fourier transform of the corresponding lower case variables). The OTF plays a major role in characterizing an incoherent imaging system and includes all lens aberrations that may degrade the object function.

To demonstrate the utility of the model let us consider an optical system that consists of the atmosphere, an imaging lens, a piece of film, a development process, and a projection system for viewing the film (Fig. 3.1).

The atmosphere introduces attenuation and random phase perturbations of the wavefront. This causes an otherwise perfect imaging system to record a distant object as a blurred image that both wanders over the film plane and changes its shape as it wanders. The effect can be modeled by considering a "frozen" atmosphere which introduces distortions $H_a(f)$ into the pupil function of the imaging lens. If the lens distortions are represented by $H_1(f)$, the image recorded on film is distorted by an OTF which is the autocorrelation of the product $H_a(f)H_1(f)$.

The interaction between the atmosphere and lens is complex and beyond the scope of the present treatment. However, for our purposes we can assume that this part of the system is adequately characterized by an OTF which is an average over the states of the atmosphere during the time the image was recorded. In particular, if the atmosphere introduces only phase distortions and these are a realization of a stationary (in f) Gaussian random process $\theta(f)$, then the average OTF becomes a product of an atmospheric OTF, $P_A(f)$, and the lens OTF, $P_L(f)$. The former is

$$P_A(f) = \exp\{-2[R_\theta(0) - R_\theta(f)]\}, \tag{3.6}$$

where $R_\theta(f)$ is the autocorrelation function of $\theta(f)$.

Further distortions may be introduced by relative motion between the object and the film planes, commonly called image motion. Let the spatial motion be a realization $a(t)$ of a random process. An otherwise perfect system will record an image

$$i(x) = \frac{1}{T_1} \int_0^{T_1} o[x - a(t)]dt, \tag{3.7}$$

where T_1 is the exposure time. The Fourier transform is

$$I(f) = O(f)M(f), \tag{3.8}$$

where $M(f)$ is the motion transfer function,

$$M(f) = \frac{1}{T_1} \int_0^{T_1} \exp[-j2\pi f a(t)]dt. \tag{3.9}$$

When the motion is linear, $M(f)$ reduces to a $(\sin f)/f$ function. When the motion is rapid compared with T_1 and is stationary (in t), (3.9) becomes

$$M(f) = \int_{-\infty}^{\infty} P_a(a)\exp(-j2\pi f a)da \tag{3.10}$$

where $P_a(a)$ is the (first order) probability density function of $a(t)$, and $M(f)$ is also known as the characteristic function of the random variable "a".

So far, the system OTF will be the product of three frequency functions $P_A(f)$, $P_L(f)$, and $M(f)$.

As the image is recorded on film it undergoes an optical spreading $h_F(x)$, which is characteristic of the film. The image is recorded by the exposure and subsequent development of randomly placed density "sites". This causes the

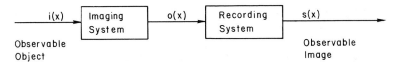

Fig. 3.2. Model for the observed image

developed density signal to be a sequence of randomly spaced pulses, with the arrival rate nonlinearly related to the noiseless effective exposure. It is usually possible to select the parameters of the development process such that the final transmission is proportional to the effective exposure over a limited range of exposure. (In some cases this may not be desirable, and we can use the nonlinearity to advantage, as we shall show later).

In the projection system the film density is translated into a transmission function, the final observable. All of the above processes are well known and can be adequately modeled.

Thus, the overall OTF will be

$$P(f) = P_A(f)P_L(f)M(f)P_F(f). \tag{3.11}$$

To complete our simple model for the observed image we consider noise—the fundamental limitation in the enhancement and restoration of an image. For most purposes we can assume that the noise is additive and is a realization of a stationary, random process with power spectral density $\Phi_n(f)$. Thus the observed image is

$$s(x) = i(x) * p(x) + n(x). \tag{3.12}$$

A block diagram of this simple model is shown in Fig. 3.2. The residual signal between $s(x)$ and $i(x)*p(x)$, the noise, is usually signal dependent. Theoretically one can benefit from this dependence, but the benefit is extracted by resorting to iterative, nonlinear techniques which are not well suited to optical processing techniques as they are now known. Thus, it suffices to assume that the noise is independent of the signal or at least to ascribe to $p(x)*i(x)$ that portion of $s(x)$ which is signal-correlated and to ascribe to noise, that which is uncorrelated with the signal.

3.3 Principles of Optical Filtering, Detection, and Estimation

In this section, we present some theoretical results on the filtering of optical scenes. We are especially interested in the interplay between amplitude and phase filtering in the presence of noise.

3.3.1 Optical Filtering

Let $p(x)$ be the point spread function associated with a given system. If the input is $i(x)$, the noiseless output $o(x)$ is given by (3.4).

To restore the scene in the absence of noise, one should divide the observed spectrum $O(f)$ by $P(f)$, and then inverse transform the result to get $i(x)$. This procedure may be inconvenient if $P(f)$ is complex. It is usually disastrous if the image is very noisy.

To describe the general problem we consider that $S(f)$, the noisy observable, is multiplied by a filter function $H(f)$ to give $\hat{I}(f)$, an estimate for $I(f)$. This filtering process is described by

$$\hat{I}(f) = S(f) \cdot H(f). \tag{3.13}$$

In the spatial domain the error signal $e(x)$ is

$$e(x) = \hat{i}(x) - i(x). \tag{3.14}$$

A system block diagram showing calculation of the error signal is shown in Fig. 3.3. The system includes an additive noise term $n(x)$.

We want to study the selection of the filter function $H(f)$ with and without constraints. To identify these constraints, we consider that $H(f)$ is the product

$$H(f) = A(f) \exp[j\theta(f)] \tag{3.15}$$

where $A(f)$ is a positive real function called the amplitude filter and where $\theta(f)$ is a real function such that $\exp[j\theta(f)]$ is called the phase filter. Specifically we consider four cases:

a) *Unconstrained Filter*

b) *Phase Filter.* Here $A(f)$ is fixed and $\theta(f)$ is optimally chosen.

c) *Amplitude Filter.* Here we require $\theta(f) = 0$ and $H(f)$ must be both real and non-negative. $A(f)$ is optimally chosen.

d) *Amplitude and Simple Phase Filter.* $\theta(f)$ is of such a form that it is easily fabricated (constants, steps, wedges, etc.). $A(f)$ is optimally chosen.

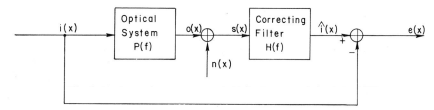

Fig. 3.3. System under study

3.3.2 Unconstrained Filter

To formulate the problem we adopt a weighted mean square error criterion. Thus, if the random error signal $e(x)$ is stationary in the spatial variable x and has a power spectrum $\Phi_e(f)$, the mean square error will be

$$E = \int_{-\infty}^{\infty} W(f)\Phi_e(f)df, \tag{3.16}$$

where $W(f)$ is a frequency weighting function. If, for example, we consider high frequencies to be more important than low frequencies, $W(f)$ would be correspondingly larger at those high frequencies.

From elementary linear system theory the error spectrum is

$$\Phi_e(f) = \Phi_n(f)|H(f)|^2 + \Phi_i(f)|1 - P(f)H(f)|^2, \tag{3.17}$$

where $\Phi_n(f)$ and $\Phi_i(f)$ are the noise and signal spectra. (We assume stationary, uncorrelated signal and noise.) If we put (3.17) into (3.16) we see that the integrand is the sum of two non-negative terms at every frequency. Thus, the optimum filter $H(f)$, evaluated at frequency f_1, will depend only on $\Phi_n(f_1)$, $\Phi_i(f_1)$, and $P(f_1)$.

By a calculus of variation argument one can show that the optimal unconstrained filter is

$$H(f) = \frac{P^*(f)}{|P(f)|^2 + \Phi_n(f)/\Phi_i(f)}, \tag{3.18}$$

where P^* denotes the complex conjugate of P. This is the well-known Wiener filter. It reduces to an inverse filter, $1/P(f)$, for small noise $[\Phi_n(f) \simeq 0]$.

The resulting error is found by putting (3.18) and (3.17) into (3.16):

$$E = \int_{-\infty}^{\infty} W(f)\frac{\Phi_i(f)\Phi_n(f)}{\Phi_i(f)|P(f)|^2 + \Phi_n(f)}df. \tag{3.19}$$

This is a "standard" error to which the error for other techniques might be compared.

3.3.3 Phase Filter

If one considers the noiseless case, $\Phi_n(f) \approx 0$, a phasor diagram can help to visualize the filtering process. First of all, note that the mean square error is, from (3.16) and (3.17),

$$E = \int_{-\infty}^{\infty} W(f)\Phi_i(f)|1 - G(f)|^2 df, \tag{3.20}$$

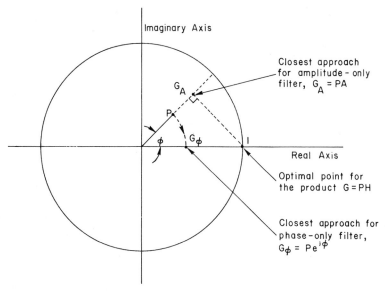

Fig. 3.4. Phasor diagram for filtering in the absence of noise

where $G(f)=P(f)H(f)$. It is evident that to minimize E one must minimize the magnitude of $1-G(f)$ at every frequency. Consider the phasor diagram of Fig. 3.4. The distorting filter is characterized by the phasor P. The optimal phase-only filter is $H=\exp(-j\phi)$. It brings $G=HP$ to the point G_ϕ on the real axis, the closest approach to the ideal, $G=1$.

The optimal phase-only filter [with $\Phi_n(f)\neq0$] is found by setting to zero the derivative of (3.17) with respect to θ,

$$\frac{d}{d\theta}[\Phi_n A^2+\Phi_i(1-PAe^{j\theta})(1-P^*Ae^{-j\theta})]=0 \tag{3.21}$$

which implies $\text{Im}\{P\exp(j\theta)\}=0$. For $P(f)=|P(f)|\exp[j\phi(f)]$ where ϕ is real, the results of (3.21) imply $\theta(f)=-\phi(f)$. That is, the optimal phase filter introduces a phase shift equal but opposite to the phase of the distorting filter $P(f)$. It makes the product HP real and positive as in Fig. 3.4.

This result is independent of the amplitudes of $H(f)$ and $P(f)$, and independent of the characteristics of either signal or noise spectra [$\Phi_i(f)$ or $\Phi_n(f)$]. It emphasizes the importance of phase correction in an optical processor.

The resulting mean square error is

$$E=\int W(f)\{\Phi_n(f)+\Phi_i(f)[1-|P(f)|]^2\}df. \tag{3.22}$$

It is clear from (3.22) that a phase-only filter provides no filtering of the additive noise.

3.3.4 Amplitude Filter

The optimal amplitude-only filter is found by setting $\theta = 0$ and by setting to zero the derivative of (3.17) with respect to A. The result is

$$H(f) = A(f) = \frac{\text{Re}\{P(f)\}}{|P(f)|^2 + \Phi_n(f)/\Phi_i(f)} . \qquad (3.23)$$

Note the similarity of this result to the Wiener filter (3.18).

To interpret (3.23), consider the noiseless case where $A(f)$ becomes,

$$A(f) = \frac{\cos\phi(f)}{|P(f)|} . \qquad (3.24)$$

From Fig. 3.4 we find

$$\cos\phi = |G_A|/1 = |HP| = A|P| . \qquad (3.25)$$

This is the same as (3.24) from which we see that A scales P to be the perpendicular projection of 1 onto P.

A difficulty arises when $|\phi| > \pi/2$. Here $\cos\phi$ is negative and $H(f)$ is no longer an amplitude-only filter. If, however, a π-phase-shifting filter is available, (3.23) can be realized.

If no π-phase-shifting network is available we must set

$$H(f) = 0 \quad |f| > \pi/2 . \qquad (3.26)$$

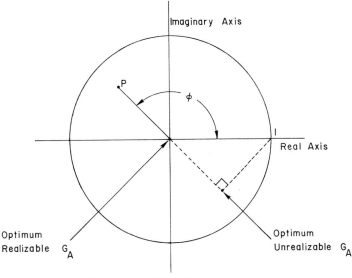

Fig. 3.5. Amplitude filtering when $|\phi| > \pi/2$

This is evident from Fig. 3.5 when one realizes that H is chosen in the noiseless case, to minimize $|1 - G|$. Equation (3.26) also applies with noise added since it minimizes the second term of (3.17) and sets the first to zero. Any other value of H causes both terms to increase. The error is

$$E = \int_{-\infty}^{\infty} W(f) \frac{\Phi_i(f)[\Phi_n(f) + \Phi_i(f)|P(f)|^2 \sin^2 \phi(f)]}{\Phi_n(f) + \Phi_i(f)|P(f)|^2} df. \tag{3.27}$$

This reduces to (3.19) if $\phi(f) \approx 0$. If $\Phi_n(f) \approx 0$ it reduces to

$$E = \int_{-\infty}^{\infty} W(f) \Phi_i(f) \sin^2 \phi(f) df. \tag{3.28}$$

Note that $\sin \phi$ is the length of the phasor from 1 to G_A in Fig. 3.4.

3.3.5 Amplitude and Simple Phase Filter

Simple phase functions can be more easily implemented for image restoration applications. Such simple functions include binary phase filters (step functions of various spatial designs such as annular shapes for defocus restoration or line shapes for linear blur restoration), linear phase functions or other step phase functions. Such functions can be produced by techniques discusssed later in Section 3.4. This surfaces the question of interest here: what is the optimum complex filter where the phase filter is constrained to a simple phase distribution?

An iterative estimation process has been developed to resolve such problems [3.5]. Simply stated, given a desired line spread function (LSF) $g_0(x)$, and its corresponding frequency response $G_0(f)$, the phase component of $G_0(f)$ is clipped to yield a new binary phase and a modified frequency function $G_1(f)$. The corresponding $g_1(x)$ will be real but may go negative, an unsatisfactory situation. $g_2(x)$ is chosen equal to $g_1(x)$ where it is positive and zero elsewhere. The phase of $G_2(f)$ is clipped as with $G_0(f)$ and the procedure continues until it converges, typically after five iterations.

An interesting example is a binary phase filter with $A = 1$. This problem has been approached for the case of an optical filter having pure π-phase steps for suppression of raster in incoherent viewing optics [3.4]. The $A = 1$ constraint is imposed to minimize the loss of image luminance through the filter and to simplify fabrication of the filter. The optimum filter $G_0(f)$ for this case was a $(\sin \pi f)/\pi f$ distribution. A binary phase filter, $G_1(f)$, with the phase component of $(\sin \pi f)/\pi f$, is initially selected. As described in [3.4], its corresponding LSF $g_1(x)$ is computed. The LSF is then constrained to be a positive function satisfying a minimum mean square fit with the optimum LSF, $g_0(x)$. This yields a new $g_2(x)$. $G_3(f)$ is constrained to be a binary, phase-only filter with the phase of $G_2(f)$ and the iterative process continues.

Another iteration technique such as this was used as a procedure to synthesize Vander Lugt filters [3.5]. A Vander Lugt filter can be generated from a mask function $g(x)$ as discussed in Section 3.5. The filter is a photograph of the Fourier transform of the mask $G(f)$ and a reference beam. As the filter is recorded on film, nonlinearities between exposure and transmittance distort the effective filter. The iterative technique was used to define the mask required to generate a desired filter, given the known film nonlinear transfer curves. The details of this example have been described in [3.5] and will not be repeated here. These techniques are ideally suited to machine calculation and to predict the performance of the resulting filter. The results are applicable to detection and filtering processes.

3.3.6 Detection

In the previous sections we discussed the filtering problem. Now we address the problem of detection. The system is described in Fig. 3.6. Here the signal $i(x)$ is known. The noise is random with power spectrum $\Phi_n(f)$, as before. The filter $H(f)$ is selected to maximize the signal-to-noise ratio (SNR) of the output $g(x)$, sampled at $x=0$,

$$\text{SNR} \equiv \frac{[\text{mean of } g(x) \text{ at } x=0]^2}{\text{variance of } g(x) \text{ at } x=0}. \tag{3.29}$$

The sample A is

$$A = g(x)|_{x=0} = \int_{-\infty}^{\infty} h(-x)s(x)dx = \int_{-\infty}^{\infty} H(f)S(f)df. \tag{3.30}$$

The mean of A is

$$\langle A \rangle = \int_{-\infty}^{\infty} H(f)I(f)P(f)df, \tag{3.31}$$

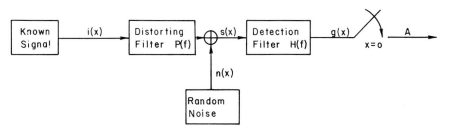

Fig. 3.6. The detection problem

if the noise has zero mean. The variance is

$$\text{var}\,A = \int\limits_{-\infty}^{\infty}\int\limits_{-\infty}^{\infty} H(f)H^*(l)\langle N(f)N^*(l)\rangle df\,dl$$

$$= \int\limits_{-\infty}^{\infty} |H(f)|^2\Phi_n(f)df, \tag{3.32}$$

since

$$\langle N(f)N^*(l)\rangle = \Phi_n(f)\delta(f-l) \tag{3.33}$$

for stationary noise. Thus the SNR is

$$\text{SNR} = \frac{\left|\int\limits_{-\infty}^{\infty} H(f)I(f)P(f)df\right|^2}{\int\limits_{-\infty}^{\infty} |H(f)|^2\Phi_n(f)df}. \tag{3.34}$$

If the phase of $H(f)$ is optimally selected, it will be the negative of the phase of the product $I(f)P(f)$. This follows since

$$\left|\int\limits_{-\infty}^{\infty} |\,H(f)I(f)P(f)\,|\exp[j\beta_H(f)]\exp[j\beta_I(f)]\exp[j\beta_P(f)]df\right|^2$$

$$\leqq \left|\int\limits_{-\infty}^{\infty}\left|H(f)I(f)P(f)|df|^2\right.\right. \tag{3.35}$$

Thus $\beta_H(f) = -\beta_I(f) - \beta_P(f)$ maximizes (3.34).

If no restrictions are placed on $H(f)$ it should be set to

$$H(f) = \frac{I^*(f)P^*(f)}{\Phi_n(f)}. \tag{3.36}$$

This is the matched filter solution which follows from a simple calculus of variation argument. The resulting SNR is

$$\text{SNR} = \int |I(f)P(f)|^2/\Phi_n(f)df. \tag{3.37}$$

A repeat of the constrained amplitude and phase cases for the detection problem is probably unnecessary. We note, simply, that for both detection and estimation, the optimal filter must provide both amplitude and phase correction.

3.4 Optical Filter Fabrication

In this section we describe techniques for fabricating optical filters for optical image processing systems. We discuss fabrication of separate amplitude and phase components of a filter and finally the fabrication of the unconstrained complex filter.

3.4.1 The Optical Filter

The optical filter is a transmission mask that controls the complex transmittance of the lens pupil function in an optical processor. The filter defines the optical transfer function of the optical processor that in turn controls the frequency distribution of information that is imaged from the input to the output of the processor. Consider the classical three-lens coherent optical processor design shown in Fig. 3.7. This is a classical design because it closely parallels the analytical description of the processing operation. The input transparency is placed in plane P_1. The transparency is illuminated by coherent light formed by a point source S of monochromatic light and a collimating lens L_c. The first lens L_1 produces a two-dimensional Fourier transformation of the complex amplitude transmittance $f(x, y)$ at the plane P_2 [3.6] described by

$$F(f_x, f_y) = \int_{-\infty}^{\infty} \int_{-\infty}^{\infty} f(x, y) \exp\left[\frac{j2\pi}{\lambda F}(xf_x + yf_y)\right] dx dy \qquad (3.38)$$

where we now describe the spatial frequency variables for two dimensions f_x, f_y, defined by $f_x = 2x/\lambda F, f_y = 2y/\lambda F$ where λ is the mean wavelength and F is the lens focal length. This first portion of the COPS is an optical spectrum analyzer. The power spectrum of input scene data can be measured at this plane for spectrum analysis purposes.

The second lens L_2 performs a successive Fourier transformation of the data described by

$$r(u, v) = \int_{-\infty}^{\infty} \int_{-\infty}^{\infty} F(f_x, f_y) \exp\left[\frac{j2\pi}{\lambda F_2}(f_x u + f_y v)\right] df_x df_y. \qquad (3.39)$$

This gives an output image $r(u, v)$ of the input transparency $f(x, y)$.

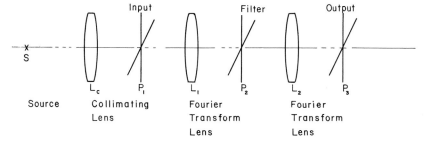

Fig. 3.7. Three-lens design for a coherent optical processor

Optical processing is performed by placing a filter function $H(f_x, f_y)$ at the frequency plane of the COPS. The filter can be a complex or real function. The complex amplitude distribution in the frequency plane is modified to $F'(f_x, f_y)$ by a multiplicative process where

$$F'(f_x, f_y) = F(f_x, f_y) \cdot H(f_x, f_y). \tag{3.40}$$

The filtering process is determined by the application (i.e., see Sect. 6).
    The filtered output $r'(u, v)$ can be described by

$$r'(u, v) = \int\limits_{-\infty}^{\infty} \int\limits_{-\infty}^{\infty} F'(f_x, f_y) \exp\left[\frac{j2\pi}{\lambda F_2}(f_x u, f_y v)\right] df_x df_y. \tag{3.41}$$

Thus, a modified image distribution is generated; that is the processed image. By using the convolution theorem we can express the output of the image processor by

$$r'(u, v) = \int\limits_{-\infty}^{\infty} \int\limits_{-\infty}^{\infty} f(u, v) h(x - u, y - v) dx dy \tag{3.42}$$

where $h(x, y)$ is the impulse response of the optical processor.
    The design described here illustrates the basic elements of a coherent optical processor. These elements are:

1) Coherent source.
2) Transillumination of the input function.
3) Production of the source image at the filter plane.
4) Filter at the source image plane.
5) Production of filtered image at the output.

The elements of optical processor design are discussed in more detail in Section 3.5. Here we consider the filter mask that is placed in the filter plane of the optical system.

3.4.2 Amplitude Filter Synthesis

The amplitude filter is a transmission mask that represents the amplitude component of the function $H(f_x, f_y)$ [see (3.15)]. There are a number of methods to fabricate the amplitude filter. Two approaches are discussed below.

Analog Filter Synthesis Techniques

The simplest means for generating the amplitude of an optical filter is with a coherent optical spectrum analyzer. The output spectrum is the exact Fourier transformation of the input amplitude transmittance function. The amplitude component of the output spectrum can be recorded on film. The film records the intensity distribution $|H(f_x, f_y)|^2$. Now consider the photographic response. The amplitude transmittance of film is related to the intensity distribution by:

$$T_A(f_x, f_y) = [|H(f_x, f_y)|^2]^{(-\gamma/2)}. \tag{3.43}$$

We assume that the spectrum is recorded on the linear part of the photographic response curve where the slope of the response curve can be considered a constant. An inverse transmittance amplitude filter

$$T_A(f_x, f_y) = \frac{1}{|H(f_x, f_y)|} \tag{3.44}$$

can be obtained by processing the film to $\gamma = +1$. This is a reversal process and produces, within the linear dynamic range of the film, the desired inverse amplitude transmittance function. Amplitude transmittances proportional to $|H(f_x, f_y)|$ can be obtained by processing the film to $\gamma = -1$, a negative image of the spectrum.

This method for generation of an amplitude filter requires an input transmission mask $t(x, y)$ whose Fourier transform yields the desired filter function $H(f_x, f_y)$. For the case of image restoration where the optical process is to remove the image degradation (sometimes referred to as deconvolution), the input transmission mask is the aberrated image impulse response. For linear image blur the aberrated impulse response can be represented by a slit whose length equals the amount of image smear. Its Fourier transform is a $(\sin x)/x$ distribution in the direction of image blur. In some situations the impulse response can be isolated in an image and used as the input transparency. Close examination of a photographic image sometimes reveals point images that represent the impulse response.

Another technique for generating the amplitude component of a filter is described by Tsujiuchi [3.7]. In this case, controlled exposure of the film is obtained from a function generator that can take a number of forms, depending on the function to be generated. For the example of an inverse sinc filter, the function generator consists of a linear motion device for smearing out a predefined aperture on film. The function generator consists of source illumination, a precalibrated binary mask on a linear motion platform, and imaging components. Calibration of the mask aperture distribution $h(x)$ is described by

$$h(x) = \frac{v T(x)}{I} \tag{3.45}$$

where I is the source radiance, v is the motion velocity and $T(x)$ is the film amplitude transmittance. The aperture shape calibration technique is illustrated in Fig. 3.8. A calibration run is first made to define film amplitude transmittance vs aperture height for the film and process selected. Then, as shown, the input mask is defined by tracing from the desired output through the film response to

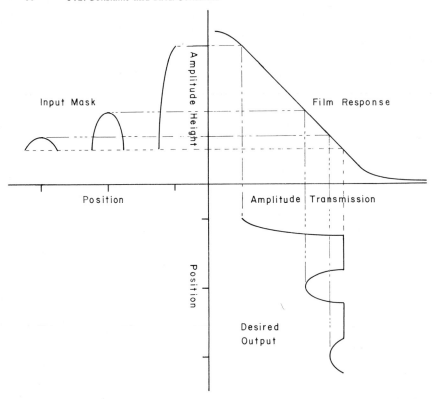

Fig. 3.8. Transfer curves for determination of a mask function

the input mask function. This technique is self-compensating for film nonlinearities.

This function generation technique can be difficult to perform. Every filter design requires a unique generation method. The linear blur filter requires a longitudinal motion device. The defocus filter requires a rotational device. More complicated spatial patterns may be impossible to effect. For this reason the spectrum recording technique is preferable. It will be expanded below as a means to fabricate the unconstrained filter holographically.

3.4.3 Phase Filter Synthesis

A photographic phase relief image can be used for a phase filter. Thus optical phase filters can be generated in a manner similar to amplitude transmission masks. A photographic transfer curve of phase transmittance vs exposure can be defined. The phase image in film is obtained by means of the phase relief image associated with the density image in a photographic emulsion [3.8, 9]. By "bleaching" of the density image, a clear phase function is obtained. Thus calibration of a film phase relief image provides an accurate means to fabricate a known phase function.

For the example of a $(\sin x)/x$ filter cited earlier, the phase component consists of levels of 0 and π phase retardation in one dimension. This can be generated by means of exposing the emulsion through a binary mask with the required transmission pattern. This two-level phase filter can be easily and accurately generated. An application of a phase-only filter is described in Section 3.6. Such fabrication techniques are generally limited to two exposure levels and are thereby constrained phase filters.

3.4.4 Synthesis of the Unconstrained Filter

The above methods for generating phase and amplitude filter components can sometimes be used to generate unconstrained filters where the filter function can be represented by such filter generation techniques. However, the more general methods for generating an unconstrained filter are holographic filter and digital filter synthesis techniques.

The Holographic (Vander Lugt) Filter

One of the foremost methods for fabrication of coherent optical filters is the holographic technique developed by *Vander Lugt* [3.6, 10]. The holographic technique enables recording of arbitrary phase and amplitude functions on a photographic transparency. The Fourier transform hologram filter is formed with an optical spectrum analyzer and a reference wave as illustrated in Fig. 3.9 [3.11, 12]. The complex transform $H(f_x, f_y)$ is combined with a reference wave of amplitude A_0 such that the output distribution is a non-negative function. An angle θ is maintained between the reference wave and the complex function. If $H(f)$ is a real function, and film transmission is proportional to intensity, then the holographic filter is described by

$$M(f_x, f_y) = A_0^2 + |H(f_x, f_y)|^2 + 2A_0|H(f_x, f_y)| \cos[2\pi\alpha f_x + \phi(f_y)], \qquad (3.46)$$

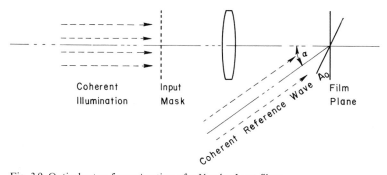

Fig. 3.9. Optical setup for generation of a Vander Lugt filter

where $\alpha = (\sin \theta)/\lambda$. The cosine frequency is phase modulated by the phase of the complex function.

A variety of filters can be generated by the above technique. The most useful filter is the matched filter [3.13] that is the complex conjugate of a function [note the third term of (3.46)]. The matched filter is the optimum Wiener filter for low SNR and can be used in detection filtering or deconvolution processing (e.g., blur removal) [3.14]. An inverse filter can be obtained by combining the Vander Lugt filter (3.46) with a second transparency of the form

$$T(f_x, f_y) = \frac{1}{|H(f_x, f_y)|^2} \tag{3.47}$$

formed by techniques described above (Sect. 3.4.2, p. 67). The combined transmittance is then described by

$$M'(f_x, f_y) = \frac{A_0^2}{|H(f_x, f_y)|^2} + \frac{1}{H^*(f_x, f_y)} \exp[-j\alpha(f)] + \frac{1}{H(f_x, f_y)} \exp[j\alpha(f)] \tag{3.48}$$

with the third term being the inverse filter. This is the optimum filter in the case of high SNR.

Transmission properties of the Vander Lugt filter can be adjusted by control of the recording film characteristic response [3.15, 16]. Two control parameters are exposure of the film and adjustment of the ratio of the reference and signal wave amplitudes. A practical means for evaluating a Vander Lugt filter is to view the regions of the interference fringe contrast. Regions of maximum contrast provide maximum diffraction. Higher contrast fringes occurring at low frequency portions of the filter (near the dc term) illustrate that the filter will function as a low frequency matched filter (often referred to as a low pass filter). A filter with highest contrast fringes at intermediate frequencies will operate as an inverse filter at low frequencies, as a matched filter at intermediate frequencies. Such a filter is optimum in the case of frequency dependent SNR. Here the signal level is high at low frequencies and low at higher frequencies, a common situation with conventional imagery. The effect of high or low pass filters is demonstrated in TIPPETT, [3.16]. The filter that emphasizes the intermediate to higher frequencies of a character function enhances edge information of a character. It is often referred to as a high pass filter. This reference also illustrates filter response when changes occur in filter scale, filter orientation and signal quality.

The frequency of the cosine term in the Vander Lugt filter is selected to obtain image format separation at the output of the processor (Fig. 3.10). For a cosine interference frequency of $2\pi\alpha$, the format separation is:

$$d = \lambda F(2\pi\alpha) \tag{3.49}$$

where λ is the wavelength of light and F is the lens focal length. The output diffraction term separation increases with the value α in the holographic filter.

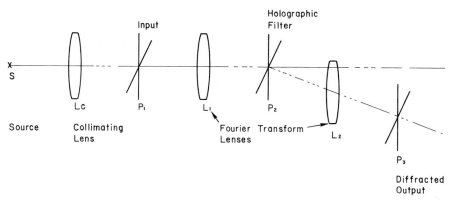

Fig. 3.10. Diffracted off-axis output using a Vander Lugt filter

However, it is advantageous to minimize the cosine frequency to just that required for output format separation. Photographic modulation response remains high at lower spatial frequencies. As diffraction efficiency is directly related to cosine modulation, the highest efficiency is obtained with the lower frequency cosine term.

Digitally Synthesized Amplitude Filters

A facsimile generator provides a flexible means for generating transmittance functions on film. There are a number of facsimile generators that can be used, including electron beam recorders (EBR), laser beam recorders (LBR), video writing devices (CRT), or opto-mechanical scanners. By such means, complicated transmission patterns can be accurately generated under digital control.

A digital facsimile printout of a function $S(f)$ is generated as sampled data. Consider a facsimile printer in one dimension with a rectangular shaped writing spot of width 2a described by $R(f/a)$. Contiguous sampling implies a sampling comb function described by $\sum_{n=-N}^{N} S(f-2na)$. The transmittance function on film, assuming linear recording is

$$F(f)=S(f)\left[R(f/a)\circledast\sum S(f-2na)\right]. \tag{3.50}$$

If such a filter is used as an optical filter in a coherent optical processor, the output amplitude impulse response of the processing system is its Fourier transform, given by

$$f(x)=s(x)\circledast\left[\operatorname{sinc}2\pi xa\cdot\sum s\left(x-\frac{n}{2a}\right)\right]. \tag{3.51}$$

The output filter contains periodic terms. In the case of a rectangular writing spot, the comb terms are very small. The writing spot shape is an important consideration as it can be controlled to reduce deleterious sampled data effects in the output of the processor. A triangular spot shape is an ideal distribution for most writing requirements. This topic has been thoroughly analyzed in the literature [3.4].

A digital printer can produce a sampled function such as a Fourier transform hologram [3.17]. A practical recording medium for digital filters is a real time transducer that can be used for quick write-read-erase operations for filter updating [3.18]. The use of these transducers can provide near real time optical processing with complex spatial filters. Optical processor design for real time processing is discussed in Section 3.5.

A digital printer can also be used to generate a binary mask that produces a desired filter function. The binary filter is a set of clear apertures set at computed positions and dimensions that, by diffraction, generate the amplitude and phase of the desired complex function [3.19, 20]. They can be generated by computer at a large scale and photographically reduced to the desired size.

Digital filter synthesis techniques provide the best potential for the future in optical processing. The digital system is required for its computational accuracy and flexibility for linear and nonlinear operations. Its interface to optical systems via real time transducers [3.21] is a prime area of importance for future applications.

3.5 Optical Processor Design

We have seen that image processing is performed by means of control of the optical processor transfer function. We have also seen that the optical processor transfer function is controlled by means of transmission masks in the pupil plane of the optics as well as by control of the source coherence. We will now consider the physical design of the image processing system.

There are many optical design configurations that can be used for optical processors. Some basic configurations that are frequently used and that illustrate fundamental considerations of the design are described in this section. However, it is important to emphasize that all optical imaging systems are candidates for use as optical processors.

3.5.1 Coherent Optical Processor System (COPS)

A basic COPS design was shown in Fig. 3.7. This three-lens processor configuration is directly related to the two sequential Fourier transform operations in optical processing [3.2]. There are other optical designs that satisfy these analytical requirements. A two-lens coherent optical processor design is shown in Fig. 3.11. This simpler design contains all the basic elements required in a coherent processor. A point source S is imaged to plane P_2 by the condenser lens L_c. A two-dimensional Fourier transformation of $f(x, y)$ at plane P_1 occurs

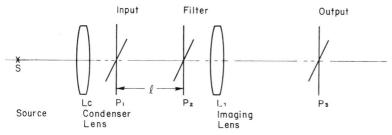

Fig. 3.11. A two-lens coherent optical processor

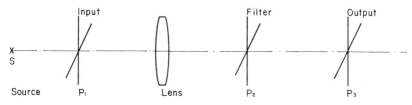

Fig. 3.12. A one-lens coherent optical processor

at plane P_2. In this design a quadratic phase factor exists at plane P_2 [3.2], but this does not affect the processing operation. A filter can be placed at plane P_2 for the optical process. The output image is produced at plane P_3. Lens L_1 satisfies the imaging condition from plane P_1 to P_3.

This design provides a distinct advantage over the three lens design. The distance l between the input transparency at P_1 and the filter at P_2 can be adjusted. Thus, a scaling of an input image to filter coordinates can be performed [3.12]. This is equivalent to tuning a filter to the frequency parameters of the input image. Another advantage of this COPS design is the ability to adjust scale at the output. The object to image distances can be adjusted, as with any imaging system, to obtain the desired output image scale.

A one-lens coherent optical processor is illustrated in Fig. 3.12. Note that it also satisfies all requirements for the COPS. The lens L produces an image of the point source at the filter plane P_2. The same lens produces an image of plane P_1 at the output plane P_3.

In addition to the flexibility of adjusting scale between input and output and between the input and the filter, the one-lens and two-lens systems are a simpler design than the three-lens system. Generally a minimum of optical components should be used in a system on the basis of image quality and component costs. Of the three designs considered above, the two-lens design is more conventional and is the recommended approach.

3.5.2 Coherent Optical Correlators

Coherent optical correlation can be performed with a COPS system. The output of the COPS is the cross-correlation between the input function and the Fourier transform of the filter function [see (3.42)]. Techniques also exist whereby the autocorrelation or the cross-correlation of input functions can be generated by means of a two-step Fourier transform process.

The autocorrelation of an input function $f(x, y)$ can be obtained by first recording its power spectrum on film using an optical spectrum analyzer (see Sect. 3.4.1). By linear processing so that the film's amplitude transmittance is proportional to $F(f_x, f_y)$, the auto-correlation is then obtained by performing a second Fourier transformation. This yields

$$r(u, v) = \int\limits_{-\infty}^{\infty} \int\limits_{-\infty}^{\infty} |F(f_x, f_y)|^2 \exp\left[\frac{-j}{\lambda F}(uf_x + vf_y)\right] df_x df_y \tag{3.52}$$

$$r(u, v) = \int\limits_{-\infty}^{\infty} \int f(u, v) f(u - f_x, v - f_y) df_x df_y. \tag{3.53}$$

Thus, the autocorrelation of the input amplitude transmittance $f(x, y)$ is obtained.

This basic optical approach can also be used to obtain cross-correlations. A design where both input and filter mask functions are placed at the input plane is called a joint transform correlator [3.22]. Consider the requirement to perform cross-correlation between a mask function $m(x, y)$ and an image of a text $s(x, y)$. By placing both transparencies at the input to the optical spectrum analyzer, their joint Fourier transform is recorded at the frequency plane. The input can be described by

$$f(x, y) = m(x - a, y) + s(x + a, y) \tag{3.54}$$

where the transparencies are displaced by $2a$ along the horizontal axis. Their Fourier transform is described by

$$I(f_x, f_y) = M(f_x, f_y) \exp(jf_x a) + S(f_x, f_y) \exp(-jf_x a). \tag{3.55}$$

The magnitude squared of the Fourier transform is recorded on film. The joint transform image is then placed at the input to the optical transform system where a second Fourier transform produces an output image described by

$$o(u, v) = m(u, v) \circledast m(u, v) + s(u, v) \circledast s(u, v) + m(u, v) \circledast s(u - 2a, v)$$
$$+ m(u, v) \circledast s(u + 2a, v) \tag{3.56}$$

where $\circledast$ denotes convolution. The last two terms describe the desired cross-correlation of m with s. These terms are shifted off-axis by a distance $2a$ where the final output is obtained.

The joint transform technique is an easy means to perform the cross-correlation operation. However, use of the COPS also provides a cross-correlation between an input function and the Fourier transform of a Vander

Lugt matched filter. The Vander Lugt filtering method provides better control of the process because filter features can be directly controlled. For example, as discussed in [3.16], high or low pass filters can be generated to control the correlation signal output. On this basis the Vander Lugt filter matched filtering approach is recommended.

3.5.3 A Hybrid Digital-Optical Processor

Digital synthesis of an optical filter and a real time incoherent to coherent transducer are fundamental requirements for the future application of optical processors [3.21]. Digital filter synthesis is ideal because it unifies the computational flexibility and accuracy of a digital system with the high data throughput of the optical system. A potential hybrid system design is shown in the diagram in Fig. 3.13 that combines a three-lens coherent optical processor with a digital system, described by the block diagram. A recorder device (e.g., LBR) generates the desired function on the input plane or the filter plane [3.23]. The incoherent to coherent transducer enables coherent optical processing of information written on the input plane transducer, with the filter written on the filter plane transducer. Complex functions can be generated at this plane by using a Vander Lugt filter [3.24]. Very high operating cycles can be effected by using scanners of video bandwidth and by multiplexing filters [3.25].

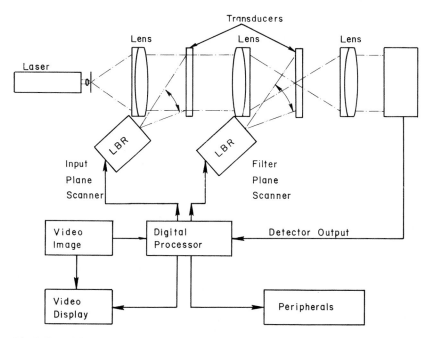

Fig. 3.13. Hybrid optical-digital processor system

3.5.4 Partially Coherent Optical Processor System (POPS)

When a coherent processor is used, essentially any complex filtering operation can be performed. However, there are some limitations in a coherent optical processor. From a practical point of view it may be desirable at times to use incoherent or partially coherent illumination. This avoids some noise problems and, since "white" light is used, the system interfaces more readily with a human observer. However, filter design becomes more complicated with a partially coherent system. The filter must satisfy the conditions of the OTF-lens pupil relationships. In this section we discuss partially coherent optical processors for correlation processing and for autocorrelation operations [3.26, 27].

The transfer function, $T(f)$ for low contrast partially coherent imaging is described by [3.28, 29]:

$$T(f) = K(f) \circledast [G(f) \cdot K^*(-f)] \tag{3.57}$$

where $K(f)$ is the complex amplitude transmittance of the lens pupil and $G(f)$ is the source image in the lens pupil. This equation provides an intuitive understanding of the response of most optical systems such as microscopes, projectors, enlargers, etc. These optical systems contain condenser optics and imaging optics. The condenser optics generally image the source into the imaging lens pupil, to obtain greatest illumination efficiency. If the source image, described as $G(f)$, is very small (a point), then (3.57) reduces to the description of a COPS transfer function, where $T(f) = K(f)$. If the source image is constant over the imaging lens pupil, then this reduces to the incoherent transfer function description, $T(f) = K(f) \circledast K^*(-f)$. A review of some conventional optical systems illustrates the use of these properties.

The most general partially coherent optical processor is a microscope system with Kohler illumination [3.30]. Figure 3.14 describes this form of illumination where C_1 is the condenser that images the source to the iris I_2, that is in turn imaged into the microscope objective L_1. Iris I_2 enables control of the source diameter at L_1. Lens C_2 is the substage condenser that images the iris I_1 to the input plane, enabling control of the illumination field diameter at the transparency. Lens L_1 (the microscope objective) images the input to the output plane, where an eyepiece is located for viewing. Note that the transfer function of this

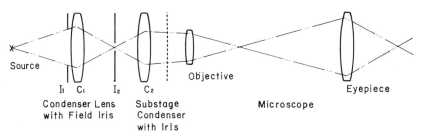

Fig. 3.14. The microscope as a partially coherent processor

optical system can be controlled by adjustment of the source diameter with iris I_2. Image contrast can be enhanced by decreasing source diameter.

A practical illumination system for effecting source size control is illustrated in Fig. 3.15. A small source S_1 is imaged to a point at S_2 by means of the condenser lens C_1. A ground glass diffuser, G, is positioned on a slide together with the condenser lens C_2. When the diffuser is in plane S_2, the effective source is a small point. As the diffuser is moved from the plane it intercepts a diverging field, providing increasing source size with increasing distance. The transparency T is transilluminated, and the source is imaged into the back focal plane P of the imaging lens L.

One application for the optical processor illustrated in Fig. 3.15 is adaptive imaging. Control of the source diameter enables control of the frequency response of the system [3.28]. The range of frequency response control is illustrated in Fig. 3.16 for several source to lens diameter ratios. The dashed line curve is obtained with a source image equal to or greater than the lens pupil diameter. The dot-dash line curve is an intermediate response where the source image diameter is 1/2 the lens pupil diameter.

Filters can be placed in the lens pupil plane for image enhancement purposes, such as high frequency or image contrast enhancement. If an absorbing disk is placed in the center of the lens pupil plane then $T(f)$ is described by the dashed line curve in Fig. 3.17. In this case the source image is a point and the absorbing disk diameter is 0.1 of the lens diameter. Figure 3.17 shows the MTF of the optical system for several other source image diameters. This example illustrates the ability to use conventional optical systems for image enhancement [3.31].

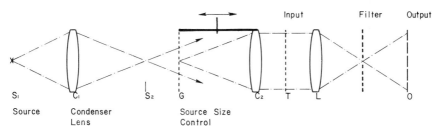

Fig. 3.15. An adaptive partially coherent optical processor

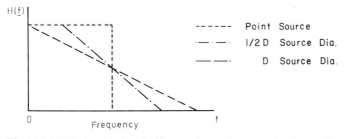

Fig. 3.16. MTF of an ideal optical system from coherent to incoherent illumination limits

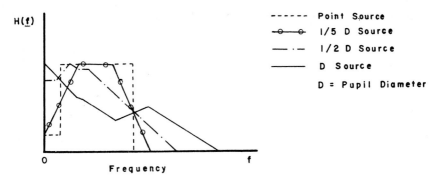

Fig. 3.17. Frequency response curves for various source diameters and a contrast enhancement filter

3.5.5 Quality of Optical Processing Systems

The quality of optical components in image processing systems is governed by two requirements, the image quality response between input and output and the fidelity at the frequency plane. In this section we consider requirements for optical components that produce an image of the source in the coherent optical processor. The COPS has a point source. To obtain a point source image requires a high quality condenser lens. As noted in the three-lens design (Fig. 3.7), the collimator lens and the first transform lens are combined to produce the source image. In the two-lens design (Fig. 3.11) only the condenser lens is used to produce the source image. The quality requirements of the source imaging lens(es) depends on the application. In many cases, high tolerance frequency discrimination is not required. As the requirements in frequency discrimination are relaxed, the requirements of the condenser lens are also relaxed.

For an optical system with a stationary condenser response, the effective frequency plane filter can be described by

$$F'(f_x, f_y) = \int_{-\infty}^{\infty} \int_{-\infty}^{\infty} S(f_x, f_y)F(f_x - f_x', f_y - f_y')df_x df_y \qquad (3.58)$$

where $S(f_x, f_y)$ is the source image and $F(f_x, f_y)$ is the input filter. This is the familiar convolution equation describing an imaging process. Here it describes the impact of the source image on the filtering process. If $S(f_x, f_y)$ is an ideal point source formed by a perfect lens, then the effective filter is equivalent to the input filter. If $S(f_x, f_y)$ is degraded by aberrations in the condenser lenses then the effective filter is modified accordingly. Condenser lenses need only be of sufficient quality so as not to distort the point source image. If the point source is large relative to the impulse response of the condenser lenses, then no lens improvement is required.

3.6 Some Applications and Examples

The potential for optical image processing far exceeds the present status of its applications. Optical systems have a space-bandwidth product capability that is ideally suited to the processing of two-dimensional data such as pictorial information. In addition, input-output transducers are being or have been developed that can interface optical and digital processing systems. The full potential of optical image processing will most likely become fully utilized in data processing as a hybrid system.

In the early stages of filter development, extensive work was required to generate a high quality filter. With the Vander Lugt filter, the fabrication task is greatly simplified. Now with new transducers, a computed filter can be generated at video rates by means of a facsimile printer (e.g., LBR). It is expected that the utility of the optical processor, thus enhanced, will become fully applied in the near future.

The simplest example of image processing is the use of blocking filters [3.31, 32], in a coherent optical processor. We have seen that there is a 1 for 1 correspondence between position and frequency in the filter plane of a coherent optical processor. By placement of an opaque filter at a particular frequency component, that component is blocked out in the image formation. By this means one can selectively perform frequency blocking for certain spatial filtering applications. One of the more popular filtering applications, frequently used with microscopes, is dark-ground illumination where the dc spot is removed. This filtering process is also known as high pass filtering. The radius required of a blocking filter can be computed from the space frequency relationship of the coherent optical processor [see (3.38)]. A radial distance r in the filtering plane and spatial frequency f are related by $r = \lambda F f$, where F is the lens focal length. For example, if all frequencies above f_0 are to be passed, a disk of radius given by $\lambda F f_0$ is required. The disk is then placed in the filtering plane, centered on the optical axis. An example of high pass filtering with a coherent optical processor is given in Fig. 3.18 where (a) is the input and (b) is the output image. Note that the background illumination has been removed and that the energy associated with high frequency components of the image (i.e., edges) are passed. This causes an inversion of the small scale components in the image.

A second example in blocking filtering is illustrated in Fig. 3.19 [3.33]. This example shows how directional information can be selectively passed for enhanced detection. Figure 3.19a shows an acoustic recording where vertical signal information is of interest. A rectangular aperture was placed in the filtering plane of a three-lens COPS. The width of the aperture in the vertical direction was narrow to block, out the horizontal line information. This is often referred to as low pass filtering. The length of the aperture passed all vertical line information. The vertical timing marks and signal information are more easily detected when the unwanted data is removed. The scale of a blocking filter for high pass or low pass filtering can be computed as described above with Fig. 3.18,

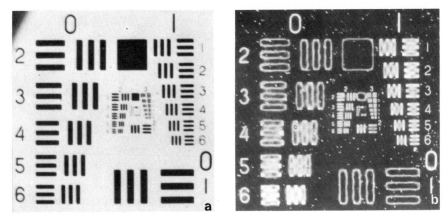

Fig. 3.18a and b. Original image of a resolution test target (a) and a high pass filtered image (b)

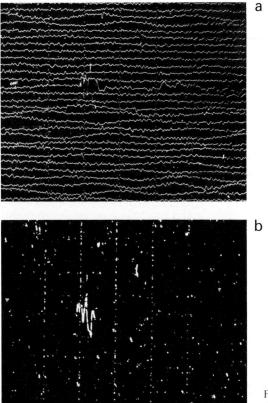

Fig. 3.19a and b. Directional separation of information with a rectangular blocking filtering

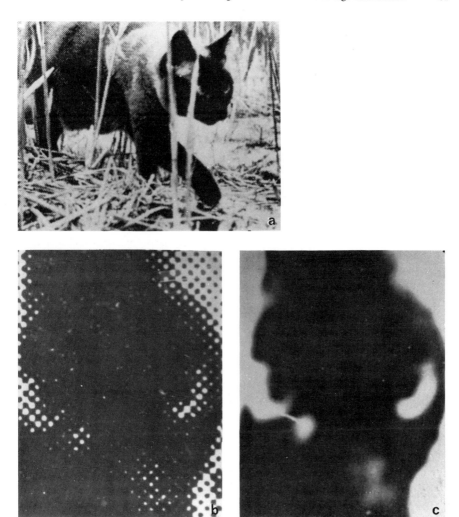

Fig. 3.20a—c. Half-tone image (a), and enlarged section (b), with half-tone removal (c) using low pass filtering

or can be determined by visual observation of the output signal. In the case of Fig. 3.19, a visual observation of the output was used while a slit aperture in the filter plane was adjusted.

Blocking filters have also been applied for removal of half-tone information in an image. This process has been described in the literature [3.33]. An example in Fig. 3.20 shows a half-tone image in (a) with an enlargement of a section of the half-tone in (b). The filtered image (c) of the enlarged section shows scene detail not observable in the half-tone case. This example of half-tone removal was obtained with a circular aperture (low pass filter) in the filtering plane. The

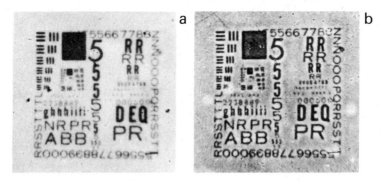

Fig. 3.21a and b. Contrast enhancement with a partially coherent processor

radius of the aperture was computed as illustrated with Fig. 3.18 where f_0 was half the half-tone frequency. This filter passed image information but blocked half-tone information. Half-tone removal can aid improved observation of image detail.

Enhancement of low contrast imagery has been best performed by partially coherent optical systems (see Sect. 3.5.4). Some spatial and temporal noise effects can be reduced with a reduction of coherence in the illumination of the optical processor. Another advantage is that white light can be used in a partially coherent system enabling a color response to colored input and a better match to the human visual response.

Enhancement of image contrast is performed by altering the dc bias term when the information is imaged through the optical processor. This is accomplished with a reduction of the dc component by means of an absorbing filter. An example of contrast enhancement is shown in Fig. 3.21 where (a) is the low contrast input and (b) is the enhanced output. This process was accomplished with the partially coherent system described in Section 3.5.4 with a dc disk of 10% transmittance and a diameter 0.1 the lens pupil diameter. This partially coherent system enabled continuous source diameter control while the output image was observed. Interactive control of an image processor provides a distinct advantage, enabling the operator to select the best transfer function for a desired processed output [3.28].

It is noted that a combined contrast and high frequency enhancement was performed in Fig. 3.21. The filter used here emphasized the high frequency terms as well as reducing the relative dc component.

Coherent in-line image restoration has been applied to many problems. The application of linear image blur filters was discussed in Section 3.4. An example of the image correction obtained with a clipped inverse sinc filter is illustrated in Fig. 3.22. Figure 3.22a is a blurred image, and Fig. 3.22b is the filtered image. The in-line coherent optical filter was fabricated according to techniques described in [3.7]. Although these filters are difficult to fabricate, excellent results can be obtained [3.33, 34].

Fig. 3.22a and b. Image blur correction with an inverse filter

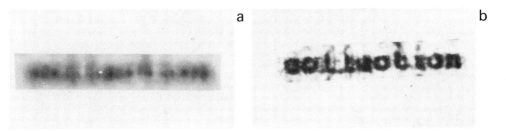

Fig. 3.23a and b. Image defocus correction of the word "collection" with an inverse filter

A second example of image restoration with an in-line complex filter is illustrated in Fig. 3.23. Figure 3.23a is a defocused image of a word that is unreadable because of the defocus aberration. A clipped inverse filter was fabricated for the filtering process. The resulting filtered image shown in Fig. 3.23b illustrates the capability for image restoration. Inverse or matched filters for image restoration can also be made using the Vander Lugt filter technique (see Sect. 3.4).

We have seen that the Vander Lugt filter can be generated in an optical interferometer (Fig. 3.9). The input mask from which the filter is made can be an alphabetic letter for text reading, a target for target detection, a feature function for feature recognition, an impulse response for image correction, etc. Matched, inverse or frequency controlled filters for emphasizing high or low frequencies can readily be generated.

As an initial example consider the smeared image in Fig. 3.24a. The impulse response is shown in Fig. 3.24b. A Vander Lugt inverse filter was generated from the impulse response using techniques described in Section 3.4. The resulting restored image obtained with the three-lens COPS illustrated in Fig. 3.7 is seen in Fig. 3.24c. This result illustrates a significant improvement in the output image.

Character detection can be implemented by recording known characters of interest as matched filters [3.10, 13], and processing unknown data with each

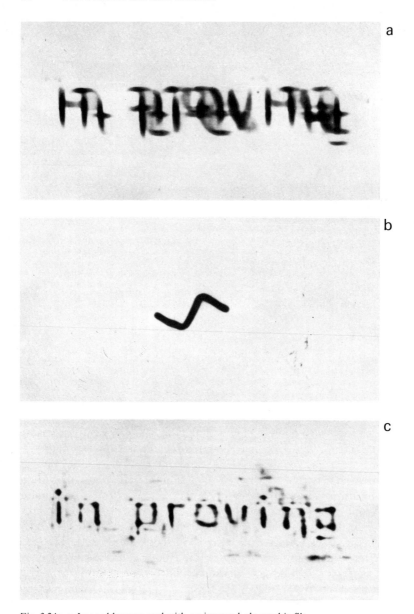

Fig. 3.24a–c. Image blur removal with an inverse holographic filter

filter. The location of autocorrelation peaks at the output defines locations of a respective character. This operation can be made more efficient by recording multiple characters on each filter [3.25] thereby using a parallel processing feature. The process is *n* times faster for *n* parallel characters on the filter.

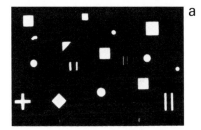

a

b

Fig. 3.25a and b. Correlation detection of circles with a Vander Lugt matched filter

Shape detection that is similar to character detection is illustrated in Fig. 3.25 where (a) shows an input transparency containing various geometrical objects. A matched filter for a circle was recorded as a Vander Lugt filter. The output obtained by photographic clipping to isolate the high energy peaks of the autocorrelation terms is shown in (b).

The field of medicine offers many opportunities for optical processing [3.35, 36]. This includes areas of enhancement of low contrast X-rays, edge and line definition for improved feature detection, and correction of optical abnormalities such as human cataracts [3.35] among others. Phase aberration balancing has been performed to cancel cataract visual aberrations. A holographic matched filter of the cataract phase field was generated to obtain results shown in Fig. 3.26. The filter is used to cancel the phase aberrations induced by the cataract. Figure 3.26a shows an image of a resolution test target formed through a cataract sample. The induced aberrations are apparent in the image. Use of phase correction by means of a holographic filter permits the image correction illustrated in (b) and (c) where (c) is an enlargement of the center of (b). This example illustrates an important application area in medical technology.

An incoherent optical filtering application of interest is the removal of periodic raster line patterns in scanned imagery. Raster scanned imagery is common in many devices where the output information is generated by a scanned spot. The raster lines can interfere with visual operations. In some cases such as a CRT, the raster can be smoothed by spot shaping or by controlled spot warble. However, in some cases such as an output generated by an array of LED elements, smoothing must be accomplished by the viewing optics. A phase-only

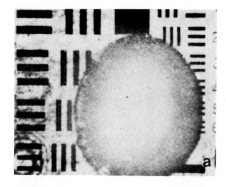 

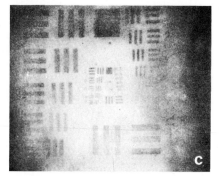

Fig. 3.26a–c. Resolution test target with superimposed cataract (a), as viewed through a holographic correction filter (b), and with the center enlarged (c). (Printed with permission of *G. Reynolds* [3.35])

Fig. 3.27a and b. Raster suppression with an incoherent viewing system and a phase-only filter

filter was generated to modify the transfer function of viewing optics in an LED scanned viewer of an image intensifier [3.4]. A binary phase filter was used because of ease of fabrication. The effect of this filtering operation is illustrated in Fig. 3.27 where the rastered image without filtering (a) is compared to the filtered image (b). This application can be relevant in raster display systems where the raster interferes with visual detection of the information. Raster removal can also be performed coherently with blocking filters as described earlier in Fig. 3.19.

3.7 Summary

This chapter has presented a brief review of optical image processing and some of its applications. The references presented here are only a sample of a copious source of available information in this field. It is recommended that the reader maintain an awareness of current literature because of the continuous developments being reported.

Optical data processing is in its early stages of utility. Present demonstrations of optical processing are essentially one-of-a kind illustrations of feasibility. The authors believe that full utility of optical processing will be realized with the development of necessary peripherals for interfacing to digital control systems. The incoherent to coherent transducer with a laser beam recorder is one significant peripheral that, when fully developed, will permit practical use of the optical processor. Data throughput rates for some processing applications may then be increased significantly. On this basis, optical processing technology should be emphasized in the coming years.

References

3.1   K.Preston,Jr.: Proc. IEEE **60**, 1216 (1972)
3.2   J.Goodman: *Introduction to Fourier Optics* (McGraw-Hill, New York 1968)
3.3   D.Gabor: Nature **161**, 777 (1948)
3.4   R.Gonsalves, P.Considine: Opt. Eng. **15**, 64 (1976)
3.5   R.Gonsalves, R.Dumais, P.Considine: On Optical Holographic Filters. In *Coherent Optics in Mapping*, Vol. 45 (SPIE Proc. 1974)
3.6   A.Vander Lugt: Opt. Acta **15**, 1 (1968)
3.7   J.Tsujiuchi: Correction of Optical Images by Compensation of Aberrations and by Spatial Frequency Filtering. In *Progress in Optics*, ed. by E.Wolf, Vol. II (North-Holland, Amsterdam 1963) Chap. IV
3.8   H.Smith: J. Opt. Soc. Am. **58**, 533 (1968)
3.9   R.Iamberts: J. Opt. Soc. Am. **60**, 1398 (1970)
3.10 A.Vander Lugt: IEEE Trans. IT-**6**, 139 (1964)
3.11 J.DeVelis, G.Reynolds: *Theory and Applications of Holography* (Addison-Wesley, Reading 1967) p. 15
3.12 A.Vander Lugt: Appl. Opt. **5**, 1760 (1966)
3.13 D.Casasent, A.Furman: Appl. Opt. **15**, 1690 (1976)
3.14 G.Stroke: J.SPIE **9**, 131 (1971)
3.15 R.Gonsalves, R.Dumais: Opt. Eng. **12**, 43 (1973)
3.16 E.Leith, A.Kozma, J.Upatnieks: Coherent Optical Systems for Data Processing, Spatial Filtering and Wavefront Reconstructions. In *Optical and Electro-Optical Information Processing*, ed. by J.Tippett et al. (MIT Press 1965) Chap. 7, pp. 125ff.
3.17 W.Lee: Appl. Opt. **9**, 639 (1970)
3.18 D.Casasent: Proc. IEEE **65**, 142 (1977)
3.19 A.Lohman: Appl. Opt. **7**, 651 (1968)
3.20 S.Lee: Pattern Recognition **5**, 21 (1973)
3.21 See *Optical Information Processing*, Vol. 83 (SPIE Proc. 1976)
3.22 C.Weaver: Appl. Opt. **5**, 124 (L), 1966
3.23 D.Casasent: IEEE Trans. C-**22**, 852 (1973)

3.24 C. Mansfield: Optical Deconvolution Using Computer Generated Filters. In *Coherent Optical Processing*, Vol. 52 (SPIE Proc. 1974)

3.25 K. Preston: *Coherent Optical Computers* (McGraw-Hill, New York 1972)

3.26 B. Thompson: Image Formation with Partially Coherent Light. In *Progress in Optics*, ed. by E. Wolf, Vol. VII (North-Holland, Amsterdam 1969) Chap. IV

3.27 H. Wilde: J. SPIE **8**, 35 (1970)

3.28 P. Considine: Opt. Eng. **12**, 36 (1973)

3.29 M. Born, E. Wolf: *Principles of Optics*, 2nd ed. (Pergamon Press, New York 1964)

3.30 L. Martin: *The Theory of the Microscope* (Blackie and Son, Ltd., London 1966) p. 109

3.31 P. Jacquinot: Apodization. In *Progress in Optics*, ed. by E. Wolf, Vol. III (North-Holland, Amsterdam 1964) Chap. II

3.32 G. Parrent, B. Thompson: J. SPIE **5** (1966)

3.33 P. Considine, R. Profio: Image Processing with In-Line Optical Systems. In *Image Information Recovery*, Vol. 16 (SPIE Proc. 1968)

3.34 B. Thompson: Coherent Optical Processing. In *Coherent Optical Processing*, Vol. 52 (SPIE Proc. 1974)

3.35 G. Reynolds, J. Zuckerman, D. Miller, W. Dyes: Opt. Eng. **12**, 23 (1973)

3.36 J. Caulfield: Medical Applications (see Chapter 7 this volume)

4. Synthetic Aperture Radar

E. N. Leith

With 14 Figures

4.1 Overview

Synthetic aperture technology has been under intensive development for more than a quarter of a century, and today has reached a high level of sophistication, particularly in the microwave region of the electromagnetic spectrum. With synthetic aperture techniques, resolution hundreds, or even thousands, of times finer than the diffraction limit of the *actual* receiving antenna can be achieved, particularly in the centimeter wavelength region, where development has been concentrated. We note that the principle has also been extended into radio astronomy, where the success has also been considerable, as well as into the optical region and into the sonic domain, although with more limited success.

We describe the synthetic aperture principle from several viewpoints, including Doppler filtering and holography, and we describe how the data gathered from a synthetic aperture radar is processed by optical means; the optical processing approach is in large part responsible for the enormous success of synthetic aperture radar.

4.2 The Range Doppler Principle

The synthetic aperture principle can be regarded as a subcase of the much broader, range Doppler principle, which is one of the basic pillars of modern radar technology. We begin by examining this important principle, then introduce the synthetic aperture as a special, and very important, case.

In a range-Doppler radar system, the transmitter radiates a signal $f(t)$, which typically is a pulse or a sequence of pulses. A portion of the signal reflected from an object is returned to the radar, which then becomes a receiver. By measuring the round-trip delay time, the range to the object is readily ascertained. By measuring the Doppler shift, the relative radial velocity between radar and object can be determined.

Let the radiated signal be

$$f(t) = a(t) \exp\{j[2\pi f_0 t + \phi(t)]\}, \tag{4.1}$$

where f_0 is the RF carrier frequency and a and ϕ are, respectively, the amplitude and phase modulations impressed on the wave. A point object at range r returns to the radar a signal

$$g(t) = \sigma f(t - 2r/c) = \sigma a(t - 2r/c)$$
$$\cdot \exp\{j[2\pi f_0(t - 2r/c) + \phi(t - 2r/c)]\}, \tag{4.2}$$

which is just the radiated signal time delayed and Doppler shifted; σ is a complex constant containing such factors as the complex reflectivity of the object and the attenuation with distance which, in the radar case, because of the round-trip factor, becomes the inverse fourth-power factor. Note that, in (4.2), $a(\ )$ and $\phi(\ )$ indicate what a and ϕ are functions of, whereas $f_0(\ )$ indicates a multiplication of two factors.

The Doppler shift is implicit in the variable r, which is a time-varying function. Let the radial velocity be v_1, which for simplicity we take to be constant; thus

$$r = r_1 + v_1 t, \tag{4.3}$$

where r_1 is the range at time $t = 0$. We insert (4.3) into (4.2) and make the customary narrow-band approximations

$$a\left[t - \frac{2(r_1 + v_1 t)}{c}\right] \cong a\left(t - \frac{2r_1}{c}\right) \tag{4.4a}$$

$$\phi\left[t - \frac{2(r_1 + v_1 t)}{c}\right] \cong \phi\left(t - \frac{2r_1}{c}\right). \tag{4.4b}$$

These are justified by the assumption that a and ϕ are narrow-band functions which are centered about zero frequency, and therefore, in a short time interval $2(v_1/c)t$, they change negligibly even if the RF carrier term changes considerably. The return signal is then

$$g(t) = \sigma a(t - 2r_1/c)\exp\{j[2\pi f_0(t - 2r_1/c - 2v_1 t/c) + \phi(t - 2r_1/c)]\}$$
$$= \sigma a(t - 2r_1/c)\exp\{j[(2\pi f_0 - 4\pi v_1/\lambda_0)t + \phi(t - 2r_1/c) - 4\pi r_1/\lambda_0]\}$$
$$= \sigma f(t - t_1)\exp(-j2\pi f_{d1} t), \tag{4.5}$$

where the bulk phase delay term $\exp[-j(4\pi r_1/\lambda_0)]$ has been incorporated into σ, the round trip delay time $2r_1/c$ has been written as t_1, and $f_{d1} = 2v_1/\lambda_0$ is the Doppler shift. We measure these and then calculate r_1 and v_1. One of the fundamental problems is to determine optimum forms for $f(t)$, since our ability to make these measurements is strongly dependent on the form of this signal.

The range-Doppler measurement is performed by cross correlating the return signal with a reference function

$$r_c(t) = f(t)\exp(j2\pi f_r t), \tag{4.6}$$

which is a frequency-shifted replica of the radiated pulse, yielding

$$u(t_r, f_r) = r_c \circledast g = \exp(j2\pi f_r t_r) \int f(t - t_r) f^*(t - t_1)$$
$$\cdot \exp[-j2\pi(f_r - f_{dl})t] dt, \tag{4.7}$$

where $\circledast$ represents the cross-correlation operation. This equation is readily placed in the standard form

$$|u(\tau', f')|^2 = |\sigma|^2 |\int f(t' + \tau') f^*(t') \exp(-j2\pi f' t') dt'|^2 \tag{4.8}$$

by the substitutions $t' = t - t_1$, $\tau' = t_1 - t_r$, and $f' = f_r - f_{dl}$. Equation (4.8) is known as the ambiguity function of f. The ambiguity function, somewhat analogous to an impulse response or a point spread function, describes how the system images the object field into a two-dimensional range-Doppler space. The waveform $f(t)$ is designed to give an ambiguity function with a sharp peak at $\tau' = f' = 0$, with low secondary responses. Note that when there are no Doppler shifts, the ambiguity function becomes just the magnitude squared of the autocorrelation function.

The simplest and most commonly used waveform is a single pulse of constant frequency,

$$f(t) = \operatorname{rect}(t/T) \exp(j2\pi f_0 t), \quad \text{where} \quad \operatorname{rect}(t/T) = \begin{cases} 1 & |t| < T/2 \\ 0 & |t| > T/2 \end{cases} \tag{4.9}$$

or a group of such pulses. The ambiguity function is then

$$|u(\tau', f')|^2 = |\sigma|^2 \left| \int_{-T/2}^{T/2} \operatorname{rect}\left(\frac{t' + \tau}{T}\right) \operatorname{rect}(t'/T) \right.$$
$$\left. \cdot \exp(-j2\pi f' t') dt' \right|^2$$
$$= \tfrac{1}{4} |\sigma|^2 |A(\tau/T)|^2 \operatorname{sinc}^2 f'(T - \tau), \tag{4.10}$$

where $\operatorname{sinc} x = \sin \pi x / \pi x$. If $f' = 0$, i.e., if the reference signal matches the returned signal, then u is just the square of the triangular function A, the autocorrelation function of the radiated pulse. The range resolution improves as the pulse is made shorter, as is well known. On the other hand, if $\tau = 0$, that is, if signal and reference match, then u is just the function $\operatorname{sinc}^2 f'T$, the Fourier transform squared of the radiated waveform, and determines the capability of the process to resolve Doppler frequencies. The Doppler frequency resolution is $1/T$, the reciprocal of the pulse duration; this, again, is a well-known result. Evidently, if the pulse is shortened to improve the range resolution, the Doppler resolution is degraded by a similar degree, so that the product of the two resolutions remains unchanged.

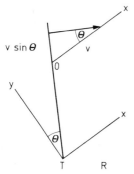

Fig. 4.1. Range-Doppler system. O is object, R is radar, v is object velocity

This result is quite general. We may design sophisticated functions $f(t)$, but we cannot improve on this limitation; the best we can do is to design functions that are relatively free from high sidelobes throughout the (f', τ) domain.

We show (Fig. 4.1) a typical range-Doppler geometry, where a ground-based radar senses an object moving with velocity v. For convenience, we introduce a coordinate system with the x-axis aligned with the velocity vector. Only the radial component, $v \sin \theta$, produces a Doppler shift; the Doppler frequency is therefore

$$f = f_0 - 2v \sin \theta / \lambda . \tag{4.11}$$

The ability of the system to resolve, i.e., distinguish between, two objects close together in angular position and in velocity depends upon resolving their Doppler frequencies. For Doppler frequencies f_1 and f_2 to be just resolved,

$$f_1 - f_2 = 1/T \tag{4.12}$$

where

$$f_1 = f_0 + 2v \sin \theta / \lambda_0$$
$$f_2 = f_0 + 2(v + \Delta v) \sin(\theta + \Delta \theta) / \lambda_0 ,$$

from which we obtain

$$2v \sin \theta / \lambda_0 + 2v \Delta \theta \cos \theta / \lambda_0 = 1/T . \tag{4.13}$$

For two objects at the same angular position and traveling in the same direction,

$$\Delta v = \lambda_0 / (2T \sin \theta) \tag{4.14}$$

is the velocity resolution. The angular position is known to within a beamwidth on the basis of antenna pointing.

Suppose, however, that we have a priori information about the object velocities. The Doppler analysis then enables their azimuthal positions to be determined, with resolution

$$\Delta\theta = \lambda_0/(2vT\cos\theta). \tag{4.15}$$

A number of interesting observations can be made from the foregoing results. First, the frequency analysis is in fact a Fourier transformation, which suggests a similarity to Fraunhofer or Fourier transform holography, in which a signal is Fourier transformed to produce an image. This viewpoint can be amplified if we choose a coordinate system in which the object is stationary and the radar system is in motion. With this viewpoint, which is fully as valid as the other, the Doppler signal sensed at the receiving antenna is indeed just the Fraunhofer diffraction pattern of the scattering object. The detection process is just one of sensing the signal both in amplitude and phase, and Fourier transforming it to obtain the object distribution, a process equivalent to Fourier transform holography. Similarly, if the integration times were sufficiently long that the angular position of the object, and hence the Doppler frequency, changed significantly, then the process would be equivalent to Fresnel holography.

This view is particularly compelling if all of the objects have the same velocity, for then the object configuration remains unchanged and can be considered in its entirety to be at rest, and the antenna then scans across an aperture equal to $vT\cos\theta$, while recording the Fraunhofer diffraction pattern.

This viewpoint is implied by (4.15), in which the distance $vT\cos\theta$ traversed by the objects during the observation time (or, viewed in an object-stationary coordinate system, the distance moved by the antenna) can be written as L, whereupon this equation becomes the well-known expression for angular resolution for an aperture L, except for the factor 2 in the denominator. This additional factor results in resolution twice as good as expected from an aperture L, and comes about because of the round-trip path of the radiation, which generates twice the Doppler frequency that would be generated if the transmitter were at the object.

The viewpoint we have just developed is that of the synthetic aperture. The small receiver, moving along the path, relative to the object field, senses the field along this path, and proper processing of the received data yields the same resolution that would have been produced by an antenna of the full aperture L, focused at infinity; indeed, the synthetic aperture does even better, by a factor 2.

The synthetic aperture process is most explicitly embodied in the geometry where the antenna is mounted on a moving vehicle, such as an airplane, and the object field is the surface of the earth (Fig. 4.2). *Wiley*, as well as *Sherwin* et al. [4.1], the earliest pioneers of this process, indeed formulated it by noting that such Doppler filtering could result in an image of the terrain with considerably better resolution than afforded by the radar beamwidth.

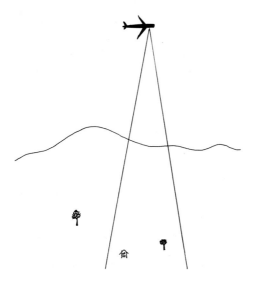

Fig. 4.2. Synthetic aperture system

There are various other range-Doppler system geometries of significance. For example, if the moving objects constitute the surface of a rotating object, a range-Doppler analysis can yield a fine-resolution image of that surface [4.2]. As another example, the moving platform carrying the radar may move in an arc rather than in a straight line. Analysis of such systems often lead to surprising results. In all cases, the systems can alternatively be modeled as a synthetic aperture, or as a holographic system, and these alternative approaches often give useful insights not readily apparent from the basic Doppler-filtering viewpoint.

In summary, we have introduced the concept of Doppler radar and showed its basic similarity to holography. We also introduced the synthetic aperture concept as an interesting way of viewing the Doppler radar process. We considered the special case where the object scene moves as a unit, relative to the sensor, as when an airborne radar senses the passing terrain, and noted that these two alternative views apply most effectively to this situation. In the remainder of this chapter, we restrict our attention to this extremely important case, which has come to be known as synthetic aperture radar.

Synthetic aperture radar, then, is a type of range-Doppler radar in which the objective is to provide resolution better than that afforded by the beamwidth. We can develop comprehensive, detailed, and complete theories of its operation from various viewpoints, including a) Doppler analysis, which is the original viewpoint [4.1, 4, 5], b) the synthesis of a large antenna from a small one, a viewpoint from which the process derives its name [4.4, 5] and c) holography, particularly when optical processing is used [4.6]. Although we have introduced these viewpoints in a context stressing their close relationship, it should be noted that each by itself forms a complete basis for describing the process. Our approach is first to present a moderately comprehensive hybrid Doppler-filtering, synthetic aperture exposition, followed by a purely holographic one, in which context we describe the optical processing. Both of these approaches, we believe, provide good physical insight, each in a somewhat different manner. Finally, we note a fourth viewpoint, that of cross-correlation [4.4, 5], which is strictly a signal-processing approach, providing little insight, but probably the best viewpoint when the data processing is to be performed digitally.

4.3 A Hybrid Doppler, Synthetic Aperture Viewpoint

In presenting a comprehensive description of the synthetic aperture process from the viewpoint of a small antenna simulating a larger one, we first consider just what the larger one does, then consider how the small, scanning antenna can duplicate this process.

Let a receiving antenna be formed of a large number of small receiving elements extending along a line. For an antenna of length L, the receiving pattern is of width $\theta = \lambda_0/L$; hence, the larger the antenna array, the better the resolution. The function of the antenna is to coherently detect the signal impinging on each element and to sum these signals, yielding

$$a = \sum_{i=1}^{n} a_i \tag{4.17}$$

where a_i is the signal received on the i-th element, and each a_i is a complex number $|a_i| \exp j\phi_i$.

The important observation to be made here is that, although all of the elements are required in order to attain the resolution and sidelobe level we expect from such an array, it is not necessary that all elements exist simultaneously. We could employ only a single element of the array, moving it in sequence to all of the positions that would have been occupied by the elements of the large antenna. At each position, the small antenna radiates a pulse and receives the reflected return, which is stored both in phase and amplitude. The stored signals are then coherently summed, thus carrying out the operation that the antenna array would have done. In the absence of the complete array, with its interconnections, which automatically produces the summation, we now require a specially constructed mechanism for the coherent summation, in addition to the previously noted storage device.

We have thus made a tradeoff, avoiding the large antenna, but requiring now a storage device and a summing mechanism. Why would such a tradeoff be considered? The motivation for the synthetic aperture development was in the area of reconnaisance radar, where the desire for extremely high resolution led to antenna sizes too large for an aircraft to carry. At X-band (about 9000 MHz) the wavelength is about 3 cm, and an antenna to duplicate the resolution capability of an aerid reconnaisance camera with 10 cm aperture would have to be about 6000 m long; evidently, we cannot carry such an antenna in an airplane.

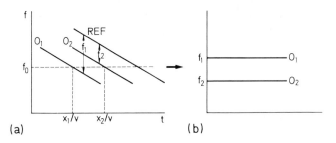

Fig. 4.3a and b. Signal histories and the conversion to constant frequencies

The viewpoint thus developed implicitly assumes that the data from an object is collected over a very short time period, so that the azimuthal position of each object changes negligibly, and the Doppler frequency from each object point is a constant. Thus, a simple Doppler analysis provides resolution, to within an angular resolution given by (4.15). If the data gathering time becomes sufficiently great, the Doppler shift from an object point can no longer be taken as constant over the time interval that it supplies data; thus, a plot of Doppler frequency as a function of time is, to a reasonable approximation, the linear function depicted by curve O_1 in Fig. 4.3a. The Doppler shift is greatest when the object first enters the beam, since at that time the radial component of velocity is greatest. The radial velocity, and thus the Doppler shift, decrease to zero when the object is abeam of the aircraft. When the object is behind the airplane, the radial component of velocity is away from the aircraft, and the Doppler shift is negative.

Another object, O_2, enters the beam at a later time and goes through exactly the same Doppler sequence, or Doppler history, but at a somewhat later time.

How should the data be processed in this more complex situation? The simple Doppler analysis no longer suffices. The simple summation viewpoint suggested by the synthetic aperture viewpoint also fails.

If the incoming signal is mixed with a reference signal which is frequency-swept at the same rate as the signals undergo their Doppler shift, each signal history is converted into a constant frequency (Fig. 4.3b), and again there is a one-to-one correspondence between a frequency component of the return signal and an object position. The frequency analysis, or Fourier transformation, approach again separates the signals originating from the various object points, thereby forming, as before, an image of the object field.

From the viewpoint of the synthetic aperture, the now much larger antenna being synthesized places the object in the Fresnel field rather than in the Fraunhofer field, as before. Therefore, the various complex numbers describing the amplitude and phase of the signals received at each sensing position from a point object now have a quadratic component, which must be compensated before summing the signals. This quadratic phase adjustment, which could be produced by means of a delay line whose length is increased quadratically with position of the small, traveling antenna, constitutes a focusing mechanism, and the aperture synthesis process thus generates a focused antenna, equivalent to a focused real antenna. The range at which the antenna is focused can be adjusted by altering the quadratic phase adjustments.

4.4 The Holographic Viewpoint

The interpretation of the Doppler radar and in particular the synthetic aperture radar as a system which detects the Fraunhofer (or Fresnel) diffraction pattern of the object field and Fourier (or Fresnel) transforms it to obtain an image, either in velocity space or in conventional space, at once suggests a similarity to holography. Why not record the radar returns as a transparency and then process this record as a hologram?

Indeed, there is a compelling reason for such storage even if holography is not considered: the amount of data to be recorded is enormous, and photographic film is even today one of the few storage media which can record such vast amounts of data in a reasonably compact manner. This statement was even more true in the 1950 s, when photographic film was first considered for such applications [4.5].

Also, the data processing problem is considerable, especially when the synthetic aperture is large and focusing factors must be included in the calculations. This consideration led to the use of optical processing [4.5], since in the 1950 s, when synthetic apertures were first considered, digital computers were still in their infancy and an all-range-focused radar would have presented a most unwieldly data processing problem if conventional electronic processors were used. Even the powerful digital computers of today are only marginally suitable for this problem. Film storage and optical processing were first considered because of these factors, not because of holographic considerations.

Nonetheless, regarding the synthetic aperture process (in combination with optical processing) as holography turns out to be immensely useful. Many aspects of the process, which otherwise are abstruse or abstract or describable primarily in mathematical terms, become very physical, elementary, and often quite obvious [4.6, 7].

To describe the synthetic aperture process in terms of holography, consider a point object at a range r (Fig. 4.4). As the radar beam passes across this object, the signal, as a function of time, is, as we have previously shown,

$$f(t) = \exp j2\pi f_0(t - 2r/c). \tag{4.17a}$$

where we have dropped amplitude coefficients. Using the customary paraxial approximation

$$r = r_1 + \tfrac{1}{2}(x - x_1)^2/r_1, \tag{4.18}$$

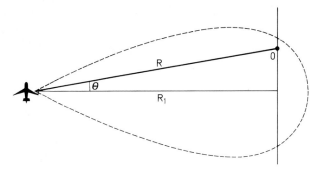

Fig. 4.4. Diagram for synthetic aperture analysis

we have

$$f(t) = \exp\{j[2\pi f_0 t - 2\pi(x-x_1)^2/\lambda r_1]\}, \tag{4.19}$$

where x_1 is the along-track component of the object, r_1 its range at closest approach, x is the aircraft position, and constant phase terms have been dropped. This expression is consistent with the Doppler viewpoint. If we would substitute $x = vt$ into (4.19), where v is the aircraft velocity, and differentiate the phase term to get frequency, we would obtain a signal whose frequency changes linearly with time, as we stated previously. In the above form, however, we recognize the signal as being the familiar quadratically varying phase function encountered in holography. Each point object forms such a signal. We reduce the microwave frequency f_0 to a conveniently low, video carrier frequency f_c, which is typically of the order of 100 Hz, and record the result as

$$s_b + \cos[2\pi f_q x + 2\pi(x-x_1)^2/\lambda r_1] \tag{4.20}$$

where $f_q = f_c/v$, and where we have made the substitution $t = x/v$, and s_b is a bias or grey-level term.

This record we recognize as the familiar zone-plate building block of holography. In this case, however, the zone plate is a one-dimensional function, or cylindrical zone plate, because the radar aperture is scanned only along one dimension. For an object consisting of many points, the hologram will similarly be a summation of many terms of the form of (4.20), each term with its own displacement factor x_1.

However, the scale of the process is far too great. The physical extent over which each signal exists is generally thousands of feet; therefore, we must introduce a scaling factor p, giving

$$s_b + \cos[2\pi f_1 x + 2\pi p^2(x-x_1/p)^2/\lambda_0 r_1] \tag{4.21}$$

where we have made the substitution $x \to x/p$, and $f_1 = f_q/p$ is the spatial carrier, after modification by the scaling process. The record now has a length of the

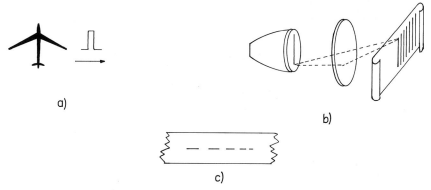

b)

c)

Fig. 4.5a—c. Recording of synthetic aperture data. (a) transmission of pulse; (b) recording from cathode ray tube; (c) resulting film record

order of a few millimeters or centimeters, and is suitable for insertion into an optical system.

This hologram is formed from a single range-resolution element. We are interested in forming a hologram from data collected over a range interval which includes hundreds or even thousands of range elements. Data from different ranges are separable through the pulsing of the radar. By appropriate recording of the radar returns, we can generate a record on which the zone plate signals from different ranges are recorded along different positions across the width of the film. The entire process is carried out as in Fig. 4.5. The return pulse is displayed as an intensity-modulated line trace on a cathode ray tube. Each spot along this line represents one sample of data from one range. This trace is recorded as a line on photographic film. The next pulse is recorded adjacently, and so on. If there is, for example, an object scatterer at range r_1, then each recorded trace will have, at the position corresponding to r_1, an intensity which departs from the average intensity in such a manner that when all traces are recorded the film transmittance at the position corresponding to r_1 will exhibit fluctuations along the x direction in accordance with the zone-plate pattern of (4.21).

The resulting hologram, in addition to comprising cylindrical-lens zone plates rather than spherical ones, differs in other ways from the conventional holograms made at optical wavelengths. First, the coordinates of the hologram are not the two lateral coordinates of the aperture plane, but rather, only one such lateral coordinate is used, with the range or object-depth dimension being the other coordinate, obtained through the pulsing process. Also, the object field, while approximately planar, lies in a peculiar orientation with respect to the aperture plane, being highly tilted; the reconstructed images therefore also lie in tilted planes. These factors influence the optical processing procedure.

If we treat the record as a hologram and illuminate it with a beam of coherent light, we obtain the customary true and conjugate image fields (Fig. 4.6). Each

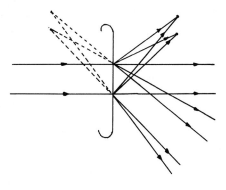

Fig. 4.6. Illumination of signal record with coherent light

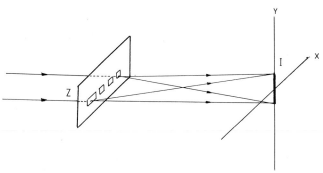

Fig. 4.7. Focusing of cylindrical zone plate Z. Image I is sharp along x, smeared along y, since rays converge along x-dimension, but fan out along y-dimension

field is an optical reconstruction, miniaturized through the scaling process, of the original radar field sensed by the radar receiver. Each image point is an optical image of an original object point which had been radar illuminated, and having resolution corresponding to the full aperture generated by the scanning antenna; thus, the holographic process reconstructs in accordance with the *synthetic* aperture, not the *actual* one. And this entire process has been carried out without any complicated computational equipment. Free space, with its propagation characteristics [4.8], results in the production of the holographic record from the original object field, and we have used the same free-space propagation characteristics, although with a different wavelength, to undo these propagation characteristics.

There are two difficulties which must be overcome. First, the zone plates have focal power in one dimension only. The image formed is sharp along the x-dimension, but along the transverse dimension, representing range, the image is not sharp at all, but smeared. Resolution in this dimension, labelled y in Fig. 4.7, resides on the signal record itself, since returns from different ranges are recorded at different positions across the film record, and therefore, the radar data has the data record itself as the focal plane for the range dimension.

The imaging process to this point is anamorphic, with the radar image being focused in the x-dimension at a position in front of (or behind) the film record, but focused in the y or range dimension at the signal record itself. This anamorphic defect must be corrected.

Examination of the focal properties of the zone plate signals reveals another complication. The signals focus a distance

$$F = \pm (1/2p^2)(\lambda_0/\lambda_L)r_1 \tag{4.22}$$

from the signal record, where λ_0 is the radar wavelength, λ_L the wavelength of the illuminating light, and p, as before, is the scaling factor; this expression is just the usual one well known in optical holography. However, we observe that signals from short ranges focus closest to the signal record, and signals from longer ranges focus farther from the signal record. The reconstructed images, under collimated illumination, then consist of two highly tilted planes, one a virtual image, the other a real image, each having a tilt corresponding to the tilt of the object plane (Fig. 4.8).

To record one of these images, we must cause all image points to focus sharply in both dimensions in a single plane, parallel or nearly parallel to the signal record. Thus, we need a compensating anamorphic system which corrects this range variation of focal lenght and causes each image point to be sharply focused in each dimension at a single location; or, stated equivalently, which untilts the tilted plane and brings it into coincidence with the plane of sharp range focus.

A number of most unusual optical systems have been devised to do this. Such optical systems are certainly among the strangest ever devised. They have little versatility, being useful for only one purpose—they carry out this compensation process. They do it, however, remarkably well, in an exceedingly cost-effective way.

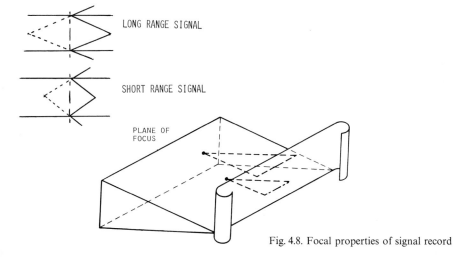

LONG RANGE SIGNAL

SHORT RANGE SIGNAL

PLANE OF FOCUS

Fig. 4.8. Focal properties of signal record

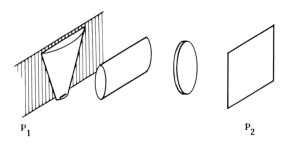

P₁   P₂

Fig. 4.9. Conical lens optical processor

One of the earliest, and most easily explainable, systems comprises a spherical lens, a cylindrical lens, and a conical lens. The conical lens is placed against the signal record (Fig. 4.9). Any segment of the lens along x is a cylindrical lens, chosen so that its focal power is equal but opposite to the negative focal length component of the zone plate signals corresponding to that range. Since these have focal length proportional to range, so must the focal length of the compensating lens vary linearly with the y, or range, dimension, hence the term *conical lens*. At each range, the virtual images are reimaged to infinity, and the tilted plane is thus erected, although it is now inconveniently located. Next, the plane of sharp range focus (the signal record itself) is imaged to infinity by means of a cylindrical lens placed so that the signal record is in the front focal plane of the lens, and oriented so that the focal power is along the y dimension. This lens then images the range focal plane to infinity. The image, now perfectly corrected, is reimaged from infinity by a conventional spherical lens.

This system is little used today, primarily because it produces range dependent magnification, a consequence of the conical lens having a different focal length for each range [4.6]. The resulting image is thus distorted by being magnified along the x dimension by an amount different for different ranges. This distortion is readily corrected by placing a vertical slit at the image plane. As the signal record moves through the aperture, the image moves past the slit, and a recording film located behind the slit moves in synchronism with the signal record, continuously recording the image falling on the slit. The more magnified parts of the image move faster, with the result that this magnification differential is eliminated, and the resulting image record is free from distortion.

However, if the image formed by the optical system were not thus distorted, the slit would be unnecessary, and the recording film could move in synchronism with the image, that is, track the image, thereby giving an exposure increase of up to several hundred. This possibility led us to seek other optical systems, which would remove the anamorphic defects without introducing the variable magnification. The most successful of these is the tilted plane optical processor [4.9]. This is a most elegant system, accomplishing all of the desired results, without any undesirable side effects. The operation of the system is more difficult to explain; however, we summarize its operation as follows. The tilted plane optical system consists of cylindrical and spherical lenses arranged in

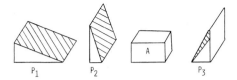

Fig. 4.10. The tilted plane processor concept. Plane P_1 images to P_3 in the x meridian, P_2 to P_3 in the y meridian. A is an anamorphic imaging system, consisting of cylindrical and spherical lenses

telescopic configurations. It has the property that any tilted plane is imaged onto another tilted plane (Fig. 4.10) with equal magnification throughout this plane. Because of the cylindrical lenses, the system has different imaging properties in the x and y meridians. In the x-dimension, a highly tilted plane P_1 is reimaged with a reduced tilt. In the y-dimension, a tilted plane P_2 is imaged into a plane with the same, or slightly different, tilt. The radar data is introduced into the aperture with some small tilt; thus, portions of the film corresponding to different ranges are at a slightly different distance from the lens system. By adjusting the various lenses, the tilt of the final image can be adjusted separately in the two meridians, and the position of the image along the z-dimension can be adjusted. Thus, the range and azimuthal image planes of the data record can be brought into coincidence (at plane P_3), but without introducing distortion. The recording film is also tilted, so as to coincide with the image.

By tracking the image, i.e., moving the recording film in synchronism with the image, the artifact noise resulting from dust, bubbles, etc., on the lenses is largely eliminated, and also, we can utilize more radar data than we could place at any one time in the aperture, assuming that the radar system has a sufficiently wide beam to acquire this excess data. The resulting incoherent integration thus reduces the speckle noise associated with coherent systems. Such speckle noise has long been known in imaging radar, since most radar systems have considerable coherence.

4.5 Pulse Compression

Although our beginning analysis of the range-Doppler principle considered the transmission of arbitrary waveforms, we subsequently considered only narrow pulses of constant frequency. By choosing more sophisticated waveforms, we gain an important practical advantage. As our analysis indicated, we may radiate long, coded pulses and cross-correlate the return signal with a replica of the transmitted pulse, obtaining resolution in range corresponding to the relatively narrow autocorrelation function of the waveform rather than to its duration (4.8). By this method, the radar can transmit a high average power level, leading to greater range capability, without incurring either the poor range resolution which would normally result from long pulses, or high peak power in the transmitter, which could result in insulation breakdown and other problems. The technique of radiating a long pulse and compressing it in the receiver is called pulse compression [4.10].

Fig. 4.11. A two-dimensional anamorphic zone plate formed by recording the Doppler shift of a sequence of chirp pulses

A commonly used waveform is the linearly frequency modulated, or chirp, pulse. This pulse is typically several hundred times longer than we would use for the uncoded case, and the frequency changes linearly with time over the pulse duration. Such a waveform, if recorded photographically, would form a cylindrical Fresnel zone plate, just as do the synthetic aperture radar signals. The compression process could then be carried out optically merely by using the zone plates as lenses [4.11–16]. Analysis shows that the structure of the focused image corresponds exactly to the result produced by forming the autocorrelation function of the pulse.

By radiating a chirp pulse in a synthetic aperture system, the return signals recorded by the radar become two-dimensional zone plates, although the focal properties are different in the two dimensions (Fig. 4.11). Such signals can be processed using any of the optical systems previously described, merely by readjusting the various lenses. This focusing operation results in simultaneous Doppler analysis and pulse compression; these two operations are treated as a single, two-dimensional operation [4.17]. By incorporating the pulse compression capability into a synthetic aperture radar system, the already powerful optical computing capability is carried a step further.

4.6 Some Optical Processors

The conical lens optical system was implemented in various forms and was the principle type of processor from the mid 1950s until 1962, when the tilted plane processor was developed.

One early form of conical lens processor used a Fresnel zone plate equivalent of the conical lens (Fig. 4.12). This system has been described previously as an optical correlator. By viewing it as a holographic system, some interesting observations follow. The zone plate conical lens R is positioned so as to be imaged onto the signal record at P_3. At the intermediate plane P_2, spatial filtering removes the zero order and one first order. If we pass the sideband corresponding to the positive focal length term, the wavefront presented to the

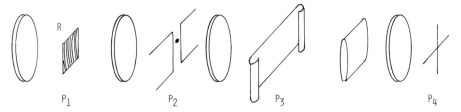

Fig. 4.12. Zone plate conical lens processor

signal record is much as if we had used the refractive conical lens described previously. There are two interesting differences, however, which become apparent when we write the expression for the zone plate conical lens,

$$\tfrac{1}{2} + \tfrac{1}{2}\cos(2\pi f_1 x + 2\pi p^2 x^2/\lambda_0 y), \tag{4.23}$$

where the coefficient of the quadratic term varies with y, thus providing the required range variation of focal length.

This zone plate is, as a consequence of the carrier term f_1, akin to a diffraction grating and is therefore wavelength dispersive. Similarly, the zone plate signals are wavelength dispersive. Since the $+1$ order (the real image term) of the conical lens is used for illuminating the signal record, and the -1 order (the virtual image term) of the signal record is used for the output image, the dispersions of the two structures cancel. This dispersion, called lateral dispersion, is present in off-axis holography, but not in in-line holography, leading to greater source coherence requirements for off-axis holography. By this compensation method, however, we have reduced the coherence requirements of off-axis holography to those of in-line holography.

But there is yet more compensation available. Both the zone plate conical lens and signal record have focal lengths which are wavelength dependent (4.22). Since we use the positive focal length of the conical lens to balance the negative focal length of the signal record, the focal powers cancel, and with them the wavelength dependence of image focal position. Thus, this optical system can be used in perfectly white light. The holographic system we have thus described, although a coherent system, has no temporal coherence requirements at all, in sharp contrast to Gabor's form of holography, which had some modest but rather definite temporal coherence requirements. Although this system was used only for the reconstruction process, the theory applies equally to the process of making an optical hologram.

Further analysis, however, reveals a limitation. The λ-compensation produced by cancellation of the quadratic components occurs at only one point in the field, namely, for that image point whose zone plate is aligned with the conical lens zone plate. At all other positions in the field, wavelength dispersion exists. Therefore, we must use a slit so as to view only one point (for each range element) at a time. As the signal record moves through the aperture, each signal zone plate lines up in turn with the conical lens zone plate, producing at that instant, for that image point, an achromatic image, which is sampled by the slit. Since a sampling slit is necessary anyway in order to remove the differential magnification, incorporating this achromatic capability does not impose any new limitations.

We note that the compensation provided by the carrier term of the zone plate conical lens, as opposed to that of the quadratic term, occurs over the entire field. We note also that the refractive conical lens described earlier provides no dispersion correction, first, because it has no carrier term, and second, because the quadratic component, being produced by refraction instead of by refraction, has a different form of λ-dependence.

Although our earliest holographic theories, developed in 1955, embodied these achromatizing techniques, we nonetheless chose not to take advantage of them. We preferred the Hg arc source to a white light source, and the coherence requirements were so slight that the Hg source provided the required coherence even if neither lateral nor longitudinal dispersions were corrected. We therefore used the refractive instead of the zone plate conical lens, because it was simpler and led to a more compact system.

The most advanced optical processors, utilizing the tilted plane concept, have been dominant since 1963. One such processor, known as the Precision Optical Processor, or POP, is perhaps the most advanced and exacting instrument ever constructed for optical processing of radar data [4.9]. It accepts film up to

Fig. 4.13a. A sample of signal film

Fig. 4.13b. A processed result

127 mm in width, gives diffraction limited performance over a 60 mm aperture, and can process 6000 separate channels, each with a space bandwidth product of 6000. The long-term film speed stability is better than one part in 20000, and the drive jitter is less than 1 μm. Film speeds can be varied over a 10000:1 range.

A radar image (Fig. 4.13), produced by the ERIM experimental synthetic aperture radar system and the POP processor, shows a suburban area west of Detroit, Michigan. Although both the radar system and the optical processor were coherent systems, the artifact noise associated with coherent illumination is absent, being eliminated by the averaging process embodied in tracking. A wide variety of object types, including lakes, trees, and subdivisions, can be seen. Of particular interest are the shadows cast by the trees; these shadows outline the shapes of the trees better than do the tree images themselves. Also note (upper left) the extremely strong point object, which has saturated the recording film. The sidelobe energy, both in the x and y dimensions, is strongly visible, even though about 20–30 dB below the primary lobe, giving this image a cross-like appearance.

4.7 Critique of the Holographic Viewpoint

The application of holographic concepts to synthetic aperture radar has been most fruitful. One might ask the question, how did the two areas merge? Their merger certainly must have been an event of low probability, since in the early 1950s the areas were extremely small and widely separated. Holography, or wavefront reconstruction as it was then called, was known to few opticists, and we doubt that any radar engineers had ever heard of it. Similarly, synthetic aperture radar was a small area, known even to very few radar scientists, and probably to no optical engineers.

There are, in fact, many misconceptions about this relationship. First, although synthetic aperture radar is most readily understood, at least by optical engineers and probably also by laymen in terms of holography and is most commonly described from this viewpoint, holographic concepts are certainly not at all necessary for either describing or understanding it, as we have already shown. Indeed, the process was conceived and developed without the aid of holographic concepts. Even the optical processing can be described without resort to holography.

On the other hand, the holographic viewpoint is helpful in understanding the process in a basic, physical way, and the physical insight thus provided has led to ideas that otherwise would have perhaps never been conceived. The tilted plane processor is one such example; certainly, one would find it quite difficult, although not at all impossible, to explain this system without the concept of the reconstructed image and its tilted planes.

Writers who have discussed the union of holography and synthetic aperture radar generally fall into two groups: those who assume that the synthetic aperture process was an outgrowth of holography, and those who believe that the similarity was first recognized after synthetic aperture systems, along with their optical processors, had already reached a high state of development. Both groups are quite wrong.

As we have noted, synthetic aperture radar was born in 1951 as a rather special but important case of Doppler radar. In 1954, the University of Michigan group (now associated with ERIM) was founded; this group introduced many new ideas, including all-range focusing and optical processing. The early optical processing ideas were based on incoherent light. Coherent optical processing methods were explored beginning in 1955. While analyzing the effects of coherent illumination, the discovery was made that if radar data stored on a transparency were illuminated with coherent light, the fields in the first diffracted orders would be optical replicas of the fields sensed at the receiving antenna. This discovery was made in a very early stage of the work, and essentially all subsequent work on the optical processing part of the radar was based on the holographic viewpoint. A theory of the radar system and the companion optical processor was developed which paralleled the earlier work of *Gabor*, which at that time was not widely known, and not known to us. Our early work was essentially theoretical; it was not until three years later that our system was completed and test flown. Our theoretical work was then verified.

Some of the significant points of our holographic theory are as follows:

1) As originally formulated, it applied to *both* synthetic and non-synthetic aperture radars. It is of course irrelevant whether the data to be formed into a hologram is recorded all at once or a portion at a time.

2) Carrier frequency, or off-axis holography, was conceived.

3) Although the chromatic compensation principles we developed apply equally to both the hologram making and reconstruction processes, our techniques were applied only to the reconstruction process, since this was the only part that was carried out optically. In the radar system, however, the lateral dispersion phenomenon is inherently absent. Indeed, the achromatic fringe systems we have described elsewhere [4.18] for making holograms, using light of limited coherence, are essentially optical counterparts of the conventional modulators and demodulators employed in electronic communication systems, including of course our radar system.

4) The novelty of holography, as applied to radar, was in some basic respects different from that of its application to electron waves and optics. In the latter areas, the possibility of recording and reconstructing a wavefield had been conceived, but a technique for doing it had not been discovered until *Gabor* introduced the holographic, or coherent background, method. The novelty lies, therefore, not in the basic concept of storing and reconstructing a wavefront, but in its accomplishment and in the theory describing it. In the electronics case, however, the recording of signals containing both amplitude and phase and the subsequent signal reconstitution had not been a problem and had been done routinely for many decades prior to holography. Wave fields could be stored, from which either the wave field or the source distribution could be recon-

stituted, for example, sound recordings, whether on photographic film or on other media, and of course, range-Doppler radar systems. In the radar domain, the novelty of the holographic viewpoint was not at all in accomplishing these operations, but in the specific way of doing it. The specific technique of sensing a wave field, recording it as a transparency, and reconstructing the field at optical wavelengths by illumination of the transparency with coherent light was quite novel. Also, there was novelty in describing in a new way processes that had long been known. The processes involved in the optical processing of the radar data were optical implementations of well known processes. What we have described as radar holography can equally well be described as correlation, matched filtering, Doppler filtering with phase adjustment, and so on. All aspects of what we had previously described in the other ways were now described in this new way. For example, the upper and lower sideband terms resulting from the multiplication of the incident light with the signal record became the conjugate image terms well known in holography.

This viewpoint can be broadened by noting that many, if not most, of the techniques of holography are optical counterparts of techniques long practiced by communication engineers; thus, in terms of basic concepts, holography represents largely a transfer of technology from one field to another. Certainly, our off-axis optical holography is an adaptation of a technique that had long been used in communication technology. It is in reality the avoidance of aliasing in situations where a signal is shifted to new spectral regions. Other methods of twin image separation, such as the single sideband technique of *Lohmann* [4.19] and the in-phase and quadrature method of *Gabor* [4.20] are likewise adaptations from other technology. To a large degree, this is true of even the basic ideas of holography. For example, in our first paper on holography [4.21], we described the process in terms of communication theory; the specific framework used was the theory of pulse compression. We indeed took the theory nearly intact and applied it to holography. Holography, then in addition to being a close analog of a Doppler radar system, is also a very close analog of a radar pulse compression system. Both radar techniques, of course, antedate holography. Adaptation of technology from one field to another, quite diverse one is certainly an innovative process and can be a highly productive one.

Finally, we raise the question, should the synthetic aperture process be regarded as a subclass of holography, or should it not. Both views are offered in the literature. We think it should not, and have described such techniques as quasi-holography. The conception and early development of this process had no connection with holography, and involved neither the adaptation nor reinvention of techniques originating in holography. Synthetic aperture radar and holography have as a common basis the sensing and storage of a diffraction field and the reconstruction of the object distribution from this sensed data; these processes, however, by no means originated in holography.

We should perhaps regard holography in the original sense, as given by *Gabor*, as the recording, on an area detector such as photographic film, of the interference between the diffraction pattern of a coherently illuminated object field and a background or reference wave, with the subsequent illumination of this record with a coherent beam so as to regenerate this field. By so doing, we may be so restrictive as to exclude some recognized forms of holography, but employment of a definition much broader than this is likely to bring in techniques which are historically unrelated to and older than holography. By this definition, we would describe synthetic aperture techniques not as holography, but as a microwave analog to holography, to which holographic techniques have been fruitfully applied. This is probably the most satisfactory viewpoint.

4.8 The Cross Correlation Viewpoint

If we formulate mathematically any of the previously mentioned viewpoints, or any hybrid combination, we can always put the resulting equations into the form of a cross-correlation of the incoming signal with a reference function which is a copy of the signal one would expect from a point object. This correlation viewpoint has been developed at length elsewhere, and we do not stress it here. However, we find it interesting that the various descriptions, Doppler filtering, aperture synthesis, holography, and cross-correlation, diverse as they are when described physically, become identical when formulated mathematically.

The cross-correlation viewpoint, however, better than any other, renders understandable the well known all-range-focusing capability of the synthetic aperture radar system, implied in our holographic viewpoint. Since the form of the recorded signal, as manifested in the quadratic phase factor, is a function of range, it is apparent that each range element must be processed differently, for example, by correlation with a reference function which is different for each range. Since the pulsing provides resolution in range, we can store the data from each range separately and process them differently, so that each range is cross-correlated with the reference function proper for that range. Thus, the synthetic antenna is in effect focused simultaneously at all ranges, a most remarkable feat when viewed in terms of the capabilities of conventional antennas [4.4].

4.9 Coherence Requirements

Since the synthetic aperture process assumes that the radiation is coherent, and since the process is a close analog of holography, we raise the question, what are the coherence requirements, and what happens if we fail to meet them? Inasmuch as we are describing the process in a holographic context, we find it instructive to compare the coherence requirements with those of conventional holography.

There is one essential difference between synthetic aperture radar and holography which bears on the coherence requirements. In optical holography,

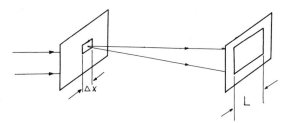

Fig. 4.14. Beam spreading in holography

as in optical interferometry, the recorded field is time averaged over a large number of cycles of the light wave, whereas in synthetic aperture radar, as well as in radio frequency technology in general, the recorded field is the instantaneous one, with no time averaging at all. Thus, a lack of coherence between the interferring beams reduces the contrast of the interference fringes, whereas a lack of coherence in the radar case does not affect the contrast, but introduces phase errors into the resulting signal, which results in an image with poorer resolution.

Despite this rather basic difference, we can establish suitable coherence criteria for the two processes and make comparisons.

The coherence requirements for optical holography have been widely discussed. We introduce here a criterion which expresses the temporal coherence requirement in terms of a single, rather basic quantity, the compression (or expansion) ratio. We assume an object transparency with resolution cell size Δx (Fig. 4.14). In producing a hologram, let the light diffracted by this cell be spread over a lineal distance L. The ratio $L/\Delta x$ we call the expansion ratio. Similarly, in reconstruction, this process is reversed, with the light from the spread function of width L being compressed into a cell of size Δx. Thus, $L/\Delta x$ is now the compression ratio.

In conventional Gabor in-line holography using transparencies, the temporal coherence requirement, that is the allowable spectral spread of the source, is readily shown to be

$$\Delta\lambda/\lambda = 4/C,\qquad\qquad(4.24)$$

where C is the compression ratio. This criterion applies to both the making and the reconstruction process. Other factors, such as object size number of resolution cells, etc., are irrelevant. This requirement is imposed by the longitudinal chromatic dispersion, which is manifested by the λ-variation of the holographic zone plate focal lengths. It is an extremely modest requirement; for example, we can set $C = 50$, in which case a resolution cell can have its energy spread in area 2500 times, while utilizing a source spectral bandwidth of up to 400 Å. Hg sources can be far more coherent than this, and are thus entirely adequate for the task.

The same coherence requirement applies to off-axis holography, provided lateral dispersion is compensated. However, for three-dimensional, reflecting objects, the situation is radically different; superimposed on the previous requirement is a coherence length equal to about twice the object depth, which translates into a $\Delta\lambda/\lambda$ typically thousands of times smaller than that given above.

How should we model the coherence requirements for the synthetic aperture process? We note, first of all, that the term frequency stability, rather than coherence, is the more conventional terminology. There are many ways in which extraneous frequency shifts (i.e., phase errors) can be introduced into the recorded signals, such as frequency shifts in the master oscillator or in the receiver local oscillator, and extraneous motions of the aircraft, including yawing, pitching, rolling and sideslipping. All effects are basically equivalent in the way they degrade the output image. An in-depth discussion of stability requirements is given by *Harger* [4.22].

A simple approach is to assume the master oscillator, which feeds both the transmitter and receiver, to execute an extraneous linear increase in frequency over the time of data collection from a point object. Ignoring amplitude coefficients, the radiated signal is

$$f = \text{expj}(2\pi f_0 t + \pi\alpha t^2) \tag{4.25}$$

where α is the frequency sweep rate in Hz s^{-1}. The return signal is $f(t - 2r/c)$, which is mixed with a reference signal $f(t)\exp(-j2\pi f_c t)$, where f_c is a video carrier term. The signal, after mixing, is of the form

$$\text{expj}(2\pi f_c t - 2\pi f_0 v^2 t^2/cr_1 - 4\pi\alpha r_1 t/c$$
$$- 2\pi\alpha v^2 t^3/cr_1 + 4\pi\alpha v^2 t^2/c^2). \tag{4.26}$$

where v is the aircraft velocity. In deriving the result, we assumed the paraxial approximation $r = r_1 + v^2 t^2/2r_1$ where $vt = x$, the aircraft position; we assumed that the term $\pi\alpha t^2$ changed negligibly in a pulse round-trip period, so that terms of the form $\pi\alpha t^2$ are removed in the mixing process, and we discarded a term in t^4.

The last three terms inside the parentheses represent the instability effects. We require that these be less that $\pi/2$ over the data collection time T. Examination shows the first of these to be the largest; neglecting the others, we can set it equal to or less than $\pi/2$, and with rearrangement we obtain

$$\pi\alpha T^2 \leq (\pi/4)(cT/2r_1) \tag{4.27}$$

where the term on the left is the phase error in the transmitted signal. In this form, we see that in a time $T = 2r_1/c$ required for the pulse to propagate to the object at range r_1 and back, a transmission distance of $2r_1$, the allowable phase error $\pi\alpha T^2$ in the transmitter is $\pi/4$. This corresponds to the coherence length criterion for reflecting-object holography, and would be exactly this if we time delayed the reference signal by an amount equal to the average delay of the radar signal. We then require stability over a propagation time corresponding to the depth of the object field.

The second term, after appropriate manipulation, can be put in the form

$$\Delta\lambda/\lambda = 1/C \tag{4.28}$$

which is the coherence requirement for transmission holography. Note that the video-carrier frequency f_c does not enter into either of the above stability conditions. Since the carrier term is introduced without change in path length, it can have nothing to do with the coherence requirement. Thus, there is inherently no difference in coherence requirements between the in-line case ($f_c = 0$) and the off-axis case. Further considerations show that the grating methods by which the coherence requirements of off-axis holography are reduced to those of in-line holography are optical counterparts of the usual procedures in electronic modulators.

4.10 Spurious Aircraft Motion

The basic theory has assumed that the aircraft flies a straight line path, to within a few mm ($\lambda/10$ for 3 cm wavelengths) and at essentially constant velocity. Of course, it generally does not. The effect of extraneous motion is readily calculated [4.22, 23]. In general, the resolution is degraded, just as when the frequency f_0 undergoes perturbation. Fortunately, spurious aircraft motions are usually of low frequency, so that over one synthetic aperture lenght, the perturbation function can be approximated as a linear or quadratic function of time. If linear, as would occur if the aircraft velocity vector were mispointed but constant, the effect would be to add a constant Doppler frequency to the expected Doppler frequency from each point object. This effect is as if the object were shifted in its angular position. Thus, whole sections of an image will be laterally shifted relative to portions where there is no extraneous aircraft motion, with the image being compressed in the transition region, where the error begins. Such a phase error gives rise to curious effects, such as curves in road images, when the road is in fact straight. Airport runways may be imaged with sharp curves, an effect which could be disconcerting. However, there will be no loss of resolution.

If the phase error is quadratic, the resulting phase error combines with the proper quadratic component of the Doppler term to give a modified Doppler term. The focal length of the resulting zone plate is thus changed, but this effect can be corrected by refocusing in the optical processor. Automatic focusing devices have been developed for such compensation. Higher order phase errors result in loss of resolution.

The complete solution lies in motion compensation systems, which sense the aircraft accelerations and introduce correcting terms into the received signals. The correcting signals may be derived either by inertial means, through the use of accelerometers mounted near the antenna, or by Doppler methods. The success of these motion compensation systems are in large measure responsible for the success of synthetic aperture radar.

If there are moving objects on the ground, their motion will add to the expected Doppler shifts. If an object (a train, for example) has a constant radial velocity as seen from the radar, the train will be imaged sharply, but in the wrong location, so that it could be found parallel to, but several hundred feet from the track. If the velocity is constant, but parallel to the aircraft flight path, the quadratic component of the zone plate signal will be altered, and the focal length will be different from that of a stationary object at the same range. Thus, not only can moving objects be imaged, but also their velocities, both radial and cross-radial, can be measured, provided we have a priori information about the object position.

4.11 Digital Methods

When the all-range-focused synthetic aperture radar was developed in the 1950s, optical processing dominated the other methods. Now that the digital computer has developed into an extremely powerful and versatile tool, its use is extending into synthetic aperture technology [4.24–26].

Digital methods have entered in two basic ways. First, there is the hybrid optical-digital technology, in which the principal task, the compression of the raw data into a high resolution image, is carried out be means of optical processing. Thus, the optical system performs the task it does best. The output image is then converted by, for example, an image converter into an electrical signal, which is then digitized and stored on tape. The various image processing operations which are normally carried out by digital computers can then be performed on the imagery. Such operations include edge sharpening, pattern recognition, level slicing, and introduction of pseudo-color. Thus the economy and speed of optical processing are combined with the flexibility and precision of the digital computer.

One such facility operates in combination with the Precision Optical Processor. The system can digitize the images which are formed at the output of the optical processor, or images from field records, or the raw data record itself, as it exists on the signal film recorded by the radar system. In the latter case, the entire data processing operation is performed digitally. One advantage of this latter mode is that the digitally stored final image can preserve the large (50–60 dB) dynamic range which is inherent in the radar data and previously was available only as a light distribution in the output plane of the optical processor.

Wholly digital methods are being developed by various groups. The advantages of an all-digital approach are:

1) In-flight processing is more readily attainable by digital means than by optical.

2) Results are more reproducible with digital methods.

3) Recently, digital methods have been developed for motion compensation, and digital processing fits naturally with digital compensation methods, to form all-digital processing systems for real-time, motion-compensated synthetic aperture imagery.

The operation to be performed has been described as a correlation, for each element in range, between the incoming signal and a reference function, a formulation well suited to the digital method. The data are gathered and a correlation is formed for each range element. When a correlation is completed, the oldest data are dumped, new data are added, and the next correlation takes place. The successive correlations are taken one azimuth-resolution element apart. The amount of data involved in each correlation determines the width of the synthetic aperture thus generated.

One of the major aims of current research is to develop algorithms which reduce the rather considerable memory and arithmetic requirements. A number of such algorithms have to date been developed which have considerably relieved the computer requirements.

We judge the optical processors to be at present more cost effective, but this situation may in time change. An effective real time capability would substantially increase the attractiveness of optical processing, and some promising work on real time correlators and transducers from incoherent to coherent light and from electrical signals to coherent light are being reported [4.27]. We expect substantial future progress in both the digital and optical technology, and at this stage we cannot predict which way the balance will tip.

In any event, optical processing and synthetic aperture radar have proved a powerful combination, with each technology deriving strength from the other. The enormus success of synthetic aperture radar would have at best been delayed, and perhaps would not have occurred, without optical processing, while optical processing technology has found in synthetic aperture radar its best application. The combination has given rise to some of the most unusual and intriguing optical systems ever developed.

References

4.1   C.W.Sherwin, J.P.Ruina, R.D.Rawcliffe: IRE Trans. MIL-**6**, 111—115 (1962)
4.2   R.M.Goldstein, R.L.Carpenter: Science **139**, 910 (1963)
4.3   L.J.Porcello, C.E.Heerema, N.G.Massey: J. Geophys. Res. **74**, 27 (1969)
4.4   L.J.Cutrona, W.E.Vivian, E.N.Leith, G.O.Hall: IRE Trans. MIL-**5**, 127—131 (1961)
4.5   L.J.Cutrona, E.N.Leith, L.J.Porcello, W.E.Vivian: Proc. IEEE **54**, 1026—1032 (1966)
4.6   E.N.Leith, A.L.Ingalls: Appl. Opt. **7**, 539 (1968)
4.7   E.N.Leith: Proc. IEEE **59**, 1305 (1971)
4.8   J.W.Goodman: *Introduction to Fourier Optics* (McGraw-Hill, New York 1968) p.60
4.9   A.Kozma, E.Leith, N.G.Massey: Appl. Opt. **11**, 1766 (1972)
4.10 J.R.Klauder, A.L.Price, S.Darlington, W.J.Albersheim: Bell System. Tech. J. **34**, 745 (1960)
4.11 E.N.Leith: New Developments in the Michigan System. In *5th Annual Radar Symposium Record* (Ann Arbor, Mich. 1959)

4.12 E.N.Leith: A Technique for Simultaneous Pulse Compression and Beam Sharpening. In *Proc. 2nd Conf. Pulse Compression* (Rome Air Development Center, Rome, New York 1960)

4.13 W.C.Curtis: Private communication (1959)

4.14 L.Lambert: Optical Correlation. In *Modern Radar*, ed. by R. Berkowitz (Wiley-Interscience, New York 1965) Chap. 3

4.15 F.Dickey: Some New Techniques in Pulse Compression. In *Proc. 2nd Conf. Pulse Compression* (Rome Air Development Center, Rome, New York 1960)

4.16 A.Reich, L.Slobodin: U.S. Patent 3 189 746. Issued June 15, 1965

4.17 E.N.Leith: IEEE Trans. AES-**4**, 879—885 (1968)

4.18 E.N.Leith, J.Upatnieks: J. Opt. Soc. Am. **57**, 975 (1967)

4.19 A.Lohmann: Opt. Acta **3**, 97 (1956)

4.20 D.Gabor, W.P.Goss: J. Opt. Soc. Am. **56**, 849 (1966)

4.21 E.N.Leith, J.Upatnieks: J. Opt. Soc. Am. **52**, 1123 (1962)

4.22 R.O.Harger: *Synthetic Aperture Radar Systems: Theory and Design* (Academic Press, New York 1970)

4.23 W.E.Vivian, L.J.Cutrona, E.N.Leith: "A Doppler Technique for Obtaining Very Fine Angular Resolution from a Sidelooking, Airborne Radar," Tech. Report 2144-5T (Univ. of Mich., Ann Arbor, Michigan 1954)

4.24 D.A.Ausherman, W.D.Hall, J.N.Latta, J.S.Zelenka: Radar Data Processing and Exploitation Facility. In *IEEE 1975 International Radar Conference Proceedings*, pp. 493—498

4.25 J.C.Kirk, Jr.: Digital Synthetic Aperture Radar Technology. In IEEE 1975 *International Radar Conference Proceedings*, pp. 482—487

4.26 W.M.Brown, G.G.Houser, R.E.Jenkins: IEEE Trans. AES-**9**, 166—176 (1973)

4.27 D.Casasent: Proc. IEEE **65**, 143 (1977)

5. Optical Processing in Photogrammetry

N. Balasubramanian

With 20 Figures

5.1 Overview

The mapping process in the broadest sense involves the acquisition of data through remote sensing, processing the data acquired, storage and display. The processing of data, which is normally termed photogrammetric data reduction, represents the work needed to convert the aerial imagery into a topographic map containing all the pertinent terrain information. During the photogrammetric data reduction process, instruments are used to measure terrain profiles and elevation contours from stereomodels reconstructed using the aerial stereo transparencies. Since the early 1960s, considerable research has been done on the application of coherent optical techniques to the photogrammetric data reduction process. This chapter reviews the applications of optical correlation techniques to photogrammetric data reduction. The optical correlation techniques applied to parallax measurement from stereo-photographs are described and an evaluation of the optical correlation schemes is presented.

The manual of photogrammetry defines photogrammetry as the "science or art of obtaining reliable measurements by means of photography". On the basis of this definition one can envisage the application of photogrammetric principles wherever it is possible to produce photograms affording adequate information on stationary objects or even real time processes. However, in the past, a major share of the photogrammetric work has been limited to topographical map-plotting of the surface, mainly because of the complexity of the photogrammetric operations. In many instances, photogrammetric data acquisition and reduction systems are totally prohibitive because of their cost and speed, and, in some specialized cases, they do not provide the desired accuracy. Coherent optical processing techniques are potentially capable of overcoming many of these problems and, hence, the application of coherent optical processing techniques to photogrammetry is an active area of research today. This review is intended to provide the reader an overall view of the basic concepts behind recent research efforts in the area of optical data processing applied to photogrammetry. It is by no means either exhaustive or complete but, however, references are provided for the purposes of obtaining additional information.

5.1.1 Principles of Photogrammetric Stereo Compilation

Photogrammetric stereo compilation refers to the methods used to determine the spatial relationships and to obtain a full three-dimensional picture of the object in terms of contours and profiles of the object photographed. By taking photographs from two view points separated by a base line, the space coordinates from the photographs can be used to solve many measurement problems in engineering and in various branches of science and technology [5.1].

The spatial relationship between the two photographs forming the stereo-pair and the three-dimensional object is illustrated in Fig. 5.1. This figure refers to the simple and ideal case of vertical photographs, in which the camera axes are parallel to each other and perpendicular to the reference plane. The transparency is a positive print of the negative and is located symmetrical to the negative about the perspective center (the camera lens). This representation avoids the problem of inversion of coordinates caused by the lens. The principal distance F is the distance between the perspective center and the image plane and for distant objects it is equal to the focal length of the lens. The distance between the perspective center and the reference plane is defined as height H and the separation of the camera axes is defined as the stereo base B. The axis of the photographs is parallel to the base line axis. The various coordinate systems are defined in the figure. The height of the object is defined with respect to the reference plane. Using similar triangles, it is easy to show from Fig. 5.1 that:

$$x_1 = fX/(H-f)$$

$$x_2 = f(X-B)/(H-h)$$

$$y_1 = y_2 = f Y/(H-h).$$

The differential x-parallax p_x is defined as

$$p_x = x_1 - x_2 = f B/(H-h).$$

As the object height h varies from object point to object point, the x-parallax also changes and the x-parallax differences are the principal cause of stereo-perception. The y-parallax defined as $p_y = y_1 - y_2$ is zero in the case of vertical photographs. The y-parallax has a definite value whenever tilt is involved between camera axes (departure from the vertical case), and it hinders stereo-scopic vision.

Data reduction from stereo-photographs can be achieved in two different ways: by direct measurement of the reconstructed spatial model of the object (double projection system) or by using a mathematical model defining the relationships between points in the image space, object space, and the perspective centers (analytical photogrammetry).

The principle of obtaining the stereomodel represents the reverse of the photographic process. The transparencies are placed in two projectors that are oriented so that the transparencies bear the exact relative angular relationship as

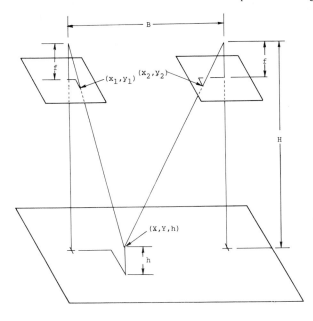

Fig. 5.1. Stereoscopic parallax for vertical photographs

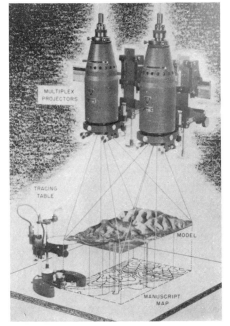

Fig. 5.2. Double projection plotter

the negative had in the camera at the instant they were exposed. Light rays are projected through the transparencies and when the rays from the corresponding images on the left and the right transparencies interact below, they create a stereomodel. The concept is illustrated in Fig. 5.2. The stereomodel is measured by bringing into coincidence a reference mark with the stereomodel point. The measurement of the planimetric position of the reference mark then provides a means of measuring the stereomodel. In contrast to the direct measurement techniques, in the analytical approach the coordinates of points in the photographs are measured independently and the planimetric position of the model point is computed analytically.

5.1.2 Optical Correlation—Its Relevance to Stereo Compilation

Stereoscopic parallax is a measurable linear distance corresponding to line segments on a pair of photographs of the same object taken from two different camera stations. This stereoscopic parallax depends on the distance between the camera stations, and the object and the focal length of the cameras. Parallax differences are caused by the variation of the distances to the camera stations from object point to object point. In the case of vertical photographs, parallax differences are directly proportional to the elevation of the object points. Parallax differences are the principal cause for stereo perception and it is through the measurement of parallax differences that photogrammetric data reduction is achieved. Hence, all photogrammetric instruments are principally used to measure stereoscopic parallax differences.

All automated stereo-compilation instruments are based on the ability to match conjugate images and automatically determine the parallax differences from object point to object point. The matching of the conjugate images involves the examination of the similarity of the spatial density variations corresponding to the conjugate images. This is the process that is referred to as cross-correlation. Mathematically, the cross-correlations can be expressed as follows. The correlation function $\varrho_{12}(x_0, y_0)$ is given by

$$\varrho_{12}(x_0, y_0) = 1/A \int\limits_A T_1(x, y)T_2(x + x_0, y + y_0)dxdy, \tag{5.1}$$

where A is the area over which the correlation is being defined, $T_1(x, y)$ and $T_2(x, y)$ represent the intensity transmittances of the two transparencies forming the stereo-pair and x_0 and y_0 represent the displacement of the image bound by area A in transparency 2 with respect to its conjugate in transparency 1, in x and y directions. The two-dimensional correlation function $\varrho_{12}(x_0, y_0)$ is generally a symmetric figure with its maximum at $x_p = y_0 = 0$ and ideally $\varrho_{12}(x_0, y_0)$ decreases monotonically as x_0 and y_0 are increased. When x_0 and y_0 are zero, the conjugate images in the two transparencies are matched; hence, the measurement of the correlation coefficient permits the detection of the conjugate image coincidence. The measurement of the displacement of transparency 2 with respect to transparency 1 to obtain maximum correlation for different sampled areas on the transparencies permits measurement of the parallax for those sampled areas. The half width of the correlation function $\varrho_{12}(x_0, y_0)$, which determines the accuracy with which the parallax can be measured, depends upon the image structure over the area being correlated [5.10].

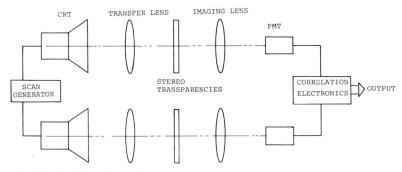

CRT   TRANSFER LENS   IMAGING LENS

PMT

SCAN GENERATOR

STEREO TRANSPARENCIES

CORRELATION ELECTRONICS

OUTPUT

Fig. 5.3. Principles of electronic correlator

It is clear from the description of the correlation function presented above that the correlation process entails selection of a section of the imagery through scanning and subsequent multiplication and integration of the intensity transmittances. This process can be accomplished using electronic, optical or digital correlation systems. In an electronic correlator, the optical transmittances of the two transparencies are converted to electrical signals by the use of a CRT flying spot scanner. If the axis of the scan coincides with the x axis, the one-dimensional correlation is given by

$$\varrho_{12}(t_0) = (1/2T) \int_{-T}^{T} f_1(t) f_2(t + t_0) dt \tag{5.2}$$

where f_1 and f_2 are proportional to the intensity transmittances of the two transparencies, t_0 represents the parallax x_0 and $2T$ represents the length of the scan. The basic principle of the electronic correlator is illustrated in Fig. 5.3. In the digital correlator, the individual transparencies are digitized independently and the correlation is performed in the computer. However, in all the optical correlation systems, the correlation is performed on a two-dimensional space without having to transfer to an intermediate domain [5.1]. It is in this context that the optical processing system plays an important role in automated stereo compilation.

5.2 Optical Correlators

The investigation of the application of optical systems to achieve correlation as an alternative to electronic correlation systems started in the early 1960s. Along with the progress in optical data processing methods and techniques came the multitude of proposals of optical systems to achieve automation of the stereo compilation process. While at the outset the optical schemes appeared to be simple, efficient and fast, the actual implementation of the optical correlation methods has given rise to many problems and limitations. Many techniques have been proposed and demonstrated, and in this section these various correlation schemes are considered in detail and some of the problem areas are outlined.

In the last few years several optical methods for generating elevation contours or profiles from stereo-photographs have been investigated and demonstrated. All of the methods utilize either coherent or incoherent optical correlation to obtain detection of imaging matching. They can be divided into three broad areas: image to image correlation, Fourier plane correlation and correlation by interferometric methods. The last two areas are a direct consequence of the progress made in coherent optical processing, and the application of coherent optical techniques to the image-image correlation systems has definitely improved the performance characteristics of such systems.

Most of the two-dimensional incoherent optical correlation schemes [5.2] described for the application of image matching and automatic parallax measurement did not prove very successful because of poor signal to noise ratio performance. The intensity transmittance $T_1(x, y)$ should actually be represented as $[T_{01} + T_{11}(x, y)]$ where T_{01} represents the average transmittance and $T_{11}(x, y)$ represents the fluctuating part. The average transmittance of the two transparencies provides a significant and constant contribution to the correlation signal which results only in increased shot noise at the photodetector. Lack of a constant power spectrum also contributed to the reduction of the maximum correlation signal obtained. By resorting to coherent optical systems, it is possible to remove the contribution due to the average transmittance and, thereby, considerably reduce the noise generated during photodetection. Spatial filtering at the Fourier plane removes the contribution to the average transmittance of the intensity distribution at the output plane and improves the signal to noise performance.

5.2.1 Image-to-Image Correlation Systems

The basic optical configuration of a coherent image-to-image correlator is shown in Fig. 5.4. Collimated light from the laser illuminates a section of the transparency 1. The transform lens 1 produces an amplitude distribution at its back focal plane which is an exact Fourier transform of the transparency 1. A dc block placed on the optical axis at the back focal plane permits removal of the average transmittance of the transparency 1 permitting only the structure information to pass through. The transform lens 2 images the transparency 1 on the transparency 2 with unit magnification (-1). The transform lens 3 produces the Fourier transform of the amplitude distribution emerging from the transparency 2. The correlation signal appears on the optical axis in the Fourier frequency plane of the transform lens 3 and this signal is discriminated from other light distributions through the pinhole. The operation of the system can be described in the following equations. The amplitude distribution in plane 1 is

$$a_1(x_1, y_1) = t_{01} + t_{11}(x, y) \tag{5.3}$$

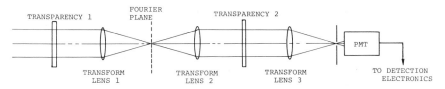

Fig. 5.4. Image-image correlation system

where t_{01} is the average amplitude transmittance of transparency 1 and $t_1(x, y)$ is the amplitude transmittance corresponding to the structure information. It is to be noted here that the amplitude transmittance $t(x, y)$ is related to the intensity transmittance $T(x, y)$ by

$$T(x, y) = |t(x, y)|^2.$$

The amplitude distribution in plane 3 is given by

$$a_3(x_3, y_3) = A_1(x_3/\lambda f, y_3/\lambda f) \tag{5.4}$$

λ = wavelength of light used; f = focal length of the transforming lens,

where $A_1(x_3/\lambda f, y_3/\lambda f)$ stands for the Fourier transform of the distribution $a_1(x_1, y_1)$. The Fourier transform of t_{01} produces a delta function centered on the optical axis in plane 3 which is removed by the dc block. The amplitude distribution on plane 5 is

$$a_5(x_5, y_5) = t_{11}(x_5', y_5')[t_{02} + t_{12}(x_5, y_5)] \tag{5.5}$$

where t_{02} is the average amplitude transmittance of transparency 2 and $t_{12}(x_5, y_5)$ is the amplitude transmittance corresponding to the image structure information. The coordinates (x_5, y_5) are in an inverted geometry to avoid the negative signs that occur because of the double transformation process (the image of transparency 1 being inverted). The amplitude distribution in plane 7 is

$$a_7(x_7, y_7) = A_5(x_7/\lambda f, y_7/\lambda f) \tag{5.6}$$

$$= T_{02} T_{11}(0, 0) + T_{11}(x_7/\lambda f, y_7/\lambda f) * T_{12}\left(\frac{x_7}{\lambda f}, \frac{y_7}{\lambda f}\right) \tag{5.7}$$

where T stands for the Fourier transform of t and $*$ denotes convolution. The first term is zero since the first dc block in plane 3 has essentially removed the information $T_{11}(0, 0)$ and, hence, the light passing through the pinhole is essentially $T_{11}(x_7/\lambda f, y_7/\lambda f) * T_{22}(x_7/\lambda f, y_7/\lambda f)$. If another lens is used to perform an additional Fourier transform, the resultant signal will be

$$a_9(x, y) = t_{11}(x, y) \cdot t_{12}(x - x_0, y - y_0) \tag{5.8}$$

where (x_0, y_0) represent the displacement of t_1 with respect to t_2.

If the area of the image being illuminated is A, then the total light intensity is

$$I_0 = \left[\int_A t_{11}(x, y) t_{12}(x - x_0, y - y_0) dA \right]^2. \tag{5.9}$$

The translation of the transparency 2 with respect to transparency 1 varies x_0 and y_0 and results in the function $I_0(x_0, y_0)$. By comparison to (5.1) it is clear that $I_0(x_0, y_0)$ is proportional to the square of the correlation function $\varrho_{12}(x_0, y_0)$ within a constant. It is to be noted that for the purpose of determining the image coincidence, there is no significant difference between the correlation function and its squared value. The integrated intensity at the final image plane or at the second Fourier plane 7 represents the cross-correlation value between the amplitude transmittances of the transparencies for the given translation between the transparencies. When the imagery corresponding to the two transparencies is identical indicating image matching, the cross-correlation becomes an autocorrelation. In practice, however, the corresponding images on the two transparencies are never identical. In electronic correlation systems this problem is solved by properly shaping the scan pattern to generate maximum correlation signal. In an optical system this can be achieved by suitably modifying one of the transparencies using spherical and anamorphic magnification systems before it is imaged on the other.

The optical configuration of an experimental image-to-image coherent optical correlator developed by Bendix Research Labs is shown in Fig. 5.5, and the system used for the detection of the output is shown in Fig. 5.6. In principle the system is identical to the basic configuration illustrated in Fig. 5.4. The first Fourier transform lens L_1 forms the Fourier transform of the area of the diapositive 1 being illuminated and the dc block permits the removal of the average background. The lenses L_1 and L_2 permit the imaging of the diapositive 1 onto the diapositive 2 through the spinning canted flat and the Pechan prism. The spinning flat permits the continued motion of the image of the transparency in a circular path at a fixed displacement from the optical axis. This action forms the basis for the alignment error measurement scheme. The Pechan prism simply rotates the image so as to permit the orientation of the two transparencies for manual stereoscopic viewing. A complete description of the system along with performance results can be obtained in [5.3].

In another modification of the system, whose configuration is identical to the basic system configuration in Fig. 5.4, the entire transparency 1 is illuminated by a collimated beam [5.4]. All the regions of the transparency, where the conjugate images are perfectly matched, give rise to an autocorrelation function centered on the optical axis. All the mismatched regions will contribute a broadened

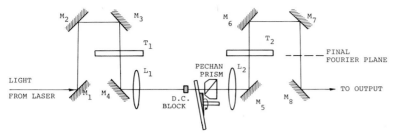

Fig. 5.5. Bendix image-image correlator

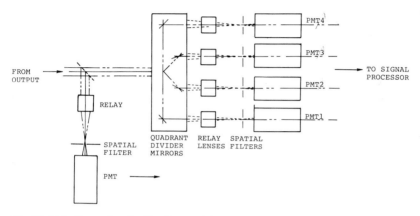

Fig. 5.6. Detection system for Bendix correlator

spatial frequency distribution dependent on the product of the two transparencies. Hence, a pinhole placed on the optical axis in plane 7 passes only the autocorrelation signal which contributes to uniform illumination of the matched areas in the final image plane. It is not possible in this system to selectively modify sections of the imagery to obtain maximum correlation signal. Also, the transparencies used must be either vertical or rectified to be vertical.

5.2.2 Frequency Plane Correlation Systems

In the image-to-image correlation systems just described, the parallax measurement was made by selection of a section of imagery in one transparency and detection of the location of the conjugate imagery on the second stereo-transparency by physical translation. The correlation signal provided the means of detection. In the frequency plane (or Fourier plane) correlation systems, as the name suggests, the correlation detection is performed in the Fourier transform plane. The basic equation representing correlation in the frequency plane can be

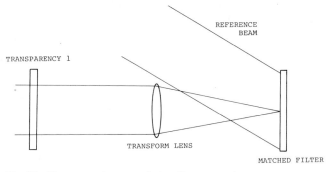

Fig. 5.7a. Frequency plane correlation filter generation system

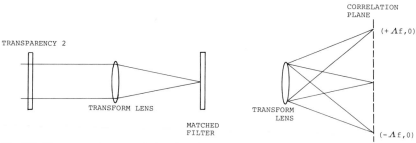

Fig. 5.7b. Frequency plane correlation detection system

written as

$$\varrho_{12}(x_0, y_0) = \iint t_1(x, y)t_2(x + x_0, y + y_0)dxdy \tag{5.10}$$

$$= \iint T_1(f_x, f_y)T_2(f_x, f_y)e^{j(f_x x_0 + f_y y_0)}df_x df_y \tag{5.11}$$

where $T_1(f_x, f_y)$ and $T_2(f_x, f_y)$ represent the spatial frequency distribution of the transparencies and f_x and f_y are the spatial frequency coordinates. It is possible to perform this operation using complex spatial filters [5.5]. A detailed description of the concept of complex spatial filtering is presented in Section 5.1. The basic optical configuration describing the concept of the frequency plane correlation is illustrated in Fig. 5.7. Figure 5.7a shows the arrangement used for making the complex spatial filter corresponding to transparency 1 and Fig. 5.7b shows the coherent optical processor used to determine the correlation between the conjugate images in transparency 1 and 2. It can be shown (see Chap. 1) that the output plane amplitude distribution of the optical processor shown in Fig. 5.6b can be written as

$$a_5(x_5, y_5) = a_0^2 t_2(x_5, y_5)$$
$$+ t_2(x_5, y_5) * t_1(x_5, y_5) * t_1(x_5, y_5)$$
$$+ a_0 t_1(x_5, y_5) * t_2(x_5, y_5) * \delta(x_5 + \alpha\lambda f, y_5)$$
$$+ a_0 t_1 * (-x_5, -y_5) * t_2(x_5, y_5) * \delta(x_5 - \alpha\lambda f, y_5) \tag{5.12}$$

where a_0 is the amplitude of the plane reference beam used to make the complex spatial filter and α is related to the angle θ between the optical axis and the plane reference beam by $\alpha = (\sin\theta)/\lambda$. (x_5, y_5) refers to the coordinate system of the final output plane. The first two terms of (5.12) are centered on the optical axis at the back focal plane of the second lens while the third and fourth terms are displaced upward and downward from the axis. The third term represents the convolution between the two transparencies while the fourth term represents the cross-correlation between the two transparencies. Thus, when the two transparencies are identical, the cross-correlation becomes an autocorrelation and is detected as a bright spot centered around $(-\alpha\lambda f, 0)$. When the transparency $t_1(x, y)$ is translated by x_0 and y_0 along the x and y directions, the cross-correlation also is translated by x_0 and y_0 about its origin $(-\alpha\lambda f, 0)$ provided that the ratio of the focal lengths of the two transforming lenses is unity. Hence, assuming that the conjugate images are identical and are aligned without rotational error, when a small section of the transparency 2 is illuminated in the configuration shown in Fig. 5.7b, the x and y displacement of the center correlation output spot from its origin $(-\alpha\lambda f, 0)$ directly represents the x and y parallax of the illuminated section of the imagery from its conjugate in transparency 1. Thus, it is possible to measure the x and y parallax between conjugate images on the transparencies without any mechanical displacement or scanning of one of the transparencies with respect to the other. Two different types of systems based on this concept of frequency plane correlation have been proposed and demonstrated.

The optical arrangement used in the one-dimensional coherent image/matched filter correlator is shown in Fig. 5.8a. Through the combination of cylindrical and spherical lenses, the frequency plane filtering and correlation are performed in only the x-coordinate. First, the frequency plane filter corresponding to a stereo-transparency 1 is made with the stereo-transparency 1 behind the cylindrical lens 1 and a high resolution photographic plate in the Fourier transform plane. The collimated beam in the second arm of the interferometer provides the reference beam for recording the complex spatial filter (matched filter of transparency 1). The filter is then repositioned in the Fourier transform plane and the transparency 2 is positioned in place of transparency 1. A narrow slit parallel to the x-axis placed in front of transparency 2 selects the y strip along which the profile is required. The Fourier transform plane, corresponding to the second cylindrical-spherical lens combination, forms the output plane in which the y-coordinate of the correlation signal spot is directly proportional to the x-parallax at that point. Thus, the focus of the correlation output coordinates represents the profile along the selected y strip. A straight line image formed by the reference beam still passing through the filter provides a convenient datum line [5.6]. While it is advantageous as well as faster to obtain the entire profile instantaneously, the use of anamorphic optics introduces problems in maintaining the geometric fidelity of the diapositives during measurement. Also, the inability to shape the conjugate images along the entire profile to overcome problems of shape and perspective distortion represents a major drawback of this approach.

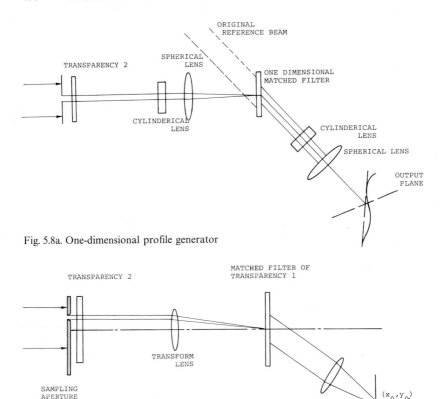

Fig. 5.8a. One-dimensional profile generator

Fig. 5.8b. Two-dimensional frequency plane correlator

A second type of image-matched filter correlation system is a direct implementation of the basic concepts of the frequency plane correlation technique and the typical optical arrangement is shown in Fig. 5.8b. First, a matched filter corresponding to transparency 1 is made using an optical arrangement similar to the one shown in Fig. 5.7a. The filter is repositioned and transparency 1 is then replaced by transparency 2. The auxiliary lens focuses the reconstructed plane wave from the matched filter as a correlation signal at the correlation plane. When transparency 2 is selectively illuminated section-by-section, the x and y coordinates of the correlation output signal directly represent the x and y parallaxes of that part of imagery on transparency 2 with respect to the conjugate imagery on transparency 1. The focal spot at the correlation plane due to the original reference beam used for making the matched filter provides a convenient origin against which the displacement of the correlation signal can be measured [5.7, 11]. An experimental prototype system based on this concept is discussed in detail later in this chapter.

5.2.3 Interferometric Correlation Systems

In all the optical correlation systems described so far the basic requirement to achieve correlation detection has been the ability to perform the multiplication of the amplitude transmittance of the two transparencies and integrate the product over the area of interest. Consider now the coherent addition of the amplitude transmittances of two transparencies $t_1(x, y)$ and $t_2(x, y)$. The superimposed intensity image distribution is given by

$$I(x, y) = |t_1(x, y)|^2 + |t_2(x, y)|^2 + 2t_1(x, y)t_2(x, y)\cos k\Delta(x, y) \qquad (5.13)$$

where $k(x, y)$ is the phase difference distribution between the two beams at the final image plane. It is clear that the coherent addition of the amplitude transmittances of the two transparencies gives rise to a term containing the product of the amplitude transmittances at the superimposed intensity distribution. The independent detection of this term forms the basis for a new class of coherent optical correlation systems which can be classified as interferometric correlation systems.

Let the amplitude transmittance of the two transparencies be $t_{01} + t_1(x, y)$ and $t_{02} + t_2(x, y)$ where t_{01} and t_{02} represent the average transmittances. At the superimposed image plane of the two transparencies, the total intensity distribution would be given by

$$I(x, y) = \{[t_{01} + t_1(x, y)]\, e^{ik\Delta_1} + [t_{02} + t_2(x, y)]\, e^{ik\Delta_2}\}$$
$$\cdot \{[t_{01} + t_1(x, y)]\, e^{-ik\Delta_1} + [t_{02} + t_2(x, y)]\, e^{-ik\Delta_2}\}, \qquad (5.14)$$

where $\Delta_1(x, y) - \Delta_2(x, y)$ represents the path difference of the beams illuminating each transparency and $k = 2\pi/\lambda$. Expanding, we obtain,

$$I(x, y) = t_{01}^2 + t_1^2 + 2t_{01}t_1 + t_{02}^2 + t_2^2 + 2t_{02}t_2$$
$$+ 2(t_{01} + t_1)(t_{02} + t_2)\cos k(\Delta_1 - \Delta_2)$$
$$= [t_{01}^2 + t_{02}^2 + 2t_{01}t_{02}\cos k(\Delta_1 - \Delta_2)]$$
$$+ [2t_{01}t_1 + 2t_{01}t_2 + 2(t_{01}t_2 + t_{02}t_1)\cos k(\Delta_1 - \Delta_2)]$$
$$+ [t_1^2 + t_2^2 + 2t_1t_2\cos k(\Delta_1 - \Delta_2)]. \qquad (5.15)$$

Terms containing $\cos k(\Delta_1 - \Delta_2)$ represent spatial fringe modulation, the fringe shape and frequency being dependent on $\Delta_1(x, y) - \Delta_2(x, y)$. In the above expression the last term containing the product $t_1 t_2$ is the only term of interest and hence represents the signal. Consider a section of imagery over which the detection of conjugate image matching is desired. The value of the last term can vary from $-2t_1(x, y)t_2(x, y)$ to $+2t_1(x, y)t_2(x, y)$, resulting in a fringe modulation amplitude of $2t_1(x, y)t_2(x, y)$. Hence, the average fringe modulation over a small area A is given by

$$I = 1/A \int_A t_1(x, y)t_2(x, y)dA \qquad (5.16)$$

which represents the correlation between the two transparencies for any given displacement. The maximum amplitude of fringe modulation corresponds to maximum correlation. Other terms that contribute to the fringe modulation do not depend upon the correlation between t_1 and t_2 and hence contribute a constant amplitude to the fringe modulation. In practice the contribution to the amplitude of the overall fringe modulation by the last term which represents the signal is significantly small. This makes it very difficult to detect small contrast changes in the fringe modulation. However, if each of the transparencies is spatially filtered through Fourier transformation and dc blocking, the contributions of average transmittances t_{01} and t_{02} in the final image plane become zero. Substituting zero for t_{01} and t_{02} (5.14) becomes

$$I(x, y) = t_1^2 + t_2^2 + 2t_1 t_2 \cos k(\Delta_1 - \Delta_2). \qquad (5.17)$$

The above equation shows that the amplitude of fringe modulation depends only upon the correlation between t_1 and t_2 and hence is a direct measure of conjugate image matching.

The optical contouring system first reported by *Krulikoski* et al. [5.6] is shown in Fig. 5.9. It essentially consists of a Mach-Zender interferometer and two *x–y* photo-carriages which hold the stereo-transparencies in each channel of the interferometer. The stereo-transparencies are then transformed and spatially filtered to remove the average transmittance from the stereo images. The filtered images are then superimposed at the output of the interferometer, and the regions of conjugate image coincidence at the superimposed image plane are detected through the existence of fringe modulation in those areas. By translating one transparency with respect to the other, different conjugate image areas can be made to coincide and the magnitude of translation then represents the parallax between the transparencies. Then, the parallax distribution over the entire transparency can be measured. Because it is necessary to detect the existence of fringes for matching the conjugate images, the system provides poor spatial and height resolutions. If the fringes are made finer in order to increase the spatial resolution, the detectability is lowered [5.8].

The second method to be described here, even though similar in concept, uses a normalized correlation signal obtained, using optical heterodyne detection to achieve detection of image matching [5.9]. The optical arrangement used in a basic experimental system is shown in Fig. 5.10. The collimated beam illuminating the transparency 1 is frequency shifted by moving (oscillating) the mirror M_1. The average transmittances of the two transparencies are removed through the dc block placed at the back focal plane of the imaging lens L_3. The

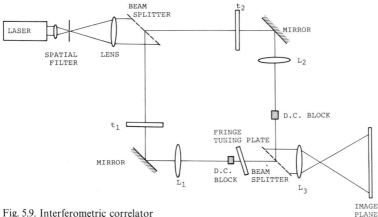

Fig. 5.9. Interferometric correlator

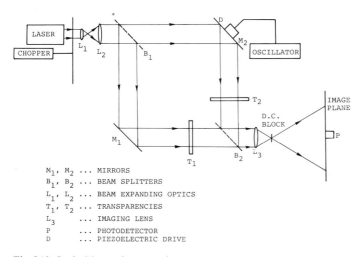

M_1, M_2 ... MIRRORS
B_1, B_2 ... BEAM SPLITTERS
L_1, L_2 ... BEAM EXPANDING OPTICS
T_1, T_2 ... TRANSPARENCIES
L_3 ... IMAGING LENS
P   ... PHOTODETECTOR
D   ... PIEZOELECTRIC DRIVE

Fig. 5.10. Optical heterodyne correlator

intensity distribution at the superimposed image plane is given by

$$I(x, y) = t_1^2 + t_2^2 + 2t_1 t^2 \cos k [\Delta \omega t + \Delta_1(x, y) - \Delta_2(x, y)] \tag{5.18}$$

where Δ_1 and Δ_2 represent the path difference distribution of the two beams at the image plane and $\Delta \omega$ is the frequency shift.

If a detector of aperture of A is placed at the point (x, y) in the image plane, the time varying part of the photocurrent is given by

$$i_{ac} = 2K \int \int_A t_1 t_2 \cos k [\Delta \omega t + \Delta_1(x, y) - \Delta_2(x, y) da] \tag{5.19}$$

(K – constant of proportionality).

It is reasonable to assume that the path difference distribution between the beams is essentially a constant over the small aperture A of the detector (the fringe spacing due to interferometer alignment or other phase errors is large compared to the detector aperture A). Hence,

$$\Delta_1 - \Delta_2 = \Delta_0, \quad \text{a constant over the aperture of the detector.}$$

Hence,

$$i_{ac} = 2K \cos k(\Delta \omega t + \Delta_0) \int\int_A t_1 t_2 dA. \tag{5.20}$$

If the beam of light from transparency 1 alone is used to illuminate the photodetector, then the value of photocurrent (dc)

$$i_1 = k \int\int t_1^2 dA. \tag{5.21}$$

Similarly for the transparency 2

$$i_2 = k \int\int t_2^2 dA \tag{5.22}$$

consider now the expression

$$C_{12} = \frac{2\int\int_A t_1 t_2 dA}{\left[\int\int_A t_1^2 dA \int\int t_2^2 dA\right]^{1/2}}. \tag{5.23}$$

C_{12} has a maximum value of 2 wherever the two transparencies are perfectly matched in the image plane. In areas where there is image mismatching, the correlation integral value drops and hence the value of C_{12} will drop also to a lower value. This system will work without the presence of a dc block but, however, the dc block helps in discrimination of image matched areas. This system can be considered as an extension of the interferometric contouring system described earlier. However, it overcomes many of the problems posed by the interferometric contouring system. A more detailed description of an experimental prototype system based on this concept can be found later in this chapter.

5.3 Experimental Prototype Systems

While many different investigators have demonstrated, within the basic research environment, the potential applications of optical correlation to the stereo compilation process, the real world applications of these concepts are yet to be realized. Two different systems have been constructed for test and evaluation. They are: a) IMF (Image Matched Filters) correlator, and b) HOC (Heterodyne Optical Correlator). The IMF correlator system is based on frequency plane correlation and the HOC system is based on interferometric correlation. In this section a brief review of the two systems is presented along with a discussion of the results obtained using the two systems.

a) *Image Matched Filter Correlator*

The IMF system is a coherent optical processor designed for the purposes of parallax measurement in stereoscopic aerial photographs. The concept is based on frequency plane correlation; detailed discussions relating to the system can be found in [5.11]. The optical configurations for the IMF system are illustrated in Figs. 5.11 and 5.12. The optical arrangement used to generate the matched filter is shown in Fig. 5.11, and the parallax measurement system using the matched filter generated is shown in Fig. 5.12. The input transparencies are held in a liquid gate and the instrument has an aperture of 100 mm · 125 mm. The Fourier transform lens has a focal length of 617 mm and a clear aperture of 217 mm. Variable attenuators placed in the unexpanded regions of the laser beam allowed the adjustment of the ratio of reference to signal beam intensity for optimum filter modulation in spatial frequencies of importance.

For parallax measurement, all of the laser power was directed into a telecentric scanner consisting of a folded telescope and two mirror galvanom-

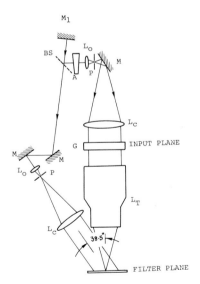

M_1 ... BEAM ROUTING MIRROR	M ... MIRROR
BS ... BEAM SPLITTER	G ... LIQUID GATE
A ... ADJUSTABLE ATTENUATOR	L_C... COLLIMATING LENS
L_O ... MICROSCOPE OBJECTIVE	P ... PIN HOLE
L_T ... FOURIER TRANSFORM LENS	

Fig. 5.11. IMF matched filter generation system

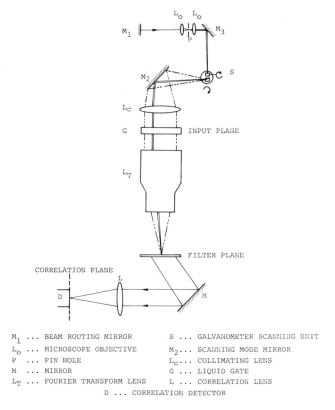

M_1 ... BEAM ROUTING MIRROR   S ... GALVANOMETER SCANNING UNIT
L_0 ... MICROSCOPE OBJECTIVE M_2... SCANNING MODE MIRROR
P ... PIN HOLE L_C... COLLIMATING LENS
M ... MIRROR   G ... LIQUID GATE
L_T ... FOURIER TRANSFORM LENS   L ... CORRELATION LENS
              D ... CORRELATION DETECTOR

Fig. 5.12. IMF parallax measurement system

eters whose axes are at right angles. Beam-forming optics focus a narrow cone of light into the first galvanometer mirror, which is in turn imaged by the telescope onto the second galvanometer mirror. This device produces a narrow, scanning cone of light which appears to originate at a point on the second galvanometer mirror. A mirror, which is not present during filter generation, directs the scanning beam into the signal beam collimator. The scanner and mirror are positioned so that the scanning beam appears to emanate from the same point as did the signal beam during the filter-making operation.

The scanning beam is driven to any point in the input gate by the signals from a pair of D/A converters coupled to a minicomputer. This computer performs the necessary corrections so that the operator can specify the scanning beam location directly in photo coordinates. It is also used to automatically step through a sequence of positions.

The correlation plane is formed by a 500 mm $f/4$ lens; the system is folded by a mirror for compactness. The correlation peak was observed by means of a small vidicon camera mounted on a horizontal and vertical translation device. A pair of electronic crosshairs was superimposed on the television display. In order to measure the location of a correlation peak, the camera was translated until the correlation peak fell exactly under the crosshairs. The position of the camera was sensed by a pair of linear potentiometers. This method, while somewhat awkward, was expedient in this circumstance and avoided problems with calibrating the vidicon scan. During the test and evaluation of this system, care was taken to optimize the filter exposure to emphasize the spatial frequency band of importance. The lowest frequency of the band was determined by the aperture of the scanning beam, and the highest frequency was determined by the resolution of the imagery used. The input photograph was preprocessed with a high gamma copy process to enhance the edge contrast present in the imagery. The evaluation of the parallax measurement process involved the use of the Canadian photogrammetric test model (scale 1:16 000), for which the ground control and elevation data were available. The parallax measurements were made along several scan lines orthogonal to the stereo base. The scans, 100 mm long, were made with a 1 mm beam in 0.5 mm steps. The parallax measurements were made manually using the vidicon camera and the electronic crosshairs. Using control points in the model, the measured parallax data was converted from the photocoordinates to the ground coordinates so that an evaluation of the data can be made. The comparative results of the data obtained using the IMF correlator and the AS-11B automatic electronic stereo compilation instrument are illustrated in Fig. 5.13. A least mean square adjustment of the data permitted the removal of the rotational and translational errors in initial

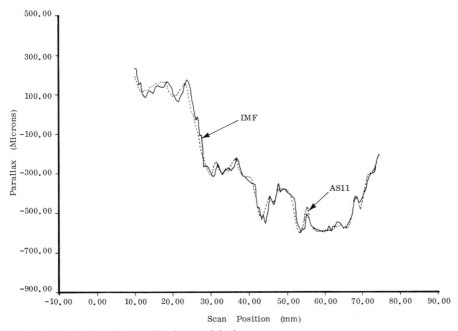

Fig. 5.13. IMF and AS11 parallax data—original

relative orientation of the transparencies. The adjusted data is exhibited in Fig. 5.13. Considering the breadboard nature of the experimental IMF correlator system, the results clearly demonstrate the potential capabilities of this optical correlation system.

b) *Heterodyne Optical Correlation System*

The heterodyne optical correlation system is a generalized optical correlation system having significant advantages in its application to stereo compilation. In the HOC system, the two transparencies forming the stereopair are relatively oriented and projected onto a common image plane where coincidence is detected. By means of heterodyne optical techniques, a normalized correlation coefficient is measured at each element of a photodiode array in the common image plane. The normalized correlation values are then used to define regions of conjugate image coincidence for a given orientation between transparencies. The principle of operation of the heterodyne optical correlator has already been presented in Section 5.2.3. However, the implementation of the concept for the measurement of stereoscope parallax is somewhat different from the optical configuration shown in Fig. 5.10.

Consider a double-projection, direct-viewing photogrammetric plotting instrument (Fig. 5.2). It represents a simple and direct solution to the problem of forming an analogic, three-dimensional, accurate stereomodel of the earth's surface from two-dimensional aerial photographs exposed as stereopairs. The basic components of this system include a powerful illumination source, a precise projection system, a discriminating viewing system for accurate observation of dual projected images, and a system for precise measurement and delineation of the images. To form the stereomodel in the system, it is necessary to construct the same perspective relationship between the pair of transparencies in the projectors as that existing in the aerial cameras at the times of exposure. This process of relative orientation is followed by mutual adjustment of the projectors to bring the model to the correct scale and relationship to a datum plane. Measurement within the projected stereomodel usually involves determining coincidence or zero parallax for a given point in the model by placing a floating mark in contact with a point on the apparent surface of the model as viewed on the platen. The horizontal and vertical position of the point can then be measured at the scale of the projected model.

Now consider the conceptual implementation of the basic HOC as illustrated in Fig. 5.14 to be analogous to the double-projection, direct-viewing photogrammetric plotting system discussed above. The basic components of this system include: a powerful illumination source, the laser; a precise projection system consisting of two image projectors; a discriminating sensing system for accurate optoelectronic viewing of selected aspects of the dual projected images; and an electronic photodiode array detector serving as a precise measurement system. A stereomodel is not formed in the HOC, however. Each projector system serves as a rectifier to correct for scale, tip and tilt, and the combined

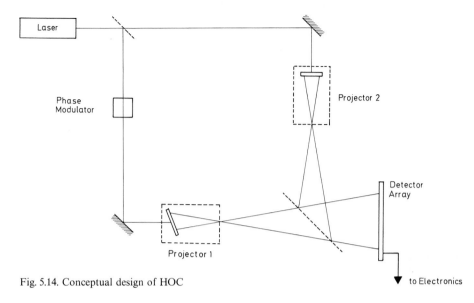

Fig. 5.14. Conceptual design of HOC

rectified images from both the projectors are superimposed in the image plane. Relative orientation of the transparencies in the projectors results in the removal of y-parallax. Then, x-parallax associated with each point in the image plane is determined by measuring the relative x-displacement necessary to obtain the maximum value of the normalized correlation coefficients. The x-parallax values can then be converted to represent terrain elevations.

In order that the two images be mutually coherent with each other, the two projectors are illuminated in an optical system configured as a Mach-Zehnder interferometer. The effect of this arrangement, when the optical system is slightly detuned, is to create a stationary fringe modulation of the superimposed images. The fringe spacing should be larger than the detector aperture to make $\Delta_0(x, y)$ constant over the aperture so that at points where the correlation is maximum, the fringe modulation has a maximum value. Measurement of this fringe modulation is accomplished in the HOC by translating a mirror in the Mach-Zehnder interferometer, as shown in Fig. 5.14 and simultaneously measuring the time-varying intensity function in the image plane. Detection of the modulated signal at any point in the superimposed image plane forms the basis for the heterodyne optical correlator and effectively increases the signal-to-noise ratio in detection by several orders of magnitude [5.10].

Changes in the normalized correlation value are caused mainly by the image structure associated with the two photographs whereas the average transmittance has a constant bias level contribution to the correlation value. The ability to locate the maximum value of the normalized correlation coefficient can be enhanced by removing this bias level contribution. In the electronic correlation systems this is accomplished by dc filtering of the video signals. In the HOC, the bias level is removed by placing a small and non-transmitting light block on the optical axis of the two projection systems to remove the undiffracted light from the transparencies. Then diffracted light, representing the image structure, is allowed to pass through to the final image plane.

For any given orientation of the two superimposed images the normalized correlation coefficient is determined at each element of the array. To accomplish this, the values corresponding to (5.21) and (5.22) are first determined for individual projectors, by measuring the intensity distribution over the image plane due to each projector when the light from the other projector is blocked. The modulated intensity value defined by (5.20) is then determined. In actuality this sequence of steps is automatically carried out by the control computer. First with the shutter in Channel II closed, the output of each element of the array is read and stored in the computer. The same procedure is repeated with the shutter in Channel I closed. Finally, the modulated intensity term is determined with the shutter in both channels open. Due to the interference between the two beams, the intensity distribution at the image plane is time modulated at the frequency determined by the modulator in Channel I of the interferometer. During this measurement, the output of the array is read sequentially over several frames. The first reading is stored in two locations to represent the minimum intensity corresponding to each element of the array. The output of the subsequent frames is compared to the maximum and minimum values stored for the corresponding element and the resulting maximum and minimum values are stored. After a large number of frames has been compared and the frequency of modulation has been read, the difference between the stored maximum and minimum intensity values provides the amplitude defined by (5.20) for each element of the array. Within the computer, the normalized correlation coefficient is then computed. This coefficient has a maximum value of 1; however, terrain slopes cause perspective differences between stereoimages which can reduce this value [5.10]. The area of correlation can be determined by projecting the elemental detector area backwards through the optical system onto the transparencies.

The optical configuration of the experimental HOC is somewhat different from the Mach-Zehnder configuration shown in Fig. 5.10. The optical configuration of the experimental HOC is schematically shown in Fig. 5.15, and a picture of the system is shown in Fig. 5.16. The basic optical configuration still remains that of a two beam Mach-Zehnder interferometer; however, the two projector optical system has been replaced by a single imaging system. This change has been necessitated by the relative sizes of the illuminated transparencies and the detector array. The modification, however, has resulted in simplicity and greater geometric accuracy during measurement.

Light from the laser (Spectra Physics Model 125, power 50 mW) is directed into the two channels of the interferometer with the 50-50 dielectric beam splitter. A linear wedge neutral density filter permits attenuation of the laser power before it enters the interferometer. Electronically operated shutters S_1 and S_2 permit selective illumination of the two transparencies. The modulator M is used to modulate the optical path difference between the two channels of the

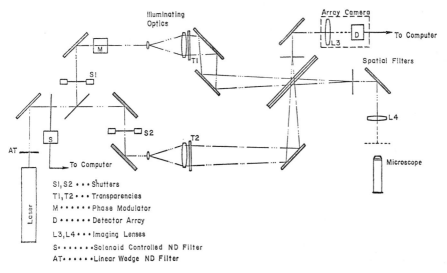

Fig. 5.15. Optical configuration of experimental HOC

Fig. 5.16a and b. Experimental HOC system

interferometer. The modulator consists of a $5 \cdot 5 \cdot 1$ mm size glass plate attached to the spindle of a Galvoscanner (General Scanning G-100). The oscillation of the glass plate in the path of the beam results in the time modulation of the optical path difference between the two beams.

The illuminating optics in each channel of the interferometer consists of a beam diverger and a condenser. The standard microscope objective ($20 \times$) and a spatial filter placed at its front focal point make up the diverging optics. The condenser consists of a combination of two collimating objectives mounted back to back so as to minimize wavefront distortion. The objectives have focal lengths of 220 mm and 540 mm, and both lenses have a clear aperture diameter of 50 mm. The two transparencies T_1 and T_2 are mounted on translation stages and are placed in the converging beam, as close to the condenser optics as possible, to obtain maximum coverage of the area of illumination at the plane of the transparency. The circular illumination area obtained in the experimental HOC has a diameter of approximately 40 mm.

The final imaging lens L_3 (EL NIKKOR Projection Lens, 85 mm/f2.8) produces superimposed images of the transparencies at the common image plane occupied by the detector array. The beam splitter, acting as a tilted plane parallel glass plate, introduces astigmatic aberration in the imaging process. However, since the beam splitter is located at the long conjugate side of the imaging lens (f # of the cone of rays being large), the aberration introduced is negligible. The beam splitter is formed by cementing together two identical plane parallel glass plates with the beam splitting coating at the cemented interface. This symmetric nature of the final beam splitter also assures that the aberrations have the same effect on both images. Thus, the aberrations produced have little effect on the correlation value.

The dc block is a circular opaque spot (0.25 mm diameter) formed with India ink on a microscope slide and is placed at the point of convergence of the illuminating beam. The dc block is located between the beam splitters and the imaging lens L_3 and hence is common to both images. Because of this fact, once again the small aberration contribution of the microscope slide has no effect on the correlation value. It is to be emphasized here that the minimum number of optical components has been introduced between the transparencies and the final imaging lens. This simplicity in optical configuration not only enhances the resolution performance of the final imaging optics but also significantly reduces geometric distortions during imaging. Hence, it is possible to maintain the geometric fidelity of the transparencies during the measurement process.

The final beam splitter has two output beam paths that are normal to each other. One of the beam paths as described earlier is directed to the array detector. Lens L_4 (EL NIKKOR Projected Lens 85 mm/f2.8), placed symmetrical to lens L_3 in the path of the other beam, also produces superimposed images of the transparencies in the common image plane. The common image is examined under white light illumination with a $100 \times$ microscope mounted on a three axis stage. The visual examination of the common image plane permits manual relative orientation of the two transparencies.

Because of the extreme geometric fidelity of the detector array, each elemental area defines a precise location on the transparency. By using a grid plate for initialization, it is possible to relate precisely the coordinate system of the array elements to that of the photo stages. The procedure for compiling a stereomodel can be listed as follows: with the use of the microscope the two transparencies representing the model are relatively oriented and the x-parallax direction is made to correspond to the x-axis of the translational stages. During the relative orientation procedure, the two transparencies are adjusted essentially for tilt, tip and scale. Also, the relative orientation of the array on the photo-coordinate system is determined. The instrument is adjusted for the coincidence of the control imagery representing the datum. The x-parallax is introduced in incremental steps, and the normalized correlation value at each

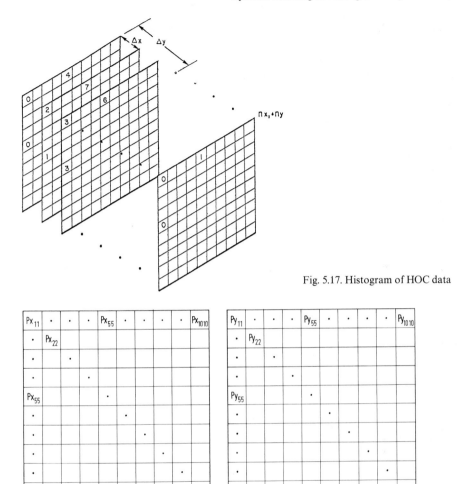

Fig. 5.17. Histogram of HOC data

Fig. 5.18. HOC output matrices

element of the array for each step is determined. The resultant data can be represented in a three-dimensional form shown in Fig. 5.17. It is clear then that by examining the histogram of the normalized correlation coefficient as a function of x-parallax steps, it is possible to define uniquely the x-parallax associated with any given element of the array. The final output of the processor is a two-dimensional matrix of x-parallax values representing two-dimensional elemental areas defined by the array (Fig. 5.18). It is to be noted here that these x-parallax values relate to the photo-coordinate system of the stationary transparency, but they can easily be transformed to elevation in the ground coordinate system. The effects of residual y-parallax and perspective slope

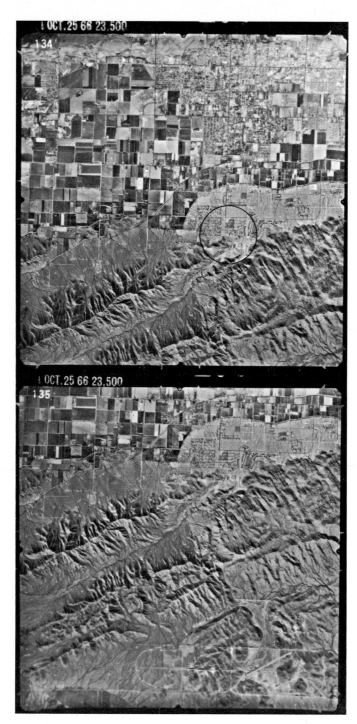

○ Area compiled

Fig. 5.19. Stereopairs
—Phoenix test
range—134/135
model

Table 5.1. HOC test results—Model 134/135

Point no.	Computed parallax	Measured parallax
1	0.459	0.457
2	0.472	0.482
3	0.495	0.482
4	0.487	0.495
5	0.579	0.596
6	0.597	0.584
7	0.575	0.584
8	0.529	[a]
9	0.660	[a]
10	0.470	0.470
11	0.693	0.686
12	0.469	0.457
13	0.484	0.457
14	0.455	0.370
15	0.432	0.381
16	0.453	0.444
17	0.831	0.609
18	1.441	1.420
19	1.415	1.420
20	0.634	0.571
21	0.463	0.431
22	0.464	[a]
23	0.473	[a]
24	0.475	0.431
25	0.569	0.558

[a] Points not in the field of view

Fig. 5.20. Contour representation of HOC output data

(within limits) are to reduce the maximum value of the normalized correlation value; however, these do not introduce errors in the x-parallax measurement.

The effects of y-parallax can be minimized by extending histogram analysis procedure to include several y-parallax steps. This data reduction approach in HOC not only enables one to overcome operational limitations such as slope effects and residual y-parallax but permits potentially high speed operation, compared to electronic correlators.

For test and evaluation of the experimental HOC system the Phoenix test range model 134/135 (scale 1:47000) (Fig. 5.19) was used. On the reference photo 135, 25 image points within the area covered by the detector array were marked and their coordinates measured using a precision stereo comparator. Table 5.1 illustrates the comparison between the HOC parallax measurement values and the computed parallax measurement values. Figure 5.20 shows the contour representation of the HOC output for the same area. The test results indicate that the accuracy of parallax measurement is about 25–50 µm without any adjustment to the raw HOC data. Once again the test results have shown the potential of an optical correlator using real world imagery.

5.4 Evaluation of Optical Correlation Systems

The factors that must be considered in evaluating the performance characteristics of the correlation systems are 1) signal to noise ratio in detection, 2) resolution in parallax measurement, 3) spatial resolution, and 4) the complexity of the system that is needed to meet the photogrammetric requirements. Theoretically, the optical correlation systems possess performance characteristics superior to those of electronic correlation systems. The optical correlation systems (essentially coherent imaging systems) have a flat frequency response (spatial frequency) and the bandwidth (which is a function of the aperture of the optical system used) far exceeds the bandwidth of the existing electronic correlation systems which are limited by bandwidth characteristics of the flying spot scanner. The major source of noise in both optical and electronic systems arises from the light detector used. However, in the case of the optical system, the noise is generated after correlation while in the case of electronic systems noise is generated before correlation. A detailed comparative analysis of optical and electronic correlation techniques can be found in an article by *Kowalski* [5.12].

While in the electronic correlation systems only the spatial frequency information along one direction is used in the image matching process, in the optical correlation systems the two-dimensional spatial frequency information is used in the image matching process. In this section, some of the basic differences between the two correlation schemes are analyzed.

For the purposes of this discussion let us consider the autocorrelation function of (x, y).

$$\varrho_{11}(x_0, y_0) \int_0^{l_x} \int_0^{l_y} t(x, y)t(x+x_0, y+y_0)dxdy \qquad (5.24)$$

where l_y is the length of the aperture along the y-direction and l_x is the length of the aperture along the x-direction. Using Taylor series expansion

$$t(x+x_0, y+y_0) = t(x, y) + x_0 \frac{\partial t}{\partial x} + y_0 \frac{\partial t}{\partial y}$$

$$+ \frac{x_0^2}{2} \frac{\partial^2 t}{\partial x^2} + \frac{x_0 y_0}{2} \frac{\partial^2 t}{\partial x \partial y} + \frac{y_0^2}{2} \frac{\partial^2 t}{\partial y^2}$$

$$+ \text{higher order terms}. \tag{5.25}$$

$$t(x, y) \cdot t(x+x_0, y+y_0) = t^2(x, y) + x_0 t \frac{\partial t}{\partial x} + y_0 t \frac{\partial t}{\partial y}$$

$$+ x_0^2 t \frac{\partial^2 t}{\partial x^2} + x_0 y_0 t \frac{\partial^2 t}{\partial x \partial y} + y_0^2 t \frac{\partial^2 t}{\partial y^2}$$

$$+ \text{higher order terms}. \tag{5.26}$$

We now consider

$$t \frac{\partial^2 t}{\partial x^2} = \frac{\partial}{\partial x} \left(t \frac{\partial t}{\partial x} \right) - \left(\frac{\partial t}{\partial x} \right)^2. \tag{5.27}$$

Using similar substitutions

$$\int_A t(x, y) \cdot t(x+x_0, y+y_0) dA$$

$$= \int_A t^2 dA - \frac{x_0^2}{2} \int_A \left(\frac{\partial t}{\partial x} \right)^2 dA - \frac{y_0^2}{2} \int_A \left(\frac{\partial t}{\partial y} \right)^2 dA$$

$$+ \frac{x_0}{2} \int_A \frac{\partial t^2}{\partial x} dA + \frac{y_0}{2} \int_A \frac{\partial t^2}{\partial y} dA + \frac{x_0^2}{2} \int_A \frac{\partial^2 t}{\partial x^2} dA$$

$$+ \frac{y_0^2}{2} \int_A \frac{\partial^2 t}{\partial y^2} dA + \text{higher order terms}, \tag{5.28}$$

where A is the area of correlation defined by (l_x, l_y). While the integrands of the first three integrals in the above expression are all positive, the integrands of all the other integrals can either be positive or negative, resulting in the integrated value being either small or zero. Thus, the first three integrals dominate the value for the correlation function. Hence

$$\varrho_{11}(x_0, y_0) = \int_0^{l_x} \int_0^{l_y} \left[t^2 - \frac{x_0^2}{2} \left(\frac{\partial t}{\partial x} \right)^2 - \frac{y_0^2}{2} \left(\frac{\partial t}{\partial y} \right)^2 \right] dx \, dy. \tag{5.29}$$

The expression represents a general case for two-dimensional correlation. Let us assume that for the electronic correlation, the scan direction corresponds to the x-direction. The corresponding one-dimensional correlation function is given by

$$\varrho_{11}(x_0) = \int_0^{l_x} \left[t^2 - \frac{x_0^2}{x} \left(\frac{\partial t}{\partial x} \right)^2 \right] dx , \tag{5.30}$$

since $\partial t/\partial y = 0$ over the width of the scan. The electronic correlation relies on the structure of the imagery along the x-direction (the scan direction) to match conjugate images. The optical correlation, however, uses the image structure in both directions to match conjugate images. The one-dimensional correlation value $\varrho_{11}(x_0)$ becomes independent of the parallax x_0 when $\partial t/\partial x = 0$ (no structure along the scan direction). However, in the optical case $\partial t/\partial x$ must equal zero over the entire correlation area before the correlation value can become independent of x_0. Additionally, the effect of y_0 (y-parallax) is to lower the maximum value of the correlation but the maximum value always occurs at $x_0 = 0$. It is clear that the optical correlation is less likely to give rise to false image matching than is one-dimensional electronic correlation.

System problems associated with the optical components' stability, phase distortion problems associated with the base and emulsion of the photo transparencies and coherent noise effects have been the stumbling blocks for the future development of optical correlation systems. System design associated with the experimental prototype systems indicates that many of these problems can be overcome and hence one can anticipate the wide-spread adaptation of the optical processing techniques to photogrammetric operations in the near future.

5.5 Summary

This chapter reviews the applications of coherent optical correlation techniques to the measurement of parallax from stereo-photographs. A brief description of the various coherent optical correlation techniques is presented and their relative merits outlined. Two experimental prototype systems are discussed in detail and their test evaluation results are presented. The potentials of coherent optical processing techniques have been demonstrated and evaluated using real world aerial transparencies. It is reasonable to expect the widespread use of coherent optical processing techniques in different facets of photogrammetric data reduction.

References

5.1   M.M.Thompson (ed.): *Manual of Photogrammetry* (American Society of Photogrammetry, Falls Church, Va. 1966)
5.2   L.I.Goldfischer, R.Vesper: Final Technical Report on Automatic Stereo Perception of Aerial Photography by Means of Optical Correlation, Contract No. DA-44-099-Eng-4966, U.S. Army Engineer CIMRADA (1962)

5.3   D.C.Kowalski: Nonholographic coherent optical correlation for automatic stereo perception. Bendix Technical Journal **5**, 24 (1972)

5.4   A.Wertheimer: "Optical Processing Techniques for Countour Generation from Stereophotographs". Ph. D. Thesis (University of Rochester 1974)

5.5   J.W.Goodman: *Introduction to Fourier Optics* (McGraw-Hill, New York 1968)

5.6   S.J.Krulikoski, D.C.Kowalski, F.R.Whitehead: Coherent optical parallel processing. Bendix Technical Journal **1**, 50 (1968)

5.7   S.J.Krulikoski, R.B.Forrest: Coherent optical terrain-relief determination using a matched filter. Bendix Technical Journal **5**, 11 (1972)

5.8   S.J.Krulikoski, J.D.Dawson, D.C.Kowalski: "Coherent Optical Mapping Techniques"; Final Technical Report, RADC-TR-70-62, AD No. 8709421 (1970)

5.9   N.Balasubramanian, V.Bennett: "Investigation of Techniques to Generate Contours from Stereopairs"; U.S. Army Engineer Topographic Laboratories, Report ETL-0029

5.10 V.Bennett: "Coherent Optical Techniques in Stereophotography". Ph. D. Thesis (University of Rochester 1974)

5.11 F.Rotz: Parallax Measurement Using Coherent Optical Processing. In *Proceedings International Optical Computing Conference*, April 1975, p. 162, IEEE Catalogue Number 75CH0941-5C

5.12 D.C.Kowalski: A comparison of optical and electronic correlation techniques. Bendix Technical Journal, **1**, 63 (1968)

5.13 N.Balasubramanian, R.D.Leighty: Heterodyne optical correlation. Photogrammetric Engineering **42**, No. 12, 1529 (1976)

5.14 N.Balasubramanian, R.D.Leighty (ed.): "Coherent Optics in Mapping"; SPIE Proceedings, Vol. 45, March 1974

6. Nondestructive Testing and Metrology

N. Abramson

With 39 Figures

6.1 Historical Background

Holography was invented by *Gabor* in 1948, but remained a scientific curiosity until a few years after the He–Ne-gaslaser was invented in 1962. *Leith* and *Upatnieks* succeeded in 1962 in making off-axis holograms with an arc lamp, later making laser holograms of diffuse light. In 1965, *Powell* and *Stetson* [6.1] discovered interference fringes in the holographic image of an object that moved during exposure of the hologram. Very soon several new methods were developed that utilized such fringes for measurement. These techniques came to be called holographic interferometry.

6.1.1 Overview

The holographic interference fringes can be used to study deformations, dimensions and vibrations of an object. As in conventional interferometry, these fringes are caused by optical pathlengths differences. In holography, however, the evaluation of the fringes is more complicated because the object might be three dimensional, and its surface scattering might be diffuse. In addition, the angles of illumination and observation usually vary over the object. Because of these differences between classical interferometry and holographic interferometry, new methods had to be found for the understanding and the evaluation of the fringes.

In holographic non destructive testing a force is applied to an object between the two exposures of a hologram of the object. The fringes seen in the holographic image are used to reveal deformations of the object surface. A defect is found if these deformations do not correspond to those expected from previous experience or from calculations. In a double exposure hologram, the fringes at the image of the object might be caused by any of the following factors, or by a combination of these factors:

1) The displacement amplitude varies over the object surface.
2) The displacement direction varies over the object surface.
3) The sensitivity to displacement varies over the object surface.
4) The sensitivity to direction varies over the object surface.

The evaluation of the fringe pattern can be divided into two steps. First, the unwanted factors 3 and 4 are eliminated. Secondly, the two useful factors 1 and 2 are separated. Factors 3 and 4 are caused by variations of illuminating and observing directions over the object surface and can therefore be eliminated by collimated illumination and observation. Usually this solution is too expensive and too complicated if the object is large, and therefore the sensitivity variation has to be compensated for. A practical way to understand the formation of the fringe patterns is to study how the object intersects interference surfaces in space.

In Section 6.1.2 we present a moiré analogy for the study of fringes caused by the interference of two beams of parallel light. In Section 6.2 this moiré analogy is expanded to include spherical wavefronts and it is demonstrated that by introducing the concept of "wavefronts of observation" the moiré analogy can be used to evaluate a great number of optical methods.

Section 6.3 describes some practical methods for the planning, making, and calculations of holograms, all of which are closely related to the moiré analogy. In Section 6.4 this moiré analogy is used in a direct way to explain a number of holographic fringe patterns. Finally Section 6.5 presents one of the latest developments in hologram interferometry—"sandwich-holography"—and some of the practical uses and advantages that result from the ability to manipulate fringes.

6.1.2 Interference Fringes Formed by two Intersecting Laser Beams

Interference fringes are formed if a laser beam is split into two beams which are directed so that they intersect at an angle. The moiré analogy to this phenomenon is demonstrated in Fig. 6.1. The two light beams are directed from A to D and from B to C, respectively. The straight wavefronts are represented by equally spaced straight lines perpendicular to the direction of the light. One dark line plus one bright line represents one wavelength (λ). The moiré pattern at the point of intersection is analogous to the interference pattern. This is true both for the separation and the direction of the fringes.

The dark parallel fringes are separated by one diagonal [$k^*(\lambda/2)$] of the bright rhombs. From Fig. 6.2 it can be shown that:

$$k^* = \frac{1}{\sin \alpha}. \tag{6.1}$$

Or if we use the angle β instead

$$k = \frac{1}{\cos \beta}, \tag{6.2}$$

where $k^*(\lambda/2)$ is the distance between adjacent fringes, λ is the wavelength of light, α is half the angle between the two beams as defined in Fig. 6.1, β is $90 - \alpha$.

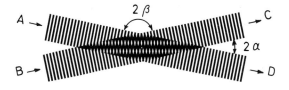

Fig. 6.1. The moiré analogy to the interference fringes created by two intersecting laser beams

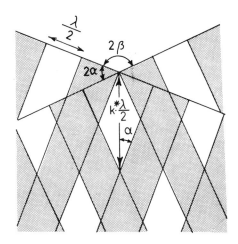

Fig. 6.2. Fringe geometry for two intersecting laser beams

The other diagonal of the rhombs represents the direction of the fringes which bisects the angle 2α because of the symmetric properties of rhombs. Because the two beams move at the same speed from A to D and from B to C respectively, if the wavelengths of the two laser beams are constant and equal then the fringes system will remain stationary. Each rhomb will move to the right invariably along the bisector of AB. Thus in spite of the high speed of light ($c \simeq 3 \cdot 10^8\,\mathrm{m\,s^{-1}}$) and its high frequency ($f \simeq 10^{15}$ Hz), slow or even static detectors can be used to measure relative changes of phase. Figure 6.1 is of course only a two-dimensional representation of the real three-dimensional space in which the interference fringes exist in the form of equally spaced, flat, parallel bright and dark sheets perpendicular to the surface of the paper.

A flat mirror placed parallel to the fringes would reflect light from A towards C just as if it had come from B. Indeed, if each fringe were replaced by a flat mirror, and if the beam from B were switched off, all the reflections of the beam from A by all mirrors would arrive in phase. The path length of the reflections from one mirror differs from those of adjacent mirrors by one wavelength. The mirrors fulfill the Bragg conditions and (6.1) and (6.2) represent the relations between the mirror distance and Bragg angle.

Let us switch on B again and see what will happen if a semi-transparent mirror is placed in the fringe system of Fig. 6.1. Experiments show that if it is placed with all of its surface within one dark interference fringe, nothing changes at C or D. If the mirror is kept parallel to the fringes but moved out into the brightness of one fringe, all the light will be thrown either to C or D. If the mirror is placed at an angle to the fringes so that it intersects, for example, five fringes, five fringes will also appear both at C and D. Dark fringes at C correspond to bright fringes at D because the energy not reaching C will reach D instead. Thus, there exist at least two methods to predict the fringes at C and D. The conventional way is to calculate the angle between the light passing through the mirror and the light reflected by the mirror and then find fringe separation using (6.1). Another way is to use (6.1) first and then count the number of intersections of the mirror surface and the interference fringes. In this chapter I will demonstrate the advantage of using the latter method. This is especially important when the semireflecting mirror is replaced in practice by an object on which measurements are to be made.

Consider now what happens if a photographic plate is placed in the fringe pattern of Fig. 6.1. After exposure, development and fixation, the fringe pattern will be recorded on the plate in the form of bright and dark lines. If the plate is repositioned and illuminated by only the beam from A, the plate will deflect light towards C as if it came from B. The deflection of the light by the grid is known as diffraction, and the grid is called a diffraction grating. The method of producing a grating using a photographic plate illuminated by two or more coherent light beams represents the basic principle of holography. When the photographic emulsion is thick the hologram is a thick hologram, or a Bragg hologram, which remembers not only the fringe spacing but also the angles of the intersecting interference surfaces.

How "real" are interference fringes? Do they exist "by themselves" or are they not formed until they illuminate a surface? Many experiments have proven that two intersecting light beams have no influence whatsoever on each other if there is no matter within the intersecting area. Therefore, it is interesting to consider what will happen when matter is introduced into the interference pattern.

Let us again study Fig. 6.1 in which two laser beams travel from A to D and from B to C, respectively. If a small particle is passed through the fringe system where the two beams intersect, it will be illuminated when it is in the bright fringes, and it will not be illuminated when it is in the dark fringes. Thus, the particle will alternatively appear bright and dark. Its scattered light can be observed by a detector placed, for example, between C and D. If the particle moves parallel to the fringes, the illumination will be uniform and no pulses will reach the detector. If it moves normal to the fringes, the pulse frequency (f in MHz) will be a measure of its speed (v in ms^{-1}) in the following way:

$$v = fk^*\lambda/2 = \frac{f\lambda}{2\sin\alpha}. \tag{6.3}$$

Instruments based on this principle are called laser velocimeters (see Sect. 6.2) and are used to measure the speed of small particles in gases or liquids. Another way to calculate the speed from the beat frequency would be to study the Doppler shift of the frequency of the light scattered by the particle. The particle moves towards the light of one of the laser beams with a speed of $v \sin \alpha$. Thus, the frequency of this light will appear to the particle to be $(v/\lambda) \sin \alpha$ higher than if the particle were at rest. The other laser beam will cause an equal Doppler shift, but the frequency will instead appear to be lower. The two Doppler shifted frequencies are scattered towards the detector placed at the bisector of CD. The difference in light frequency will produce a beat signal hacing the frequency

$$f = v \frac{2 \sin \alpha}{\lambda}. \tag{6.4}$$

Thus, the use of Doppler shift produces exactly the same result as the use of the interference fringes in the object space. However, in this chapter the use of the latter method is recommended because of its simplicity and generality.

Let us finally study the more conventional type of laser Doppler meter where only the laser beam BC of Fig. 6.1 exists. The observation is made by a detector at D which is made phase sensitive by receiving some direct laser light from B. The beat frequency at D caused by a pointlike object moving downwards along the bisector of BD can be calculated using the Doppler shift. The frequency of the light from B will appear to the particle to be $(v/\lambda) \sin \alpha$ higher than if the particle were at rest. Its component of motion towards D will cause still another Doppler shift of the same sign and amplitude to the light received at D. Thus the beat signal will for this example be identical to the one calculated for the two intersecting laser beams (6.3).

If the detector D is large, the only way to make it phase sensitive is to let it be illuminated by a reference beam in the direction A–D. Therefore we can for the evaluation of our one-beam Doppler experiment introduce an imaginary reference beam A–D and use the imaginary interference fringes, caused by the two crossing beams, to calculate the beat frequency from the number of imaginary fringes in the object space that are intersected per second (6.3).

Instead of the imaginary beam A–D traveling towards D, it is sometimes useful to think of a beam (D–A) traveling out from the phase-sensitive detector D. This we call a "beam of observation" which is mutually coherent to the beam of illumination. If a beam of illumination intersects such a beam of observation, imaginary fringes are formed that are identical to those that would be produced if the beam of observation had been an ordinary beam traveling in the opposite direction. In this way one single unifying method of evaluation can be used for a large number of optical measurement methods.

We have until now studied the moiré analogy to the interference effect of two intersecting coherent beams of parallel light. In the next section we will study the moiré analogy to the interference patterns formed by the divergent light from two points of coherent light. In that case the wavefronts will be spherical and the interference fringes will consist of surfaces in space that are neither flat nor parallel. We will in Section 6.4 study how the new concept "beams of observation" can be utilized to calculate the shape of these three-dimensional interference surfaces for the study of how interference fringes are formed when they intersect objects.

6.2 Calculation of Resolution Using the Holo-Diagram

We will now use one unifying method for the study of the interference fringes formed if A and B are either two pinhole sources of light or two pinholes through which the observation is made, or if one pinhole source of light is combined with one pinhole through which the observation is made. Let A and B be the centers of two sets of circles in a bipolar coordinate system (Fig. 6.3). The radii of the circles around A and B are labelled R_A and R_B, respectively. The separation between two adjacent concentric circles is $0.5\,\lambda$. If the wavelength λ is infinitesimal, the intersections of the two sets of circles will form a set of rhombs (see Figs. 6.2 and 6.3). The rhombs form one set of ellipses $(R_A + R_B = n\lambda)$ and one set of hyperbolas $(R_A - R_B = n\lambda)$. In Fig. 6.3, every second rhomb has been painted black except in one quadrant where only two chains of rhombs have been painted to emphasize the ellipses and hyperbolas. A similar effect can be produced by the moiré of two sets of concentric circles each with the circular areas alternately polarized in orthogonal directions or alternatively painted red and green. Using the moiré effect it is easy to demonstrate in real time how the elliptical and the hyperbolic patterns change shape as A or B is moved around.

From Fig. 6.4 it is possible to show that the length of the diagonal CE (the separation of the ellipses) is $0.5\,\lambda/\cos\alpha$ and that the diagonal DF (the separation of the hyperbolas) is $0.5\,\lambda/\sin\alpha$. The angle between R_A and R_B is 2α, and k and k^*

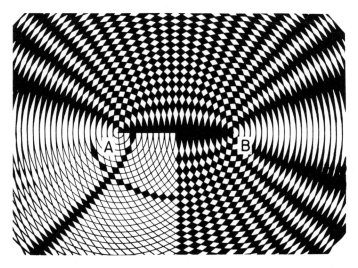

Fig. 6.3. *A* and *B* are the centers of two sets of concentric circles in a bipolar coordinate system. The moiré fringes form one set of ellipses and one set of hyperbolas

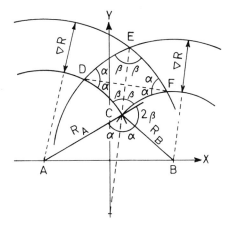

Fig. 6.4. The angles of one of the rhombs of Fig. 6.3 are studied and the diagonals are calculated. The statements in the figure are true only if λ is infinitesimal

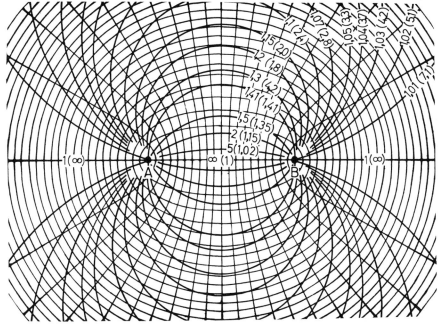

Fig. 6.5. The holo-diagram, based on one set of ellipses and one set of hyperbolas with common focal points. The arcs of circles represent the loci of constant separation between the ellipses (k value without parentheses) and the hyperbolas (k^* value within parentheses). The hyperbolas might represent Young's fringes or the diffraction-limited resolution of Abbe if the foci are two light sources or two points of observation, respectively. The ellipses might represent imaginary interference fringes, or the "interference-limited" resolution of, for example, holographic interferometry, if the foci represent one light source and one point of observation

are defined as $1/\cos\alpha$ and $1/\sin\alpha$, respectively. α is constant along the periphery of a circle through A and B and, therefore, it is possible to produce Fig. 6.5 where the arcs of circles represent the loci of constant separation between the ellipses (k-value without parentheses) and the hyperbolas (k^*-value within parentheses).

This "holo-diagram" was introduced in 1968 as a practical device for the production and evaluation of holograms (described in Sect. 6.3). However, only the ellipses and the k-values were used for that purpose. Figures 6.3 and 6.5 represent cross-sections of a three-dimensional body produced by rotation of the figures around the AB axis. In the three-dimensional case the circles are transformed into spheres, the ellipses into ellipsoids, the hyperbolas into hyperboloids, and the k-circles into toroids.

These surfaces have many properties of interest. Every hyperboloid reflects light so that a virtual image of A is formed at B. The reflected wavefronts add coherently because the Bragg conditions are fulfilled everywhere on the surface of the hyperboloids. Every ellipsoid reflects light so that a real image of A is formed at B. All the wavefronts arrive in phase at B because the Bragg conditions are also fulfilled everywhere on the ellipsoid surfaces.

Another feature of the hyperboloids is that they remain stationary in space if the circles around A and B represent the spherical wavefronts of light that move outwards from two mutually coherent light sources. The ellipsoids, however, will move outwards with a speed that is $k \cdot c$ (where c is the speed of light). Thus the hyperboloids represent stationary interference surfaces which, when intersected by an object on its surface, produce the ordinary interference fringes caused by two divergent beams of coherent light. The ellipsoids will remain stationary in space if the circles around A represent spherical wavefronts that move outwards while those around B move inwards, or vice versa. The hyperboloids, however, will move in a transverse direction with a speed that is $k^* \cdot c$. Thus the ellipsoids represent stationary interference fringes caused by one divergent and one convergent beam of light. If, finally, the light converges towards both A and B, the stationary interference surfaces will once again form a set of hyperboloids.

Let us study what happens when a phase-sensitive observation is made, e.g., when an object is compared to its own holographic image (real-time hologram interferometry) [6.4]. The observation is made through the processed hologram plate and the reconstruction beam is identical to the reference beam used during exposure. The observation may be recorded from one point, e.g., through a camera lens somewhere behind the plate. This camera will only react to light that converges towards the lens and has a certain phase relation to the beam which reconstructs the holographic image. Thus we could introduce a set of imaginary spherical "wavefronts of observation" that are mutually coherent to the beam of illumination but moving outwards from the camera lens as in Section 6.1.2. When this beam of observation intersects the beam of illumination, imaginary interference surfaces are produced in the object space; these surfaces are identical to those that would be formed by ordinary light waves moving inwards, towards the lens. These surfaces form a set of ellipsoids which, when intersected by the objects, produce imaginary interference fringes that can be used for the understanding and evaluating of holographic interference fringes.

We may define resolution as the shortest possible distance corresponding to the formation of one interference fringe. Figures 6.3 and 6.5 then may be said to represent the resolution limit of any optical system using a corresponding geometric configuration. The diffraction limited resolution and the "interference limited resolution" are represented by the separation of the hyperboloids and the ellipsoids, respectively; the resolution is thus $0.5\lambda k^*$ and $0.5\lambda k$.

The following examples are presented in order to compare the resolution as given in Fig. 6.5 with corresponding values from different quoted references in which other methods of calculation have been used. If there is a discrepancy, the reference value of the resolution is noted.

6.2.1 Example 1: A and B are two Mutually Coherent Points of Illumination

The hyperboloids represent interference surfaces in space. A point passing through these surfaces will produce a beat signal. Any measuring system based on this configuration will have zero sensitivity parallel to the hyperboloids and maximal sensitivity normal to the hyperboloids (parallel to the ellipses). The resolution in this direction is represented by the separation $(0.5\lambda/\sin\alpha)$ of the hyperboloids. This case can be utilized for the application and understanding of the following optical phenomena:

1.1 Conventional interferometry (Ref. [6.5], p. 261)
1.2 Young's fringes (Ref. [6.5], p. 261)
1.3 Bragg angle [6.6]
1.4 Fresnel zone-plate producing a virtual image (any cross-section of the hyperboloids) (Ref. [6.5], p. 371)
1.5 Two-beam Doppler velocimeter [6.7]
1.6 Two-beam radar [6.8]
1.7 Ordinary and Lippman holography (A is the point on the object. B is the reference point) [6.9]
1.8 Holographic interferometry (fringes seen on the hologram plate when studied from the real image of a displaced point on the object) [6.10]. Identical to the results of 2.6 and 3.4
1.9 Two-beam holographic interferometry (measurement of in-plane displacement) [6.11]
1.10 Objective speckles. Speckle size: $0.61\lambda/\sin\alpha$ [6.12]
1.11 Speckle photography for in-plane measurement (A–B is the lens diameter). Resolution is $0.61\lambda/\sin\alpha$ [6.13]
1.12 Two-beam speckle photography (measurement of in-plane displacement) [6.14]
1.13 Projected interference fringes (sensitivity direction is normal to object surface and the resolution corresponds to the movement of a surface point from one hyperboloid to the next) [6.15, 16]
1.14 Focused spot size (A and B are two diametric points on the lens). Resolution is $0.61\lambda/\sin\alpha$ (Ref. [6.5], p. 397). If the lens could focus to a spot smaller than one dark fringe, the law of energy conservation would no longer apply

1.15 Resolution of any optical system. Necessary condition for resolution of an object of size AB is that the lens used for observation crosses at least one bright and one dark hyperboloid. Identical to the result of 3.6 in Example 3

The moiré of two cross-sections of the hyperboloids represents the difference between the two interference patterns. If the two cross-sections are identical but one is displaced, the moiré fringes also represent the loci of constant resolution in the displacement direction. If one of the focal points is fixed while the other is displaced, the resulting moiré pattern forms a new set of hyperboloids. Their foci will be the two positions of the displaced focal point. This new pattern is independent of the position of the fixed focal point. (A rotation of one of the original spherical wave fronts of Fig. 6.3 produces no moiré effect.) Therefore, hologram interference fringes are independent of the position of the point source of the fixed reference beam.

6.2.2 Example 2: A is a Point of Illumination; B is a Coherent Point of Observation

B is the center of "spherical wavefronts of observation" and has been brought to coherence with A by receiving a direct reference beam. The ellipses represent imaginary interference surfaces in space. A point passing through these surfaces will produce a beat signal. Any measuring system based on this configuration will have zero sensitivity parallel to the ellipsoids and maximal sensitivity normal to the ellipsoids (parallel to the hyperbolas). The resolution in this direction is represented by the separation $(0.5\lambda/\cos\alpha)$ of the ellipsoids. This case can be utilized for the application and understanding of the following phenomena:

2.1 Conventional interferometry and interferometry using oblique illumination and observation [6.17, 18]

2.2 Bragg angle

2.3 Fresnel zone-plate producing a real image (any cross-section of the ellipsoids) [6.19]

2.4 Holography (utilizing the coherence length, controlling the sensitivity to unwanted movements) [6.20, 21]

2.5 Hologram interferometry (evaluating displacement, selecting the resolution—one interference fringe is formed each time an ellipsoid is crossed by a point on the object) [6.1, 20]

2.6 Hologram interferometry using two points of observation (identical to the results of 1.9 and 3.4) [6.22]

2.7 Hologram contouring using two-frequency illumination [6.23]

$$\text{Resolution} = \frac{\lambda_1}{\lambda_1 - \lambda_2} \cdot \frac{0.5\lambda_2}{\cos\alpha} \tag{6.5}$$

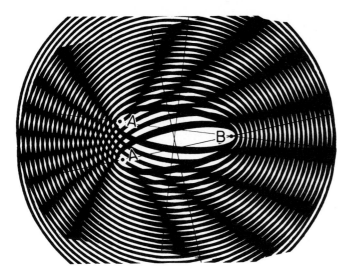

Fig. 6.6. Two identical sets of ellipses, one of which has been rotated around the common focal point B. Moiré fringes form a set of hyperbolas, their foci being the two positions of the displaced focal point A

2.8   Gated viewing (the ellipsoids represent surfaces of constant time delay)

$$\text{Resolution} = ct/\cos\alpha \qquad (6.6)$$

where c is speed of light and t is pulse width

2.9   Doppler velocimeter [6.24]

2.10   Doppler radar [6.25]

The moiré of two cross-sections of the ellipsoids represents the difference of two imaginary interference patterns. It also represents the interference fringes in holographic interferometry [6.26]. If the two cross-sections are identical but one is displaced, the moiré fringes also represent the loci of constant resolution in the displacement direction. If one of the focal points of the ellipsoids is fixed while the other is displaced, the resulting moiré pattern forms a set of hyperboloids. Their foci will be the two positions of the displaced focal point as shown in Fig. 6.6. This new pattern is independent of the position of the fixed focal point. (A rotation of one of the original spherical wavefronts of Fig. 6.3 produces no moiré effect.) Therefore, the movement of holographic interference fringes, when studied from different points of observation, is independent of the position of the fixed point source of illumination.

6.2.3 Example 3: A and B are two Mutually Coherent Points of Observation

The information from A and B is brought together in a coherent way, for example by a semi-transparent mirror or by the use of a reference beam. A and B could even be two points on a lens. The hyperboloids represent imaginary interference surfaces in space. A point passing through these surfaces will produce a beat signal. Any measuring system based on this configuration will have zero sensitivity parallel to the hyperboloids and maximum sensitivity normal to the hyperboloids (parallel to the ellipses). The resolution in this direction is represented by the separation $(0.5\lambda/\sin\alpha)$ of the hyperboloids. This example can be utilized for the application and understanding of the following optical phenomena:

3.1 Doppler velocimeter using two points of observation [6.24]
3.2 Subjective speckles (A and B are two diametric points on the observation lens). The number of subjective speckles seen on the object is equal to the number of objective speckles projected onto the lens. Therefore, 3.2 and 1.10 in Examples 3 and 1 give identical results
3.3 Speckle photography where the camera lens is blocked except for two diametric holes (measurement of in-plane displacement) [6.27]
3.4 Holographic interferometry using two observation locations. The number of fringes passing a point on the object when the observation location is moved from A to B is equal to the number of hyperboloids passed by that point between the two exposures. This number is also equal to the number of hyperboloids between A and B in 1.8. The results of 1.8 and 2.6 and 3.4 in Examples 1, 2, and 3 are identical
3.5 Stellar interferometry (A and B are the two mirror systems in front of a telescope objective or the two antennae of a radio telescope). The resolution for double star system is $0.5\lambda/\sin\alpha$, and for large star is $0.61\lambda/\sin\alpha$ (Ref. [6.5], p. 275)
3.6 Diffraction-limited resolution of, for example, a microscope (A and B are the two diametric points on the objective lens). Maximal resolution is $0.61\lambda/\sin\alpha$ (Ref. [6.5], p. 418)

Conclusion

In the beginning of this section we introduced "wavefronts of observation" which may produce imaginary interference fringes in the object space. We also defined the resolution as the shortest possible distance in object space corresponding to the intersection of one interference fringe. Finally some 30 examples show a good agreement between the accepted values of resolution found in the literature and the fringe separation found by the use of the holo-diagram in Figs. 6.3 and 6.5. The discrepancies found when a circular illuminating or observing area such as a lens is involved are caused by the fact that the total area of the lens, not just two diametric points, is used. In order to produce one single image, some of the resolution has to be sacrificed. The "holo-diagram" represents the fundamental resolution of any optical system, and thus, is a tool that concentrates a large amount of information into one single method.

6.3 The Holo-Diagram: A Practical Device
for Making and Evaluating Holograms

In a hologram, the object information is recorded in the form of interference fringes on a photographic plate. These fringes are formed when light from the object and an easily reproducible light beam (the reference beam) fall upon the same place at the same time. For fringes to be recorded on the photographic plate they must be in a fixed position[1] in relation to the surface of the plate during most of the exposure time. In other words, the phase relation between the two light beams has to be constant during this time. Two conditions must be met for phase relation constancy. First, in order for the phase relation to be constant, the difference in path length between the two light components must be less than the temporal coherence length of the light in use; second, this difference must be constant during most of the exposure.

If any part of the object moves, so that the corresponding lines on the photographic plate are wiped out, no light will be deflected to this part when the finished hologram is illuminated with laser light (reconstructed). Therefore, this part looks dark in the reconstruction. The hologram can be exposed twice, with half of the exposure time used for recording the undeformed object and the other

---

[1] Here we neglect holograms of vibrating objects.

Fig. 6.7. Photograph of the image produced by a double exposed hologram of a 10 liter pressure vessel deformed by a slight pressure. The depth of the recorded scene is limited by the coherence length of the light

half for recording the deformed object. When this is done, the reconstructed wavefront will give a picture of the object with dark sections on all those parts that have made a movement such that corresponding interference fringes have moved half the fringe separation or a multiple of this (Fig. 6.7). In this way we get an interference hologram with dark fringes which, like the contour lines on a map, show the amplitude of displacement of any part of the object [6.1, 28–31].

If the object is illuminated and viewed in a direction parallel to the direction of the deformation, the distance between two dark fringes will correspond to a displacement of half of the wavelength of the light used. In all other cases the corresponding displacement is greater than this value [6.32]. The following diagram (Fig. 6.8) has been constructed to provide a simple and practical way to evaluate the correlations between the position of the fringes and the amplitude of displacement and also to simplify the making of the hologram [6.20].

6.3.1 Construction of the Diagram

A is the point (Fig. 6.8) from which the divergent laser beam originates (e.g., a spatial filter). B is the point on the photographic plate that is to be examined after the exposure of the hologram (e.g., the center of the plate). Locate the object C in the diagram so that its position with respect to A and B corresponds to its real position in the arrangement used for making the hologram. Light radiates from A and some of it illuminates C and is reflected from there to B. Let the object C be a mathematical point. The pathlength for the light rays from A to B via C is constant if C is moved along an ellipse with the focal points A and B. This distance changes, however, as soon as we move C in a direction perpendicular to

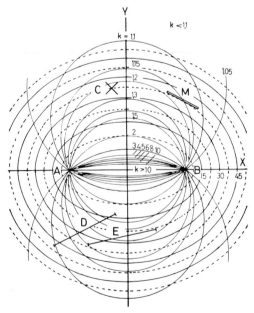

Fig. 6.8. The holo-diagram used in holography. *A* is the point from which the divergent laser beam originates. *B* is the center of the photographic plate recording the hologram. *C*, *D* and *E* are different objects. *M* is the mirror producing the reference beam

the periphery of the ellipse. In reality, the ellipses of the diagram are intersections of ellipsoids by the plane in which we are working.

Let us now place a mirror M somewhere along the ellipse on which C is situated. If the surface of the mirror is parallel to the periphery of this ellipse it will reflect light from A to B. This reflected light forms the reference beam. The pathlength of the light via object C is the same as via mirror M. Therefore, the light rays are in phase and there will be a maximum of light at point B on the photographic plate. If the object C is moved in a direction perpendicular to the periphery of the ellipses, the intensity of light at B will alternate between a maximum and a minimum value.

Let us assume for a moment that the ellipses in the diagram are so closely spaced that they intersect the x axis in points separated by a distance of only half a wavelength. If a point object is moved anywhere within the area of the diagram and illuminated from A, the phase angle at B will change by 360° each time an ellipse is crossed. If, for instance, ten ellipses are crossed, there will be ten cycles of light intensity variation (if B is also illuminated by a reference beam). The greatest number of cycles corresponding to a given movement is produced when the movement is perpendicular to the ellipses with the maximum at the x axis to the right side of B. The nearer to the center of the diagram the point object is situated, the greater is the movement required to produce one cycle. The implications of this result for the hologram follow.

Along the x axis on the right side of B the distance between two dark fringes represents a displacement of $\lambda/2$. In all other places the distance represents a greater displacement. Let us name the displacement $k(1/2)\lambda$. The value of k increases near the center of the diagram and is infinite in the center. The position line of constant k value is formed by arcs of circles, which are drawn in the diagram with the k-values printed near the y axis. If the object is large, the light reflected from its different parts must travel different distances to reach the holographic plate. Larger objects require greater temporal coherence length. When the difference in distance for the light to travel via the object and via the mirror is greater than the temporal coherence length, no interference fringes will be created at B.

The diagram of Fig. 6.8 is constructed in such a way that if a reference mirror is placed anywhere along one ellipse, the coherence length is just enough that an object placed on a second, adjacent ellipse can be recorded in the hologram.

6.3.2 Optimal Utilization of the Coherence Length

The light travels from A to B via the object C. Locate C in the diagram (Fig. 6.8) so that its position with respect to A and B corresponds to the real position. The distance between two ellipses corresponds to a difference in light path from A to B of 15 cm (when the real distance between A and B is 100 cm). Usually the coherence length from a long He–Ne gas laser is at most 30 cm. Therefore, the object may at most fill the space within four elliptical areas, or in other words, it

Fig. 6.9. Double exposed holographic image of a steel bar that is bent and twisted by a force acting on its middle. Using the holo-diagram the bar (which was about 2 meters long) could be recorded even with laser light that had coherence length of only 30 centimeters

may cross four but not five ellipses. The object D shown in Fig. 6.8 is too large to be recorded in the hologram, but if it is moved to position E, it can be recorded.

If the real distance between the spatial filter and photographic plate is, for example, 50 cm, there is a scale factor of two. The object may then cut at most eight ellipses. It is possible to record an object many meters long in a hologram by using the diagram (Fig. 6.9). Interference fringes are formed only if the difference in pathlength for the two light components is shorter than the coherence length of the light. To a mechanical engineer, the coherence length of light [6.5] is a rather mysterious expression and the author has found that is is often better to use the following explanation. Light which originates from a laser longer than about 10 cm contains a number of separate bands of frequencies (axial modes), all of which are within the limit of the Doppler width (within one spectral line). When these different frequencies are mixed, a frequency is formed that is a function of the difference between the original frequencies. As a result of this, the light is intensity modulated with a frequency of about 10^8 Hz. When the outermost frequencies within the Doppler width are mixed, the highest frequency of intensity modulation is formed. This intensity modulation creates a wavelength corresponding to the coherence length of the laser. When adjacent frequencies are mixed, the corresponding wavelength of the intensity variation is twice the length of the laser cavity (which is approximately equal to the length of the laser housing).

When a hologram is made, the light is divided into two components traveling different distances to the photographic plate. Interference fringes can be formed only if the two components illuminate the plate at the same time. The fringes, of course, cannot form if the difference in distance is such that one component has maximum intensity while the other is completely dark. When looking at the coherence problem in this way, one might think that if the difference in path length of the two light components is increased the possibility of forming a hologram should repeat. Experiments have shown that this is often the case and that holograms can be formed if this difference is an even multiple of the laser cavity [6.33, 34].

6.3.3 Selection of Fringe Separation

If the coherence lenght of the light in use presents no problem, the object can be positioned with regard only to the wanted fringe separation. If the k value is 3, for example, the distance between two fringes will correspond to a displacement of about 1 μm if a He–Ne-gas laser is used. If extreme accuracy is needed, we must determine exactly which part of the photographic plate corresponds to B. The simplest way to utilize the diagram is to use a permanent foundation with the diagram outlined directly on the surface on which the holographic equipment is placed. Then one can see at once where to position the object to optimize the conditions.

The diagram (Fig. 6.8) is valid for only a single point B on the photographic plate used for the hologram. When we study the finished hologram, we can position our eye or a camera lens close to this point. In this case we see a picture of the object with fringes that reveal the displacement and which can be evaluated with the aid of the diagram. If, however, we move our eye or camera lens along the surface of the plate the position of B is changed and corresponds to a movement of C in the diagram. Consequently, this may cause the value of k to change and the fringes that show displacement to move accordingly. The position of the fringes that corresponds to zero displacement will remain fixed while those fringes that correspond to an increasing deformation will move an increasing distance. If too large of an aperture is used in the camera, some of the fringes will disappear because different parts of the lens see them at different positions.

If the lens is moved backward from the surface of the plate, the focal point B̃ leaves the plate and follows the center of the lens. This occurs because an area of the plate is now used instead of just a single point. In this case the diagram must be modified and, for the evaluation of the fringes, the position of the object in the diagram has to be changed to correspond to the new position of B. This method works, however, only if the source of the laser beam A has the same position with respect to the plate during the reconstruction as it does during the exposure.

To get full use of the coherence length, it is necessary to position the reference mirror at the optimal place. The best position is anywhere along the ellipse that intersects the middle of the object, or if the coherence length is adequate, at the place where highest resolution is wanted. Note that this is only strictly true if the object and reference mirror use the same divergent laser beam. The surface of the mirror should be parallel to the ellipse on which it is placed. If the resolution of the photographic plate is low, the angle separating the mirror and object (as seen from B) should be kept as small as possible.

6.3.4 Evaluation

Count the number of dark fringes between a fixed (not displaced) point on the object and the point whose displacement is to be evaluated. Multiply this number by the k value of the object. This gives the displacement in the number of half wavelengths. The evaluated displacement is the projection of the real displacement onto the normal of the ellipse that passes through the object. One way to find this normal is to look for the intersection of the k circle through the object and the negative y axis. The normal passes through this intersection.

Assume that the object is so large that a stationary point on it has one value of k and that the point whose displacement we want to evaluate is positioned at a quite different k value. Which k should be used? The following reasoning and experiments indicate that only the latter k value should be used.

Let us imagine that no fringes are formed on the object during the deformation. What really happens is that every point that is displaced causes one cycle of brightness and darkness every time the pathlength of light from A to B (Fig. 6.8) is changed by one wavelength. We can tell the total number of cycles any point has experienced because this number is contained in the number of fringes between the deformation point and a fixed point. The number of cycles depends on the continuity of the object's surface since the fringes move along the object in the direction of the fixed point much like pearls on a string. The number of cycles is thus a function only of the deformation of the point we want to study and the k value at this point. An example of this is shown in Fig. 6.10.

The object is a 2 m long steel bar (Fig. 6.10). It is positioned between A and B and just underneath the x axis in Fig. 6.8. The k value in the middle of the bar is about 11, and in the far end about 7 (Fig. 6.11). The hologram was exposed once. Then the bar was given a minute rotation around its long axis and a second exposure was made. The bar was not bent during this process. The surface down the long axis of the bar has made no displacement and, therefore, is bright. Displacement increases with distance from the axis, and the first dark fringe is formed at the point where the intersection between the bar and the half wavelength ellipsoids has moved from one ellipse to the next. Where the

Fig. 6.10. Double exposed holographic image of a steel bar that, between the two exposures of the hologram, has been given a slight rotation around its long axis

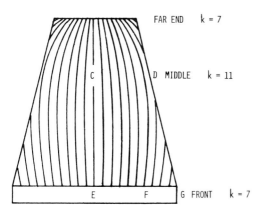

Fig. 6.11. The fringes of Fig. 6.10 are not straight because the sensitivity to displacement varies along the bar. A high k value represents a low sensitivity. The calculated displacement of D must, of course, be the same if the fringes are counted along CD, along $CEFD$, or along $CEGD$

intersection has moved three ellipses, the next fringe forms, etc. The distance separating the fringes is greatest in the middle of the bar where the k value is greatest.

The displacement of any point on the surface of the bar can be evaluated as follows. Starting at any point along the long axis (e.g., C of Fig. 6.11) we can trace any continuous path to the point that is to be studied (e.g., D) counting the number of fringes (6) that are crossed on the way. The displacement of D, normal to the ellipsoids of the holo-diagram, can be found by multiplying this number by the k value (11) at D. We must be careful not to count the same fringe twice with the same sign. The number of fringes should always be independent of the chosen path. For example, the fringes along the path CEGD should be counted in the following way. $CE = 0$, $EG = +9$, $GD = -3$. The sum, 6 fringes, is identical to the result when tracing directly CD. This rule of sign is obvious when the continuous fringes of Fig. 6.10 are studied, but the sign of the fringes might be difficult to find if only fractions of the fringes are visible, e.g., only those along the edges EGD of Fig. 6.11.

If one makes the mistake of multiplying by the k value at the point where a fringe is crossed, the value of displacement will depend on the chosen path. Let us for example follow the path CEFD which produces the following counts. CE $=0$; $EF = 6$; FD (along one fringe) $=0$. The counted fringes (6) should be multiplied by the k value (11) at D not the k value (7) at EF where all the fringes were crossed.

6.3.5 Minimizing the Sensitivity to Unwanted Movements

If the object moves or vibrates, the hologram may be destroyed. Therefore, one should try to position the object in the diagram in such a way that the sensitivity to movement is as low as possible. This is the case if the object is positioned so that the direction of displacement is parallel to the ellipse that intersects the object. If the unwanted displacement has no preferred direction, the object should be positioned where the k value is as high as possible.

6.4 The Moiré Analogy to Hologram Interference Fringes

6.4.1 Introduction to Moiré Simulation

In Section 6.2 we showed that two sets of equally spaced concentric circles produce one set of ellipses and one set of hyperbolas. These new sets could be looked upon either as just moiré patterns formed by two sets of circles or as an analogy representing the interference fringes patterns formed by two sets of spherical wavefronts. In this chapter we want to introduce general terms that include both moiré and interference phenomena. Any two sets of fringes that, combined, produce a new set of fringes are called primary fringes, and the new fringes are called secondary fringes. A combination of two sets of secondary fringes might also produce fringes named difference fringes of the third order, etc. The higher order fringes represent the difference of two lower order fringe

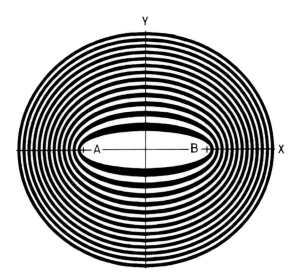

Fig. 6.12. The primary fringes that represent a cross-section through the axis of a set of ellipsoids with the common focal points A and B. A represents the point of illumination and B the point of observation

patterns [6.15]. Thus, the term "primary fringes" refers, for example, to those fringes on a hologram plate that produce the holographic image. The dark fringes in holographic interferometry that represent displacement, deformation, vibration, or changes in refractive index are all secondary fringes. Ordinary moiré fringes are secondary fringes (e.g., when produced by placing two transparencies of primary fringes on top of one another). As both moiré patterns and hologram interference patterns are secondary fringes, there might be reason to believe that useful analogies exist between these two phenomena [6.35].

A double exposed hologram can be made in the following way. The object is illuminated by a spherical coherent wavefront originating from a point source A (Fig. 6.12). The observation is made from another point B at the distance $2L$ from A. In order to record all of the optical information from the object, a photographic plate is placed between C and B (to accomplish this the plate must also be illuminated by a reference beam) (see Fig. 6.8). The laser light is turned on for the first exposure and then extinguished. Then the object is deformed so that parts of it are displaced while other parts are in a fixed position. When all movement has settled, a second exposure is made, and then the photographic plate is processed and brought back to its original position where it is again illuminated by the reference beam. If the object is taken away, its reconstructed holographic image will be seen exactly where it was during exposure. When the image of the object is studied from the observation point B we find, covering its surface, interference fringes that represent the displacements of each surface point. The fringe pattern can be interpreted in the following way.

Let A and B represent the common focal points of a set of rotationally symmetric ellipsoids, each representing a constant pathlength for the light transmitted from A to B via any point on the ellipsoidal surface. Let the difference in pathlength be half of the wavelength (λ) if the reflection is changed from one ellipsoidal shell to an adjacent one. Number the ellipsoidal shells $S_1 S_2 \ldots S_n$ and the corresponding pathlengths, $2L + \lambda/2$, $2L + 2(\lambda/2), \ldots 2L + n(\lambda/2)$. Any point on the object surface that has moved from one ellipsoid (S_k) to another (S_{k+q}, where q is an odd number) between the two exposures will look dark in the reconstruction. A point that has moved so that q is zero or an even number will cause a bright reconstruction. Thus $q/2$ dark fringes are formed on the object surface between the displaced point and a fixed point (if no extreme point exists in between).

The moiré equivalent to the described fringe formation is quite simple in theory. Fill every second space between the adjacent imaginary ellipsoids with an imaginary ink that is in an inactive state. Place the object in the space occupied by the set of ellipsoids that it intersects. Activate the ink so that it blackens the object surface on all those parts that are in contact with the imaginary ink. This process corresponds to the first exposure of the hologram plate. The object is now covered by black fringes that are so closely spaced that they cannot be seen by the naked eye. These fringes can be called primary fringes.

Deform the object and once more activate the ink. A new set of primary fringes is formed on the object surface. This process corresponds to the second exposure of the hologram plate. If the displacement between the two exposures is only a few wavelengths, the two sets of primary fringes will cause a moiré effect, and a new fringe pattern is formed that can be seen on the object surface. These moiré fringes, which can be called secondary fringes, represent the displacement of each surface point and are identical in number and shape to the holographic interference fringes.

6.4.2 Generality of the Method

The analogy given is truly independent of the type of motion (translation, deformation, or extension). It is also independent of the type of holographic setup or the shape of the object. The only restriction on the use of the moiré method is that illumination and observation have to be made from apertures that are sufficiently small compared to the distances to the object. This restriction, however, also applies to holographic interference fringes. Larger apertures of illumination and observation produce less distinct interference fringes.

The process equivalent to real time observation [6.4] of holographic fringes (live fringes) is the following. The imaginary ink should be transparent, but even in its inactive state it should appear black where it contacts the object surface. The exposure of the hologram plate corresponds to an activation of the ink so that the object becomes covered by primary fringes fixed to its surface. Thereafter, the ink is made inactive again, and a second set of primary fringes is formed on the object on all those parts where its surface contacts the ink, but only for the duration of contact. The fixed and the latter, live set of primary fringes from secondary fringes that are analogous to those live interference fringes that are seen in real time holography. If this analogy is to be absolutely strict, between the first exposure and the observation, the ink should be moved from the filled spaces between the ellipsoidal shells into those that earlier were empty. This process corresponds to the development of ordinary photographic plates where the illuminated areas become dark.

When an interference hologram is studied, the interference fringes move as the observer moves his head. The moiré analogy is based on just one fixed point of observation (the focal point B). Consequently, if that point of observation is to be changed, the whole process of making the two sets of primary fringes has to be repeated. An instrument has, however, been presented that simulates the fringe parallax [6.26]. The equivalence to time average holography consists of a single activation of the ink with a duration of many vibration periods. The darkening properties of the ink should in this case be time dependent so that those parts on the object surface that have the longest exposure time to the ink become darkest.

6.4.3 Uses

The moiré method described is, of course, only a theoretical experiment that cannot be realized in practice, but it certainly can be used to simplify the understanding of holographic interferometry. If, however, we accept some limitations to the exactness of the analogy, the proposed method can be used in a very practical way. Let us make the difference in pathlength for the light reflected from adjacent ellipsoidal shells 10000 times longer than 0.5λ. For $\lambda = 0.6328\,\mu m$, this will give a difference in pathlength of about 3 mm. Let us study only the intersections between the ink-filled ellipsoidal shells and a flat surface, for instance, a cross-section through the axes of the ellipsoids as demonstrated in Fig. 6.12. We make two transparent copies of a diagram similar to that of Fig. 6.12 and place one on top of the other, so that A and B coincide.

With these two transparencies representing two sets of primary fringes, a simulation of holographic interferometry is easily performed. Let us, for example, move one transparency in the y direction (Fig. 6.13). The resulting moiré pattern (the secondary fringes) is an almost exact copy of the holographic interference pattern that would be formed on a large surface (D) that is displaced in the y direction and placed just *under* and almost in contact with A and B. The sensitivity of this moiré method is only 10^{-4} times that of its holographic equivalent, and therefore some slight error may be introduced in the vicinity of A and B (to form the same number of fringes the displacement has to be 10^4 times larger). The main structure of the fringe pattern is, however, easily studied. The displacement of the translated set of primary fringes is constant over its whole area and therefore the secondary fringes of Fig. 6.13 represent at the same time the loci of constant sensitivity. It is, for example, easy to find out that a long object placed at D will have a surprisingly constant sensitivity to displacements in the y direction over its whole length.

The secondary fringes of Fig. 6.13 represent the solution to

$$K = \frac{2}{Y} \frac{[y^2+(L+x)^2]^{1/2} \cdot [(y^2+(L-x)^2]^{1/2}}{[y^2+(L+x)^2]^{1/2} + [y^2+(L-x)^2]^{1/2}} \tag{6.7}$$

where K is an integer and the x values of A and B are $+L$ and $-L$, respectively.

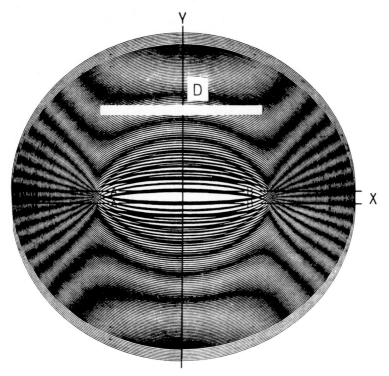

Fig. 6.13. Two transparent copies of a pattern similar to that of Fig. 6.12 have been placed on top of each other so that *A* and *B* coincide. Then one transparency has been translated in the *y* direction. Any object (e.g., the long bar at *D*) in a corresponding holographic setup that is translated in the *y* direction between the two exposures will have a fringe pattern represented by the intersection of the moiré pattern and a cross-section of the object

The two transparencies can just as easily simulate the displacement in any arbitrary direction in the *xy* plane. They can also simulate rotation around any point in that place. To find the fringes formed at other cross-sections of the ellipsoids, other transparencies have to be made. It should be pointed out that the intersection of the set of ellipsoids and any surface forms a zone plate that diffracts light from A to B (this type of zone plate is not restricted to a flat surface but might have any arbitrary curvature).

6.4.4 Examples of Moiré Simulation

When the displacement of the object surface in a hologram is a combination of rotation and translations in both *x* and *y* directions, the mathematical solution is complex and rather complicated to work out. However, all of the possible fringe patterns can be found using only the two transparencies. In this way the two sets of primary fringes represent hundreds of diagrams that can be used for the study of the main structure of the fringe patterns and the variations in sensitivity to object displacements in any direction over the whole studied area.

Sollid [6.36] described an experiment in which a studied object was translated first in a direction normal to its flat surface, and secondly in the plane of the surface. The displacement was equal in both cases and the arrangement was such that the projection of the displacement onto the bisector of the direction of illumination and observation was also equal for the two experiments. *Sollid* pointed out that these two experiments are equivalent as far as the existing theory for reducing fringes to displacements is concerned. Yet, in the first experiment there were only a few fringes to interpret, and in the second experiment there were a great number of fringes.

The equivalent moiré experiment is easily performed using the two transparencies, and produces exactly the described result. Only those fringes that are positioned on parts of the object surface that can be illuminated from A and studied from B can be seen. The holographic interference fringes are represented by the intersection of that object surface and the secondary fringes. Figure 6.14 demonstrates a translation normal to the surface (two fringes) and Fig. 6.15 a translation of the same amplitude parallel to the surface plane (12 fringes). In Figs. 6.14 and 6.15, the directions of sensitivity are portrayed in a very detailed

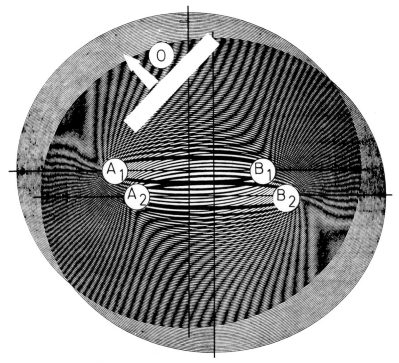

Fig. 6.14. A flat object *O* has been translated perpendicular to the plane of its surface. Only two interference fringes are seen from *B* because the object intersects only two moiré fringes

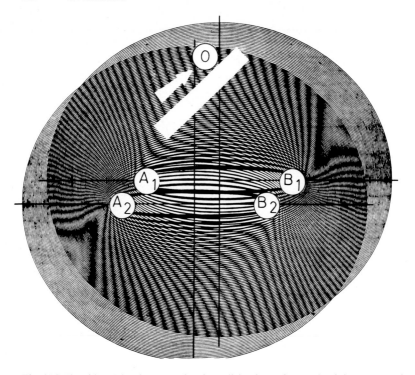

Fig. 6.15. The object *O* has been translated parallel to its surface so that it intersects no less than 12 moiré fringes. Thus 12 interference fringes are seen from *B* in spite of the fact that the translation and its projection onto the bisector of illumination and observation are equal to those of Fig. 6.14

and compact way. Figure 6.16 is a photograph of the fringe pattern formed on the surface of a disk that was given a small rotation between the two exposures of the hologram. The disk is seen from an oblique angle. The center of rotation is marked by a cross (+). The point where one of the imaginary ellipsoids is tangent to the disk surface is marked by a small circle.

Figure 6.17 demonstrates the moiré equivalent to that experiment. The sets of primary ellipses represent the locus of intersection of the ellipsoids and the flat surface of the disk. The two transparencies have been rotated with respect to one another about an axis marked by a cross. The tangential point is marked by a small circle. The secondary fringes of Figs. 6.16 and 6.17 are surprisingly well correlated considering the great difference in sensitivity. One of the transparencies of Fig. 6.17 was rotated about 10000 times more than the disk of Fig. 6.16.

The author has tested the moiré equivalence twenty times and never found any marked discrepancy between the moiré pattern and the corresponding interferometric fringe pattern. Figure 6.18 shows those cross-sections of the ellipsoids that have been studied. The corresponding moiré patterns are seen in Fig. 6.19. Each pattern is marked in the right-hand corner by figures relating to the different cross-sections of Fig. 6.18 that have been used for producing the

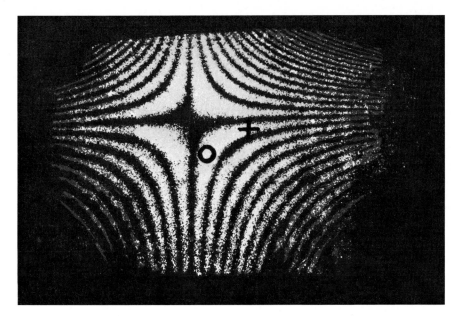

Fig. 6.16. Image of a disk that has been rotated by a small amount between the two exposures of the hologram. The disk is seen from a very oblique angle. The center of rotation is marked by a cross. The point where one of the ellipsoids is tangent to the disk surface is marked by a small circle

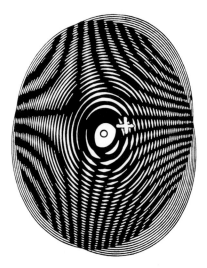

Fig. 6.17. The approximate moiré analogy to the interferogram of Fig. 6.16

moiré fringes. An arrow indicates the direction of the displacement that caused the interference fringes. This arrow also indicates the direction in which one of the cross-sections was displaced in relation to the other to form the moiré pattern.

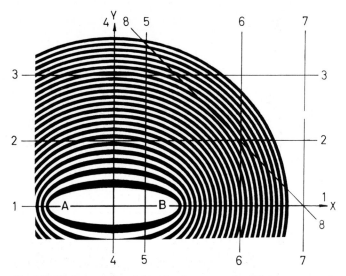

Fig. 6.18. The lines numbered from 1 to 8 represent the different cross-sections through the ellipsoids that have been calculated and used as primary fringes in moiré experiments

All of the patterns in Fig. 6.19 are similar to those predicted in [6.37]. The points A and B are represented by white dots. The pattern I(a) in row I is formed on a flat surface placed just behind ($d = 0$) A and B, rotated around the normal to the surface (through the cross). This pattern has been partly verified holographically. I(b) and I(c) demonstrate the patterns formed on a surface placed at distances of 0.5 AB and AB behind A and B. In these two cases the center of rotation was the normal to the surface through B. Both patterns have been verified holographically.

The patterns in rows II and III are the result of an in-plane translation in a vertical and a horizontal direction, respectively. Pattern (a) can be only partly studied holographically, while (b) and (c) are easy to verify. Pattern IV(a) has no secondary fringes at all. This demonstrates that a plane passing through A and B is insensitive to a translation in a direction normal to its surface. The two primary patterns are identical as they represent two parallel cross-sections made at each side of the axis AB and at the same distance from this axis. This insensitivity has been verified holographically. The two sets of circles around A and B that can be seen in IV(b) are rather difficult to see in the holohraphic image. A small fixed aperture has to be used for the observation because the fringes move very rapidly between A and B when the observer moves his head. The pattern of IV(c) is again easy to verify holographically.

The patterns of Fig. 6.19 represent the hologram fringe patterns formed on object surfaces placed in the vicinity of A and B. Moving the object surface further from A and B will cause each cross-section of the ellipsoids to become more and more like an ordinary circular zone plate. Outside a sphere with radius AB with its center halfway between A and B, the primary pattern could well be approximated as Fresnel zone plates. Thus, in-plane translations anywhere

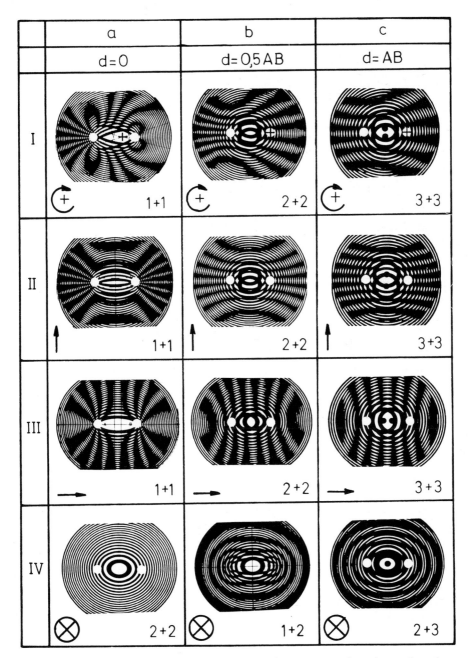

Fig. 6.19a—c. The basic moiré patterns representing interference patterns formed on surfaces that have been given a small displacement between the two exposures of a hologram. The surfaces are supposed to be placed at a distance *d* behind the axis *AB* of the holo-diagram. *A* and *B* are fixed while the surfaces are displaced. I, rotation. II and III, translation in the plane of the paper. IV, translation normal to the paper. (a) Surface in the plane of the holo-diagram. (b) Surface at a distance of 0.5 *AB*, behind the place of the diagram. (c) Surface at a distance *AB* behind the plane of the diagram

outside this sphere will produce approximately straight fringes perpendicular to the direction of translation. Translations normal to the plane will produce approximately circular fringes and, if the center is far out of sight, these fringes may also give the impression of being straight lines.

Let us study an example of the use of Fig. 6.19. A hologram is exposed using a laser beam that is widened by a positive lens to illuminate the object. The focal point of the lens is the center of spherical wavefronts and thus, as described in Section 6.2, it will represent the focal point (A) of the ellipses of Fig. 6.12. The other focal point of the ellipses (B) represents the point of observation, e.g., the eye of the observer, which for simplicity is assumed to be close to the center of the hologram plate. Let us finally position the object in the diagram of Fig. 6.12 so that the angles of illumination and observation over its whole area will be identical to those of the real setup. Thus Fig. 6.12 represents a demagnified map of the real holographic setup. (If the refrence mirror is not moved during the experiment its position will not influence the fringe pattern formed in the reconstructed image.)

Let the studied object be a flat surface positioned along the line 2 of Fig. 6.18 at a distance $d = 0.5$ AB from the x-axis. To study the holographic interference fringes formed on the object, we use the moiré fringe patterns formed by two transparencies made of two intersections of the ellipsoids along the line 2. Thus we use Column b of Fig. 6.19 which represents $d = 0.5$ AB. This is further confirmed by the numbers in the lower right-hand corner of each pattern of this column which indicate that transparencies of cross-section 2 have been used. When the object has been given a rigid body motion between the two exposures of the hologram, one of the transparencies should be displaced in relation to the other in the same direction as was the object motion. This direction is indicated by an arrow in the lower left-hand corner of each moiré pattern.

If the object is rotated around an axis that passes through B and is parallel to the y-axis, hyperbolic fringes will appear on its surface as seen in I(b) of Fig.6.19. The larger the distance d is, the more the fringes will be transformed into straight horizontal lines parallel to the x-axis. If the object had instead been rotated around the y-axis of Fig. 6.18, the fringes would form a fringe pattern similar to Fig. 6.16. This pattern is formed if the center of rotation is close to the point where the ellipsoids are tangent to the object surface.

If the object is translated perpendicular to the x- and y-axes of Fig. 6.18, the fringes on its surface would again appear hyperbolic as seen in II(b) of Fig. 6.19. The larger d is, the more the fringes again would be transformed into straight horizontal lines parallel to the x-axis.

If the object is translated in a direction parallel to the x-axes of Fig. 6.18, the fringes would once more appear hyperbolic as seen in III(b) of Fig. 6.19. The larger d is, the more the fringes would be transformed into straight vertical lines perpendicular to the x-axis.

Finally the object surface could be translated parallel to the y-axis of Fig. 6.18 (normal to its surface). To present the moiré analogy to this motion, we have to place two transparencies that represent different cross-sections on top of each other. Let us first place cross-section 3 on top of cross-section 2, which results in the elliptic pattern of IV(c) of Fig. 6.19. If we instead add cross-sections 1 and 2, the result will be found in IV(b) which shows that the inner ellipses have broken up into two sets of small circles. Thus the fringe pattern caused by out-of-plane motion changes drastically when d is varied from zero to AB. Exactly when this change appears could in this way be found only if transparencies representing a large number of cross-sections were studied.

Instead of facing the object and looking for the pattern directly on its surface let us study this surface from the side and see where it intersects the secondary interference surfaces in space. Pattern II(a) of Fig. 6.19 was produced by placing a transparent copy of Fig. 6.18 on top of Fig. 6.18 and translating it parallel to the y-axis. The intersection of the object surface (placed along line 2) with the moiré fringes thus formed represents the fringes seen on the object surface along the line where it intersects the $x - y$ plane. From II(a) of Fig. 6.19 it can be seen that for large d there is only one tangential point between fringes and object surface: thus only one set of rings is formed. For d shorter than 0.5 AB, however, there are two tangential points and thus two sets of rings are formed. The value of d for which this change appears is perhaps best found from Fig. 6.13 and is around 0.7 AB.

There are two slight drawbacks to the moiré method. One disadvantage is that the transparencies must be deformed to demonstrate the pattern resulting from deformation or extension of the object surface. The other disadvantage is that the principle described does not demonstrate in a simple way how the fringes move around and change as the observer moves his head (the dynamic properties of the fringes). Therefore, it is difficult to demonstrate the possibility of discriminating between the different types of object motion that might produce identical stationary patterns.

6.4.5 Contouring by Translation

Contouring is a method used to reveal the three-dimensional shape of an object by producing on its surface fringes similar to the lines of constant elevation that are used on ordinary maps. These fringes can be thought of as formed where the object is intersected by a set of equally spaced, flat, parallel surfaces. From Fig. 6.20 it is found that the interference surfaces in the vicinity of C are surprisingly flat and that they intersect the line of sight (radius from B) by an angle that differs from zero. This suggests that contouring fringes can be produced not only by double exposure using two wavelengths but also by a simple translation. A setup similar to that of Fig. 6.20 ought to be able to produce contouring fringes that are perpendicular to the line of sight and which also represent intersecting surfaces that are more flat than would be expected with regard to the curvature of the wavefronts or the ellipsoids.

The holographic setup used for the experiment of Fig. 6.20 was the following. A and B are the focal points of the ellipsoids of the holo-diagram representing

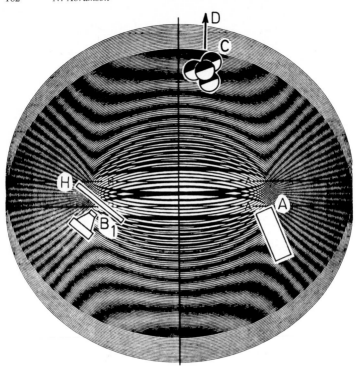

Fig. 6.20. In a holographic contouring experiment *A* and *B* are the focal points of the ellipses of the holo-diagram. The object (*C*) consists of four balls placed in the form of a pyramid which is illuminated by divergent light from a laser at *A*. Dark parts of the balls represent shadows. Between the two exposures of the hologram, *C* was displaced in the direction of the arrow *D*. The reconstruction is photographed by the camera B_1, placed close to the hologram *H*. The intersection of the object (*C*) by the moiré fringes, caused by the displacement of one of the elliptic patterns in the direction of *D*, represents the intersection of the real object by imaginary interference surfaces in space

the point of illumination and the point of observation, respectively. The object (C) consists of four white table tennis balls placed in the form of a pyramid, which is illuminated by divergent light from the laser at A. Dark parts of the balls represent shadows. Between the two exposures of the hologram the object (C) was displaced in the direction of the arrow D. During reconstruction, the camera (B_1) was placed just behind the holographic plate (H). The reference beam and the identical reconstruction beam are excluded from the figure. One advantage of this new contouring method was that a motion of the point of observation backwards away from the plate during reconstruction influenced the moiré pattern of Fig. 6.20 so that the interference surfaces rotate and at a certain distance become perpendicular to the line of sight. This is demonstrated in Fig. 6.21 which was made as follows. The first set of ellipses was placed with one focus A at the spatial filter in the same way that Fig. 6.20 was made. The other focal point, however, was placed at B_2 instead of B_1. The moiré pattern was once more produced by displacing a transparent copy in the direction of the arrow D.

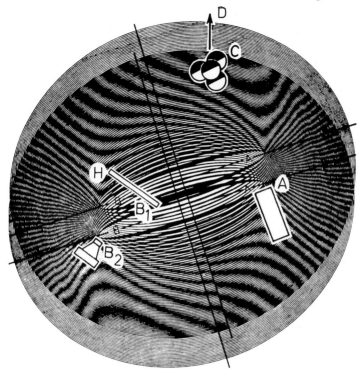

Fig. 6.21. When the camera during reconstruction is moved backwards from B_1 to B_2 the focal point B of the elliptic pattern should follow while the other focal point A is fixed to the laser at all times. As before, one pattern is thereafter displaced in the D direction and the moiré fringes formed represent the holographic contouring fringes as photographed from B_2. These fringes are now perpendicular to the line of sight (B_2C)

Fig. 6.22. Photograph of the reconstructed object taken with the camera at B_1 of Fig. 6.20. Observe the similarity to the pattern one would see from B_1 of Fig. 6.20 if the object (C) were intersected by the moiré fringes

Results of these experiments demonstrated that the practical results were in qualitative agreement with the visual experiments using the moiré analogy [6.38]. The photograph of Fig. 6.22 shows the result with a camera at B_1 of Fig. 6.20.

If our studies are limited to an object placed in the vicinity of the x-axis of Fig. 6.18, the relation between object displacement normal to the ellipsoids (d) and the separation of the contouring surfcaes (D) will be as follows:

$$d = (k)^3 \frac{L}{D} \frac{\lambda}{2} \qquad (6.8)$$

where $k\lambda/2$ = the separation of the hyperboloids of the holo-diagram, L = half the distance from A to B, and λ = the wavelength of the illuminating light.

6.5 Sandwich Holographic Interferometry: An Analog Method for the Evaluation of Holographic Fringes

Real time holography has the advantage that object changes can be studied as they appear without any time delay from the processing of the hologram plate. After just one exposure the hologram plate is processed and relocated with high precision to the position where it was exposed. Interference between the real object and its reconstructed image produces the desired fringes which can be manipulated during the evaluation, e.g., by moving the object. A disadvantage of this method is the need for interferometric precision during the reconstruction. Double exposure holography is much easier to use but has the disadvantage that the fringe pattern is fixed and cannot be manipulated during reconstruction. Sandwich holographic interferometry combines some of the advantages of both methods. In the following we will present some of our recent results.

6.5.1 Making the Sandwich Hologram

One hologram plate was placed in a special plate holder equipped with three contact points that locate the plate surface while three pins locate two sides of the plate. A second hologram plate was then placed in contact with the first covering its surface. Both plates have their emulsions towards the object (Fig. 6.23). The emulsions were therefore separated by the glass base of the front plate. When the plates were exposed simultaneously both the object beam and the reference beam reaching the back plate passed through the front plate, which was not covered by any anti-halo layer. The two exposed plates were removed and two new plates were placed in the plate holder.

The object consisted of three vertical steel bars (Fig. 6.25) that were fixed by screws at their lower ends to a rigid frame which surrounds the bars and functions as an undeformed fixed reference surface. The middle bar was also supported at the top end. A force was applied to the middle of the bars. After the deformation of the three objects the second pair of plates was exposed.

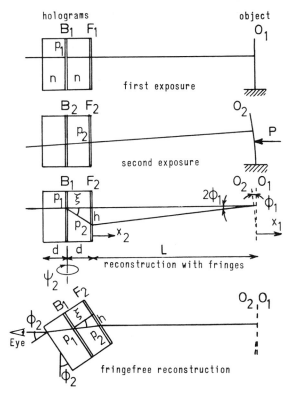

Fig. 6.23. The top of the object O is tilted by an angle ϕ_1 by the force P. Therefore a speckle ray from one object point is moved the vertical distance h from P_1 to P_2. B and F are the emulsions of back and front hologram plates, respectively. Glass plate thickness is d and refractive index is n. ϕ_2 and ψ_2 represent sandwich rotation around a horizontal and a vertical axis, respectively. The identical reference and reconstruction beams are excluded in the figure

Thereafter all four plates were processed and the back plate of the first exposure (B_1 of Fig. 6.23) was repositioned in the plate holder behind the front plate of the second exposure (F_2). The two plates were bonded together to form a sandwich hologram. The image was reconstructed by a laser beam, the direction and divergence of which were identical to those of the reference beam used during exposure.

6.5.2 Elimination of Spurious Fringes

Strange looking fringes were seen on all bars (Fig. 6.24). It was very difficult to find any correlation between this fringe pattern and the expected deformation. Straight, inclined fringes that covered the supposedly fixed frame disclosed the situation. The total object, including the frame, had made unwanted rigid motion. Even after this fact had been found, it was difficult to evaluate the fringes on the steel bars. If the hologram had been an ordinary double exposure,

Fig. 6.24. Rigid motion of the total object has hidden the information concerning deformations. If this hologram had been an ordinary double exposure it would have been judged a failure

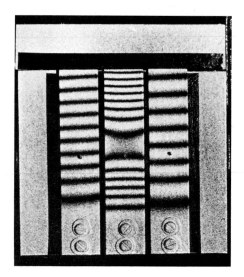

Fig. 6.25. The same reconstruction as that of Fig. 6.24 but a small tilt of the sandwich hologram has eliminated the fringes on the rigid frame. The fringe pattern now correlates well with the expected deformations. The object consists of three bars, the lower ends of which are screwed to a rigid frame. The middle bar is also supported at the top end. Between the two exposures, forces were applied at the middle of the bars. The right bar is deflected away from the observer. The other two bars are deflected towards the observer

it would simply have been considered a failure. The sandwich hologram, however, has the property that its fringes can be manipulated by tilting it in relation to the reconstruction beam. By holding the sandwich by hand and tilting it in different directions it was easy to find the reconstruction angle that made the rigid frame appear fringe free (Fig. 6.25). The fringe pattern on the three bars which now represented the deformation of the bars in relation to the frame correlated well to what could be expected from their preknown load situation. Thus we had now changed our failure into something that almost any holographer would consider a successful hologram.

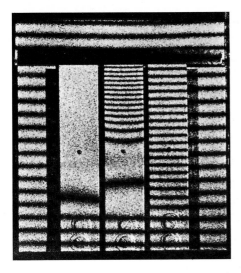

Fig. 6.26. The same image as that of Fig. 6.25 but the sandwich hologram has been tilted so that its top is moved towards the observer. At a certain tilt angle (ϕ_2) the top of the left bar (which was deflected by the angle ϕ_1 towards the hologram) is fringe free

6.5.3 Sign and Magnitude of Object Displacement

But considerable information is still missing. From Fig. 6.25 we cannot determine which bar was bent forwards or backwards. What has happened to the bar in the middle? Should we add all fringes from the top to the bottom to find the deflection? Or should we let the fringe number change sign halfway? When the sandwich hologram was tilted so that its top moved towards the observer, the number of fringes on the left bar decreased while the number on the right bar increased (Fig. 6.26). At a certain sandwich angle, the top of the left bar became fringe free. The rigid frame was now covered by fringes having the same spacing and direction as those that had been eliminated from the left bar. From this rather large sandwich tilt the much smaller tilt angle of the bar could be calculated [6.39]. As both the magnitude and sign of the sandwich tilt are analogous to the object tilt, we could conclude that the left bar had tilted towards the hologram while the right bar had tilted away from it. The number of fringes on the lower part of the middle bar decreased while those on the top increased, thus proving that its lower part had tilted towards the hologram while its top had tilted in the opposite direction.

6.5.4 Maximal Strain by Fringe Rotation

The sandwich hologram was once more tilted so that the rigid frame appeared fringe free. Then it was slightly rotated around a vertical axis (ψ_2 of Fig. 6.23). The rigid frame became covered by vertical fringes, the fringes of the left bar were inclined to the right, the fringes of the right bar were inclined to the left and the fringes of the middle bar bent into a "spoon-like" shape. This reconstruction (Fig. 6.27) presents in one single view much more information than can be found from Fig. 6.25 which represents the information content of a conventional double exposed hologram. The inclination of the fringes at each part of the

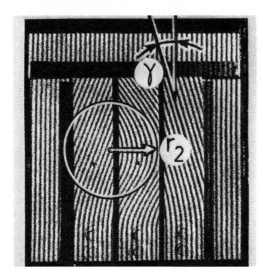

Fig. 6.27. The same image as that of Fig. 6.25 but the sandwich has been rotated by the angle ψ_2 around a vertical axis. The angle (γ) between the fringes and a vertical line is a measure of object tilt angle (ϕ_1). The radius of curvature of the fringes (r_2) is a measure of the object bending radius (r_1), from which the bending moment and maximal object strain can be calculated. Observe the large information content of Fig. 6.27 compared to Fig. 6.25

object is a measure of both the sign and magnitude of the object tilt. The fringes are curved over those parts of the object where the tilt angle varies. Thus the curvature of the fringes represents the derivative of the conventional fringe frequency and is a measure of the amount of object bending. There exists a simple relation between fringe curvature and object bending moment from which object strain can be evaluated [6.39].

6.5.5 Contouring

Sandwich holography can be applied to any contouring method, but we have concentrated our investigations on the method where the point of illumination is

Fig. 6.28. The three-dimensional shape of three objects is studied using a holographic contouring method. Between the two exposures of the hologram, the point of illumination is given a small lateral displacement causing fringes that are directed towards the illumination. Fringes perpendicular to the line of sight would be much more useful, but with this method they can be produced only in combination with large shadows

Fig. 6.29. The same reconstruction as that of Fig. 6.28 but a small tilt of the sandwich hologram has rotated the intersecting interference planes so that they become perpendicular to the line of sight

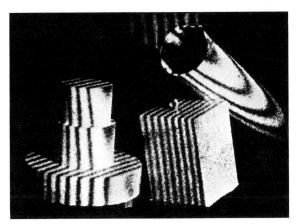

Fig. 6.30. The same reconstruction as that of Fig. 6.28 but a tilt of the sandwich hologram has rotated the intersecting planes so that they become parallel to one side of the cube

Fig. 6.31. The same image as that of Fig. 6.28 but the intersecting planes are now parallel to the top side of the cube

displaced laterally between the two exposures. This lateral shear was produced by tilting a plane parallel glass plate introduced into the illumination beam near its source. Each of the two hologram plates of the sandwich represented one exposure, and a tilt of the sandwich resulted in a tilt of the interference fringe planes that intersected the object. Figure 6.28 demonstrates the original fringe system with no sandwich tilt and therefore the fringes are parallel to the illumination direction. In Fig. 6.29 a small tilt of the sandwich hologram has rotated the intersecting planes until they are perpendicular to the line of sight. In Figs. 6.30 and 6.31 the sandwich has been tilted until the interference fringe planes became parallel to one side and the top side of the cube, respectively [6.40].

6.5.6 Theory and Calculations

Double exposure holographic interference fringes are caused by the difference of two fringe patterns that are recorded on one hologram plate. Each object point is represented by an interference fringe pattern corresponding to the intersection of the hologram plate by a set of hyperboloids, their common foci being the studied object point and the source of the reference beam, respectively. If any part of the object is displaced between the two exposures so that the corresponding fringes on the hologram plate are wiped out, no light will be diffracted to this part which consequently looks dark during reconstruction. Thus, the interference fringes seen in the reconstructed object space are caused by the moiré of the two interference patterns recorded on the plate.

The intersection of the hologram plate by the hyperboloids can be represented in the object space by the intersection of the object by an imaginary set of ellipsoids. The common foci of these ellipsoids are the point of illumination and the point of observation, respectively. The first exposure represents one set of intersections. Object displacement causes the second exposure to produce a new set of intersections that differ from the first recorded. The difference causes imaginary moiré fringes on the object surface that are equivalent to the interference fringes [6.35].

We have already pointed out that the intersection of the hologram plate by the hyperboloids is in the object space equivalent to the intersections of the object by the set of imaginary ellipsoids. If the moiré on the hologram plate can be manipulated during reconstruction, for example, by sliding one of the two plates of a sandwich hologram, the interference fringes on the object will change. If the moiré fringes on the plates are eliminated, the interference fringes on the reconstructed object will disappear too. The fringe motion caused by sandwich tilt can be explained by the study of one single speckle ray which reacts to object movements as if it were reflected by a small mirror fixed to its surface (Fig. 6.23). Object bending will cause the speckle to be recorded at different positions on the two exposed hologram plates. Any shearing or tilt of the sandwich that (during reconstruction) repositions the two recordings of the speckle along the line of sight towards the object eliminates the effects of the original speckle displacement and thus also eliminates the fringes indicating object motion. Thus fringes on the reconstructed object are, depending on tilt direction, either subtracted from or added to, the original fringe pattern. The spacing and direction of the resulting fringes are analogous to a moiré effect of the original fringe pattern and the fringe pattern caused by sheared observation.

The following equations [6.39] are limited to the study of displacements caused by object tilt that is parallel to the direction of illumination and observation. It has also been assumed that the sandwich tilt angle ϕ_2 is so small that $\sin\phi_2$ is equal to ϕ_2.

$$\phi_1 = \frac{d}{2Ln}\phi_2. \tag{6.9}$$

$$\phi_1 = \frac{d}{2Ln}\psi_2\tan\gamma. \tag{6.10}$$

$$r_1 = \frac{2Ln}{d}\frac{1}{\psi_2}r_2. \tag{6.11}$$

$$\sigma = \frac{d}{2Ln}\frac{\psi_2 Et}{2}\frac{1}{r_2}. \tag{6.12}$$

The symbols are defined in Figs. 6.23 and 6.27 where

ϕ_1 object tilt
ϕ_2 sandwich tilt
d thickness of gologram glass plate
L distance from object to hologram plate
n refractive index of hologram plate
ψ_2 sandwich rotation around vertical axis
γ fringe inclination to vertical
r_1 object bending radius
r_2 fringe radius of curvature
σ object stress
E modulus of elasticity
t object thickness.

The contouring method is described by the following equations.

$$y = \frac{xd}{\sqrt{d^2 + x^2 - 2xd\cos\beta}} \tag{6.13}$$

$$\sin\xi = \frac{\sin\beta}{d}\cdot y \tag{6.14}$$

where

y distance between resulting intersecting interference planes
d distance between interference planes caused by illumination shearing
x distance between interference planes caused by observation shearing
β angle between illumination and observation directions
ξ angle between intersecting interference planes and direction of observation.

The back plate of a sandwich hologram is both exposed and illuminated for reconstruction through a front plate. If all plates were identical, there would be no difference in optical pathlength when the front plate is exchanged. The effect of differences in thickness and amount of parallelism of the glass plates is to a high degree compensated for by the fact that the virtual image from the front plate is seen through approximately the same plate area through which the reconstruction beam passes to illuminate the back plate. Thus only the local variations in thickness have any appreciable aberration effects that cause false fringes. When the sandwich hologram is studied from a distance of only a few centimeters, the error is usually less than a quarter of a fringe.

If higher accuracy is needed, e.g., for contouring purposes, the ordinary glass base of hologram plates can be replaced by special optically flat plates. We also recommend that the equations presented in this chapter be used only as a guide. Calibrating methods should be used whenever possible. If, for example, contouring with high accuracy is to be performed, reference objects with known dimensions and angles ought to be placed near the object.

6.5.7 Moiré at the Image Plane

Manipulating the holographic fringes (e.g., by tilting a sandwich hologram) results from a moiré effect between two sets of intersections of hyperboloids and the hologram plate, which usually is situated in the Fourier plane. It is just as well possible to manipulate the fringes by producing a moiré effect in the image plane between two sets of intersections of ellipsoids and the object surface [6.41]. If we want to study the difference of two interference patterns, the two patterns could simply be recorded on two transparencies placed one on top of the other. The resulting moiré pattern represents the difference of the two patterns. If one transparency represents rigid object motion while the other represents deformation plus rigid motion, the moiré will represent deformation alone. If rigid motion produces approximately straight fringes, one transparency simply is covered by straight lines. For the result to be clear, the rigid motion should be large compared to deformation.

A double exposure hologram was made of a centrifugal pump. Between the two exposures the internal pressure was changed. Figure 6.32 demonstrates the result. A large rigid motion, rotation, has caused a great number of more or less vertical fringes. The desired information concerning the deformation of the center plate is hidden by these fringes. A grid of straight lines representing the fringes caused by the rigid motion was placed over Fig. 6.32. Thus moiré fringes were formed that represent the difference between the actual pump motion and rigid motion (Fig. 6.33). The unwanted fringes were eliminated and only the wanted fringes representing deformation are left. In Fig. 6.34 a sandwich hologram of the centrifugal pump is reconstructed. To study the deformation of the center plate, we tilted the sandwich during reconstruction until the interference fringes of Fig. 6.35 arose. These are almost identical to the moiré fringes of Fig. 6.33.

Fig. 6.32   Fig. 6.33

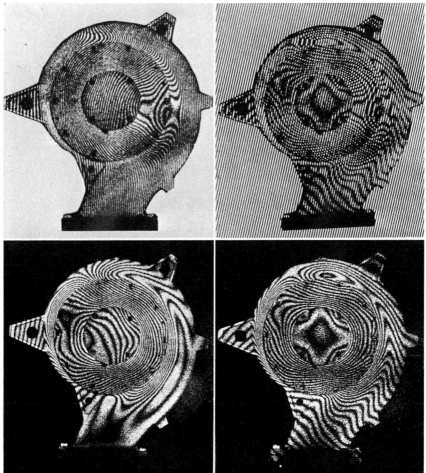

Fig. 6.34   Fig. 6.35

Fig. 6.32. A double exposed hologram was made of a centrifugal pump with a height of about 1 meter. Between the two exposures the internal pressure was changed. A large rigid body motion, rotation, was also introduced to the pump, producing a great number of almost vertical straight fringes. The desired information concerning the deformation is almost hidden by unwanted fringes

Fig. 6.33. A grid of straight lines representing the fringes caused by the rigid motion has been placed over Fig. 6.32. Thus, the moiré fringes represent the difference between the actual pump motion and the rigid motion. The unwanted fringes have been eliminated and only the wanted fringes representing deformation are left

Fig. 6.34. A sandwich hologram was made of the pump of Fig. 6.32. This time the rigid motion was smaller because no extra rotation was introduced

Fig. 6.35. The same reconstruction as that of Fig. 6.32 but the sandwich hologram was tilted until the rim of the center plate was intersected by as few fringes as possible. In that way the rigid motion of the center plate was eliminated and only the wanted fringes representing its deformation were left. (The center plate was fixed by four bolts). Observe the high degree of similarity between these fringes and the moiré fringes of Fig. 6.33

This example demonstrates that unwanted fringes can be eliminated in two ways. Either in the object image plane by a moiré effect or in the plane of the hologram plate. The first method, however, is limited because the moiré patterns are not coherent and therefore dark coarse fringes cannot be eliminated. The moiré on the hologram plate does not have this limitation and that is one of the reasons why sandwich holographic interferometry is expected to have great significance.

6.5.8 Holographic Studies of a Milling Machine

Finally we will describe another practical example of an industrial measurement which would have been quite difficult to make without the use of sandwich holography. The stability of a milling machine was tested holographically. The machine was 2 m high and weighed approximately 2 tons. The distance between the machine and the sandwich hologram was 10 m. The milling machine, standing directly on the floor of the workshop, was painted white and a dark tent of black plastic film was built around it to shut the daylight out and to prevent unwanted air turbulence. The reference beam was reflected by a mirror which was placed close to the milling machine. To make holographic imaging of the total object possible in spite of the 15 cm coherence length of the laser, we used the holo-diagram to plan the holographic setup (Sect. 6.3).

The source used was a Spectra Physics model 125 He–Ne laser with an output of some 60 mW. The exposure time was 10 s. A pneumatic membrane placed between tool and workpiece produced a simulated horizontal cutting force. First one pair of holograms was exposed with the machine at rest. Thereafter air pressure was applied to the membrane producing a force representing a low cutting force. Another pair of holograms was exposed whereafter one plate from each exposure was put together to form a sandwich hologram. The result is seen in Fig. 6.36. A heavy piece of steel was placed on the floor to the right of the machine as a fixed reference surface against which the motions of the machine could be defined. When the sandwich hologram was tilted during reconstruction, the eliminated fringe pattern could be moved from any part of the milling machine to this reference surface.

Figure 6.36 displays the motions of the milling machine with reference to the floor. Because of the large distances, illumination and observation were almost normal to the total surfaces studied and therefore each fringe represents a displacement of about 0.32 μm along the line of sight. Areas that are fringe free have not moved in this direction (the base of the machine, the reference surface). Areas covered by straight parallel lines have tilted rigidly without deformation (the table has mainly tilted). Areas covered by curved fringes have been deformed (the main body has been deformed by the force acting between the tool and table).

From Fig. 6.36 it is difficult to judge the deformation of the head of the milling machine because its fringe pattern is mostly caused by the large torsion of

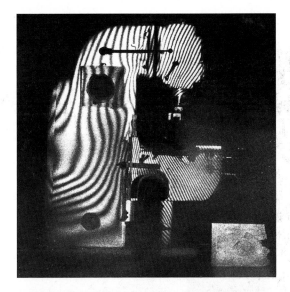

Fig. 6.36. A milling machine has been loaded by a static force representing the cutting force. Every fringe represents a displacement of about 0.3 μm normal to the plane of the photograph. Straight lines represent a tilt around an axis parallel to the lines. Curved lines represent deformation. Displacements forwards or backwards can be distinguished directly

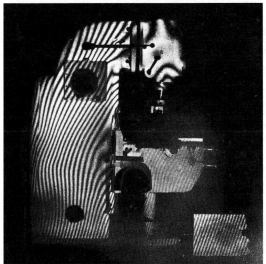

Fig. 6.37. The sandwich hologram has been tilted so that the deformation of the machine head can be studied without any influence on the fringe pattern from the deformation of the total machine

the main body. After tilting the sandwich hologram until the number of fringes crossing the head was as low as possible, it was easy to study the deformation of the head without any disturbances from the motions of the rest of the machine (Fig. 6.37). From the angles by which the sandwich hologram had to be tilted to change the picture from that of Fig. 6.36 to that of Fig. 6.37, the tilt of the machine head could be evaluated with regard to magnitude, direction and sign.

The deformation of the table of the milling machine could, however, not be studied because the force used was too low. Thus the force was increased until it

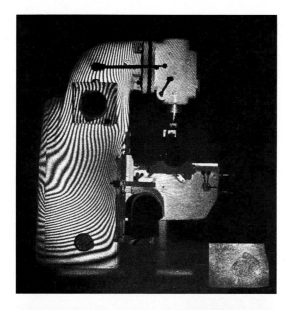

Fig. 6.38. The load has been increased so that it is four times larger than in Fig. 6.36. The motion of the machine table becomes so large that the fringes cannot be properly resolved

Fig. 6.39. The same hologram as in Fig. 6.38 but the sandwich hologram was tilted so that the deformation of the machine table is easy to study. From the tilt of the hologram the magnitude, direction and sign of the table tilt can be evaluated

was approximately four times larger and the hologram of Fig. 6.38 was made. The tilt of the table was so large that the fringes are not quite resolved. After a tilt of the sandwich hologram during reconstruction, fringes appeared on the table and after some further tilt the number of fringes crossing it was set at a minimum (Fig. 6.39). Now it was possible to measure the deformation of the table of the milling machine in spite of the fact that the deformation was so small that it had produced only about eight of the nearly one hundred fringes that theoretically should have existed on the table. From the angles through which the sandwich hologram had to be tilted to transform Fig. 6.38 into Fig. 6.39 it is also possible to calculate the magnitude, directions and sign of the table tilt, in spite of the fact that the fringes originally were so closely spaced that they could not be numbered.

We have found that it is possible to measure at least ten times larger deformations with sandwich holography than with ordinary holography. In the experiment described we increased the force still more and managed to eliminate about 500 fringes. In that case we used an extra glass plate to separate the hologram plates so that the distance between the emulsions was approximately 9 mm.

References

6.1   K.Stetson, R.Powell: J. Opt. Soc. Am. **55**, 1694 (1965)
6.2   N.Abramson: Appl. Opt. **11**, 2562 (1972)
6.3   N.Abramson: Optik **39**, 141 (1973)
6.4   B.Hildebrand, K.Haines: Appl. Opt. **5**, 172 (1966)
6.5   M.Born, E.Wolf: *Principles of Optics* (Pergamon Press, New York 1965)
6.6   G.Freier: *University Physics* (Meredith Publishing Company, New York 1965) p. 537
6.7   L.Lading: Appl. Opt. **10**, 1943 (1971)
6.8   W.M.Farmer: Appl. Opt. **11**, 770 (1972)
6.9   J.Collier, C.Buckhardt, L.Lin: Optical Holography (Academic Press, New York 1971)
6.10 J.Gates: Opt. Technol. **1**, 247 (1969)
6.11 J.Butters: In *The Engineering Uses of Holography, Glasgow* 1968 (Cambridge U.P., Cambridge 1970) p. 163
6.12 D.Gabor: IBM J. Res. Develop. **14**, 509 (1970)
6.13 E.Archbold, A.Ennos: Opt. Acta **19**, 509 (1970)
6.14 J.Leendertz: J. Phys. E**3**, 214 (1972)
6.15 N.Abramson: Laser Focus **23**, 26 (1968)
6.16 R.Brooks, L.Heflinger: Appl. Opt. **8**, 935 (1968)
6.17 N.Abramson: Optik **1**, 56 (1969)
6.18 J.Briers: Appl. Opt. **10**, 519 (1971)
6.19 J.Lit: J. Opt. Soc. Am. **62**, 491 (1972)
6.20 N.Abramson: Appl. Opt. **8**, 1235 (1969)
6.21 R.Kurtz, H.Loh: Appl. Opt. **11**, 1998 (1972)
6.22 E.Aleksandrow, A.Bonch-Bruevich: Soviet Phys.-Tech. Phys. **12**, 258 (1967)
6.23 B.Hildebrand: In *The Engineering Uses of Holography, Glasgow* 1968 (Cambridge U.P., Cambridge 1970) p. 410
6.24 R.M.Huffaker: Appl. Opt. **9**, 1026 (1970)
6.25 E.Leith: Proc. IEEE. **59**, 1305 (1971)
6.26 N.Abramson: Appl. Opt. **10**, 2155 (1971)
6.27 D.Duffy: Appl. Opt. **11**, 1778 (1972)
6.28 J.Burch: Proc. Eng. **44**, 431 (1965)
6.29 R.Collier, E.Doherty, K.Pennington: Appl. Phys. Letters **7**, 233 (1965)
6.30 R.Brooks, L.Heflinger, R.Weurker: Appl. Phys. Letters **7**, 248 (1965)
6.31 K.Pennington, L.Lin: Appl. Phys. Letters **7**, 56 (1965)

6.32 E. Archbold, J. Burch, A. Ennos: J. Sci. Instr. **44**, 489 (1967)

6.33 K. Stetson, R. Powell: J. Opt. Soc. Am. **56**, 1161 (1966)

6.34 F. Arecchi, A. Sana: *Quasi-Optics*, ed. by J. Fox (Polytechnic Press, Brooklyn 1964) p. 623

6.35 N. Abramson: Nature **231**, 65 (1971)

6.36 J. Sollid: Opt. Commun. **2**, 282 (1970)

6.37 N. Abramson: Appl. Opt. **9**, 2311 (1970)

6.38 N. Abramson: Appl. Opt. **15**, 1018 (1976)

6.39 N. Abramson: Appl. Opt. **14**, 981 (1975)

6.40 N. Abramson: Appl. Opt. **15**, 200 (1976)

6.41 N. Abramson: In *Electro-Optics International Conference in Brighton* 1974 (Kiver Communications Ltd., Surrey, England 1974) p. 35

7. Biomedical Applications of Coherent Optics

H. J. Caulfield

With 22 Figures

7.1 Overview

Coherent optics can perform two basic types of operations in biology and medicine. First, it can perform functions already being performed in other ways. Thus it can be used to process data, recognize pathological tissue, or detect object motion. Of course not everything which can be done by coherent optics ought to be done by coherent optics. The burden of proof lies in showing that coherent optics offers an advantage over incoherent optics (which is often cheaper, more convenient, and more artifact free) or over digital techniques when processing is involved. Coherent optics will succeed only where the need for it is well established. Second, it can perform new functions unrivaled by competitive methods. Examples of this are holographic imaging and holographic detection of minute motions. The problem here is to demonstrate that the job needs to be done.

In passing from concept to routinely used product, any application of coherent optics must pass through three stages. We will label those stages "proof", "engineering", and "acceptance". In the proof stage we must determine not "Can this function be done by coherent optics?" but "Ought this function to be done by coherent optics?" That, in turn, is two questions. First, "Is the proposed function really worth performing?" Second, "Is coherent optics the best way to do it?" Unless the function needs doing, it will not progress far. Does medicine really need to record three-dimensional images of people? If not, holographic whole-body imaging will not be a successful product. Even if the function is needed, coherent optics may be only one of the ways to perform it. For processing of transaxial tomography images, digital processing and incoherent optical processing look like formidable alternative approaches. Coherent optics must prove that it is the best way (by some criterion). If a coherent optical technique passes both tests in the proof stage it may (with backing) enter the engineering stage. The problem here is to reduce the very high technology coherent optical system to a reliable instrument operable without knowledge of coherent optics. The third stage (acceptance) is the last hurdle and the hardest since many nontechnical factors enter.

The vast majority of coherent optical techniques is in the first stage. This is not to say they will not lead to ultimate acceptance. Certainly some will and others will not. This chapter is an attempt to survey all of the types of applications currently being investigated.

We will start with the most obvious applications and progress to the less obvious ones. Thus we begin with coherent optical image formation (microscopic, macroscopic three dimensional, and two dimensional) and proceed to non-optical image formation utilizing coherent light in image formation (in acoustics and radiology). Because so much of this involves three-dimensional image formation and various forms of tomography, an appendix relating all of those concepts is attached. Signal processing is the next area we will examine. This includes image improvement and processing of data acquired by other means (e.g., ECGs, EEGs). Next we look at image display—a very important use of coherent optics. Coherent optics can be used to extract or display certain features of an object (dimensions, contours, motion, etc.), so a section is devoted to this. The final type of application considered is pattern recognition. There is much to cover, so detail is avoided in favor of breadth of coverage.

7.2 Coherent Optical Imaging

Biology and medicine involve the study of objects which we want to study at leisure. When the object is not convenient to keep around, we want to record its image in a form which is easy to keep. Coherent optical methods prove especially useful in this regard. The appendix on three-dimensional imaging and tomography will prove most useful after reading the entire section on coherent optical imaging.

7.2.1 Optical Microscopic Imaging

Microscopy has had a long and profound influence on the history of biology and medicine. Not surprisingly, it was microscopy which led to both coherent optical image processing by *Abbe* [7.1] in 1873 and holography by *Gabor* [7.2] in 1948. The use of phase manipulation in microscopy is so well known and so fast developing that it would require a full review chapter in its own right. The developments stemming directly and indirectly from *Gabor*'s wavefront reconstruction method are only now being assimilated into biomedical practice. We will review these in some detail.

Holography can have any of three relationships to microscopy. First, it can be a means for microscopy. Second, it can be an aid in ordinary microscopy by providing a stationary copy of a fast changing optical object for subsequent examination. Third, it can be combined with ordinary microscopy to form a hybrid system with some advantages of both.

Microscopy by holography was first suggested by *Gabor* [7.2], who proposed recording the wavefront at short wavelengths and reconstructing it at longer (visible) wavelengths. The images so formed would be magnified laterally by the ratio of the wavelengths. Later *Leith* and *Upatnieks* [7.3] realized explicitly that this form of holographic microscopy is but one example of the general approach of recording a wavefront under one set of conditions (wavelength, position of reference point source, etc.) and reconstructing it under another. Thus by varying the recording and reconstructing geometries, the image magnification can be controlled and varied at will even if only one wavelength is used for both operations.

Microscopy of holographically recorded wavefronts is an attractive concept for a variety of reasons. The object may be changing so fast that leisurely examination by ordinary microscopy is difficult or impossible. In such cases holography may be a necessity. The image can be examined by any known microscopic technique (bright field, dark field, phase contrast, interference, etc.) at the user's convenience. That is, such choices can be made *a posteriori*.

Ordinary microscopy has some difficulties which may be relieved by marriage to holography. For instance, the lens correction limits the image quality in ordinary microscopy. In holography any such lens problems, once they are measured, can be corrected. Thus, holography can be used to achieve diffraction-limited imaging through low focal number, low quality microscope objectives. One way to do this is to use a hologram as a corrector element to convert the actual point spread function into the desired one. A second way [7.4] is to pass the reconstructed wavefront back through the low quality lens to form a diffraction-limited unmagnified image of the object for subsequent examination by ordinary microscopes with better objectives.

Having looked at these three areas of holo-microscopy in sufficient depth to show their purposes and relationships, we will treat a few illustrative examples in detail.

How are objects recorded by holography for subsequent microscopic examination? The answer is: "Any way that records the object with a low enough focal number to provide the required resolution". This is not always easy. Two approaches have been used.

First, holograms of images formed at low f-numbers by microscope objectives have been recorded. This gives some relief on the f-number of the hologram. To record a high resolution image, we must see the object from a wide angle or low f-number. The f-number is the object distance divided by the system aperture. The lateral resolution is then about $N\lambda$, where λ is the imaging wavelength. The achievement of high resolution, then, requires low f-numbers. Figure 7.1 illustrates the situation. The reconstructed wavefront can then be viewed with an ordinary eyepiece if the reconstructing beam duplicates the reference beam or is passed back through the objective for automatic correction if the reconstructing beam reverses all rays in the reference beam. Automatic lens correction also occurs if instead of a general object, the object imaged is a point. The hologram thus formed converts each single point in the object to a duplicate of the reference point. Thus, the resulting image is formed of sharp rather than blurred points. All of these techniques have been used with success in holography laboratories. One of the most intriguing applications has been microcine-holography [7.5] in which motion picture holograms are taken through a microscope objective. Since focus adjustments can be made *a*

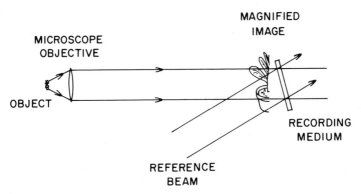

Fig. 7.1. Schematic diagram of holographic recording of a magnified image

posteriori, objects which would ordinarily drift out of focus can be followed. Indeed the focus control necessary gives three-dimensional information on the object position. Figure 7.2 illustrates some of the advantages of microcineholography. That is, we can have both fast frame rates and time to adjust the focus on each frame, because focusing can occur at leisure *a posteriori*.

Second, lensless imaging at low *f*-number can be used. This simply requires the object to be very close to the holographic recording medium, so a reasonable size of recording medium can contain the low *f*-number information from any region. This, in turn, raises problems of positioning the reference beam and object illuminating beams without affecting the recording medium. Many techniques for achieving this have been devised. Figure 7.3 shows how normal holograms of objects are recorded. The problems of moving the recording medium close to the object are not evident. Figure 7.4 shows how both the object beam and the reference beam (but not the illuminating beam) can be incident on the recording medium even though the object and the recording medium are in the way. Clearly the normal setup (Fig. 7.3) cannot be used to accomplish the desired result as there is no way to illuminate the object or insert a reference beam. A variety of solutions to this problem were reported by *McMahon* and *Caulfield* [7.6] in introducing an improved solution.

Another, even simpler method was developed by *Thompson* et al. [7.7] for studying microstructure in fog particles but is applicable to biological objects as well. A pulsed laser beam is incident on particles near a photographic plate. The diffracted light from the particles interferes with the undiffracted light to form a hologram. In this as well as in *Gabor*'s original holograms [7.2], the reconstruction step provided three overlapping wavefronts corresponding to the undiffracted reconstructing beam, a virtual image of the object, and a real image of the object. Often, the viewing of one of these images was confused by the out-of-focus image of the other (conjugate image). *Thompson* et al. showed that, with a collimated reference and reconstructing beam and the hologram in the far field of the particles, one image could be put at infinity, i.e., so far out of focus as to be of negligible hindrance in viewing the other image. With one exposure to the

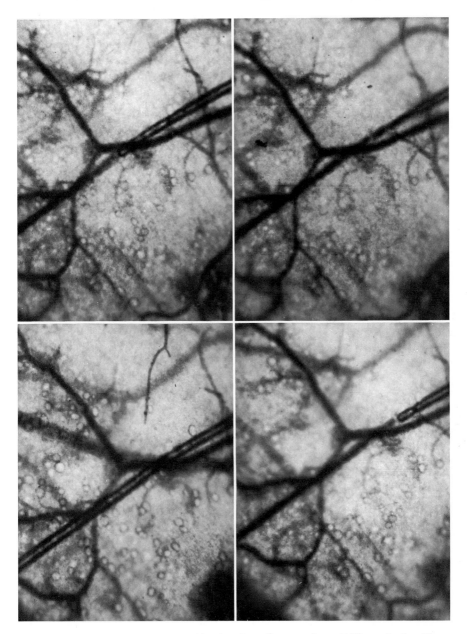

Fig. 7.2. Photographs from one holographic microcine-microscope frame. Different depths of focus are shown as can be noticed by watching the capillaries pop in and out of focus. Bubbles can be seen passing through the central artery. Courtesy of *M.E.Cox*, University of Michigan-Flint

laser pulse, the user records the shapes and locations of all particles in the vicinity of the recording medium. For essentially technical reasons (see Appendix), we cannot view all of these particles at once. We can, however, interrogate them one

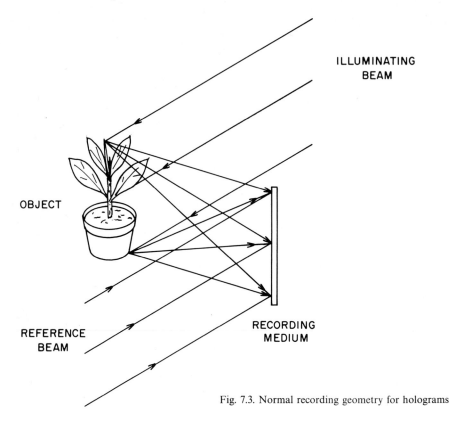

ILLUMINATING
BEAM

OBJECT

REFERENCE
BEAM

RECORDING
MEDIUM

Fig. 7.3. Normal recording geometry for holograms

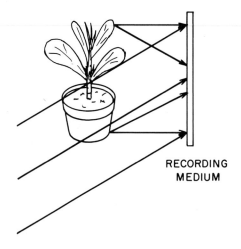

RECORDING
MEDIUM

REFERENCE
BEAM

Fig. 7.4. Desired recording geometry for holograms

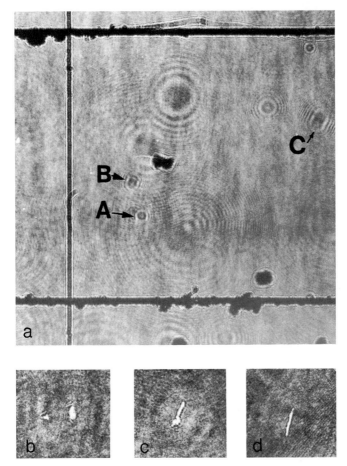

Fig. 7.5. A Fraunhofer hologram (a) of fibrous particulate matter in the respiratory range and selected images b, c, d produced from regions *A*, *B*, and *C* respectively of the hologram (after *Boettner* and *Thompson* [7.8]). By permission from the authors

plane at a time. In replay, the image of a particle is visible both in and out of focus. By moving a viewing screen or vidicon through various distances from the hologram, we can watch each image go into and out of focus. It is in focus when it has minimum size and minimum "sidelobes".

A number of applications of biomedical interest have been made. One of the most graphic illustrations derives from the work of *Boettner* and *Thompson* [7.8] on fibrous material in the size range not filtered out by our respiratory tract and hence of potential toxicity. Figure 7.5 shows a single hologram. The letters A, B, and C indicate the $x - y$ locations of three of the particulates at different depths. The inserts b, c, and d show the particulates themselves in their planes of best focus. Figure 7.5 thus provides a guide as to how holographic microparticle analysis works. Each pattern on the hologram is indicative of a particle that was on-axis with the reference beam at the instant of the laser pulse. By illuminating that pattern (itself the hologram of that individual particle) with a duplicate of the reference beam except reversed in direction, we form an accurate real image of the particle (subject to the diffraction limitations imposed by the size of the hologram, the size of the particle, and the distance of the particle from the plate). If the object were a mathematical point a distance d from the recording medium, its hologram would resemble a Fresnel zone plate of focal length d. Thus it would have concentric rings of radii

$$r_n = \sqrt{n\lambda d},$$

where n is an integer and λ is the laser wavelength. The effective diameter D_e of the hologram is limited because at some n, the distance between adjacent rings becomes too small to resolve. In reconstruction, diffraction limits us to a lateral resolution of

$$\Delta\xi = 2.44\,\lambda d/D_e\,.$$

For practical cases we can resolve features comparable to λ. Smaller particles can be detected, but their shapes cannot be determined. Their images are simply circles of diameter $\Delta\xi$. Unfortunately the image goes out of focus in such a way that at depths other than d we still see a pattern. We know we are at the proper depth when the pattern has minimum size and, ideally, no concentric ring structure. Thus one runs a viewing screen or vidicon through various depths to seek the true d. This judgement operation can be automated readily.

Fig. 7.6. The same image with and without severe speckle

All of these techniques require laser illumination, and laser illumination leads to the peculiar artifact of laser speckle. The nature and combatting of laser speckle have been studied widely for many years and many "solutions" (varying widely in complexity and practicality) exist [7.9, 10]. While many of those solutions work well for the special cases for which they were conceived, none works well universally to eliminate speckles. Perhaps these ubiquitous mottles are the primary barrier to wider acceptance of holographic microscopy. Figure 7.6 shows a speckled image before and after a speckle removal operation. In this case the speckle was removed (minimized) simply by imaging with a high numerical aperture. Speckles are essentially diffraction limited so they become smaller at the numerical aperture increases.

7.2.2 Three-Dimensional Optical Macroscopic Imaging

To us humans the most interesting biological objects are macroscopic—namely ourselves and our major "components". We want to form images and make measurements. Coherent optics does both. The measurements can be separated from the imaging. In this section we deal solely with coherent optical formation of optical images. Here the competitor is ordinary photography.

Holography is the obvious approach to biological imaging. A detailed description of a device to record and measure accurate three-dimensional information on large objects was provided by *Gara* et al. [7.11]. An ordinary pulsed laser hologram was recorded. In order to produce an image which is dimensionally accurate in three dimensions, we must use the same wavelength in reconstruction that we used in recording. The reason is easy to understand. The hologram, like a lens, is limited by certain basic laws of diffraction. Thus if R is the ratio of the wavelength of the reconstructing light to the wavelength of the recording light, the lateral magnification of the system is R but the depth magnification is R^2. This means that the two magnifications are equal only if $R = R^2$, i.e., if $R = 1$. Thus, to produce an undistorted real image, we must illuminate the hologram with a reconstructing beam which is identical to the reference beam in all respects but one: each ray is reversed in direction of travel. *Gara* et al. [7.11] recorded with a pulsed laser to "freeze" any object motion and then replayed the real image with a continuous wave laser of the same wavelength. Finally that image was scanned in three dimensions to describe the object as a surface at a distance $S(x, y)$ away from the plane of the hologram at each point (x, y) in that plane. The usefulness of this technique for whole body imaging is obvious. The need for such detailed whole body imaging has not been equally obvious, so this powerful tool awaits a need which would make its expense worthwhile. The biomedical usefulness of this technique was demonstrated by imaging skull models and then extracting profiles. Figure 7.7 shows horizontal profiles of the model as taken by *Gara* et al. [7.11]. Both micrometer and holographic measurements of the location of "landmarks" scratched onto the skull were made. The rms difference between coordinates indicated was about 40 μ.

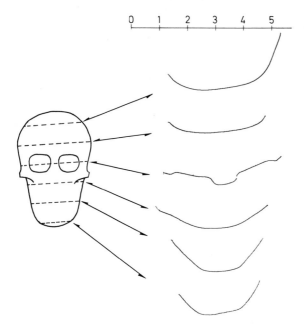

Fig. 7.7. Profiles of a skull model as derived by the holographic technique of *Gara* et al. [7.11]. By permission of Research Laboratories, General Motors Corporation

This same goal of extracting three-dimensional surface coordinates from free-standing objects has been attacked by other essentially non-coherent methods. We can call that goal "stereometry". Stereometry does not imply classical stereo photography or "photogrammetry". Rather, it is the general name given to any three-dimensional measurement (not necessarily imaging) technique. The most popular form of stereometry is computer or even coherent optical interpretation of stereo photographic pairs [7.12]. A new technique using time delays to encode range information [7.13] directly produces stereometric information on several thousand points per second. The depth accuracy of this latter technique (called "laser stereometry") is an order of magnitude worse than that of *Gara* et al., but it is essentially real time and avoids the need for a computer. As laser stereometry does not utilize the coherence of the laser, we will not review it here. It is mentioned to place holographic stereometry in realistic perspective. It is a slow method requiring great care to carry out, but it gives better accuracy than any of its competitors. Again the non-holographic alternatives to holography have proved almost as good and considerably simpler.

Of course less elaborate holographic methods can be used to good effect. The chief advantage appears to be recording in three dimensions. The question is not "what can be done?" but "where does this technology fit in?" What is it that needs to be recorded in full three-dimensional accuracy? A rare pathological object? The procedure of a uniquely skilled surgeon in a rare operation? The last carrier pigeon? Whatever it is must be rare enough to warrant recording at all and important enough to warrant the trouble and expense of holographic recording. To date only one answer has emerged. Holography through the body's optical window (the lens) is coming to be a widely used means for recording retinal and interoccular structures [7.14].

7.2.3 Two-Dimensional Image Formation

While no objects—biological or otherwise—are strictly two-dimensional, there are real advantages to recording two-dimensional images in biology and medicine as well as real advantages to using holography to do the recording. Let us consider first the applications and then the use of holography to serve those applications.

There are two broad categories of two-dimensional images of interest: symbolic recordings and images of objects. Symbolic recordings include charts, graphs, printed pages, etc. Here the problem for biomedical research is the volume of information. What is needed is a cheap, compact, conveniently accessed, readily copied, damage-invulnerable storage technique to permit better use, storage, and exchange of raw data. Two-dimensional images are common because they are the easiest to record and, more often than not, the easiest to interpret. The requirements are identical to those of two-dimensional symbolic image storage with the one additional requirement that a large number of "shades of gray" are useful for continuous tone images. Thus, for the case of two-dimensional imaging, holography is to be viewed not as a direct means of recording an image but as a means for archival storage of images recorded in other ways (e.g., by photograph, computer printout, typewriter). The simple ability to store and distribute data easily, cost-and-space efficiently, and with great invulnerability to loss due to damage would enhance the usefulness of all present research efforts.

Holography has some very pronounced advantages as a storage technique. We envision Fourier transform holograms recorded on some readily available medium such as photographic film. Many holograms of full pages of data are stored side by side. The advantages are obvious. First, the focusing problem in recording (very severe in ultrafiche) simply vanishes. Since the wavefront (not just an image) is recorded, the hologram cannot be out of focus. Second, the focusing problem in replay (a great annoyance in ultrafiche) virtually vanishes because the hologram is so small that every character is projected with a high focal number (and hence a very large depth of focus). Third, the replay equipment is simple and cheap, comprising a He–Ne laser to illuminate each hologram, a mechanical carriage to move the film so that the selected hologram into the beam, and a viewing screen. Fourth, copying is easy, noncritical, and cheap. Fifth, the record is compact. A readable version of this page could be stored in a spot 2 or 3 mm in diameter. Fifth, the record is somewhat invulnerable to damage or dirt. The information is stored in distributed form, so obscuring part of the hologram may degrade the whole image slightly, but it does not obliterate entire parts of the image. Furthermore scratches not essentially parallel to the hologram fringes do not contribute light to the image. Details of this technique can be found elsewhere [7.15].

7.3 Non-Optical Image Formation

Because tissues respond differently to non-optical radiation than they do to optical radiation, imaging outside the optical regime is useful. Of necessity, the output must be visible although the input is invisible. Coherent optics plays two major roles in non-optical image formation. First, it provides useful analogies (e.g., optical holography) which are readily extended to non-optical domains. Second, it provides readout to produce the required visible images.

7.3.1 Acoustic Holography

Acoustic holography provides good examples of both operations in the non-optical domain derived by analogy from the coherent optical domain and the use of coherent optical readout. We will summarize some results. An excellent monograph on the subject is available for those interested in more detail [7.16]. The aim here is to emphasize results which can be accomplished rather than methods for accomplishing them. Acoustic holograms are often formed and read out continuously. Two popular hologram media are liquid surfaces (ripple tanks) [7.17] and liquid crystals [7.18]. Alternatively we can use a *Bragg* diffraction cell [7.19]. In all of these cases, coherent light readout provides a real time image of the object as it is "viewed" by sound. A variety of recording media are available for delayed (not real time) viewing as well [7.16].

The images contain depth information on the object, but this information is not so easily perceived as is the scene depth in "ordinary optical holography". The reason for this is clear and an important illustration of a more general problem is applying coherent optics to biomedical problems. With an ordinary optical Fresnel hologram, we usually view the scene through the hologram which may be 10–20 cm in its linear dimensions. A typical film records $2 \cdot 10^4$ lines per cm or about $2 \cdot 10^5$ to $4 \cdot 10^5$ fringes in a visible-light hologram. Thus the whole hologram may contain about 10^{11} resolvable spatial elements or pixels. Figure 7.8 shows how an object may be viewed through such an optical hologram. The fraction of the total hologram contributing to the image seen by either eye is very small, but the number of pixels involved may still be 10^6 or more depending on where the viewer's eyes are situated. Typical acoustic holograms simply do not contain 10^{11} pixels. As a result, they cannot be used like the optical holograms just described. Instead of viewing the three-dimensional scene through a large window, we view it through a keyhole! Without the perspective changes available through a wider aperture, we lose our sense of three dimensionality. We cannot see a three-dimensional picture through a keyhole.

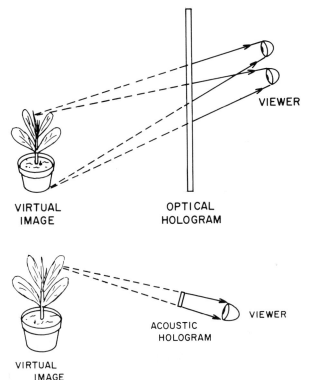

VIEWER

VIRTUAL
IMAGE

OPTICAL
HOLOGRAM

Fig. 7.8. Viewing the image
through an ordinary opti-
cal hologram

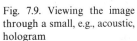

VIEWER

ACOUSTIC
HOLOGRAM

VIRTUAL
IMAGE

Fig. 7.9. Viewing the image
through a small, e.g., acoustic,
hologram

Figure 7.9 illustrates the point. That is, we must use the whole hologram to derive the image. Parallax clues vanish, but there remain depth of focus limitations on the image formation. We can, therefore, focus on successive depth planes subject only to the usual depth of focus constraints applied to the acoustical imaging situation. That is, a hologram of aperture A viewing an object at distance d at an acoustic wavelength λ has a depth resolution of about $d^2\lambda/A^2$. Often the various depth "planes" are focused in succession on a vidicon for convenient TV readout. The general problem illustrated here is the realitive paucity of data usually encountered in biomedical images. Thus, if convenient and fast $10^3 \cdot 10^3$ transducer arrays were available, these might replace the directly formed holograms and the images could be formed not by diffraction but by computer Fresnel transformation. Coherent optics is employed in acoustic holography not for its strongest point (high data handling capacity) but simply because it is (for the moment) cheaper and more convenient. Such happy circumstances do befall coherent optics but they do not lead to a stable advantage. Digital transducer arrays and digital processors will become cheaper and faster. Coherent optical means will have to improve also to hold their place.

Taking an acoustic hologram is a complex task beyond the scope of this chapter (see [7.16] for more detail), but we can outline those details which bear on the method of choice for any application. The first choice is whether the hologram must be "real time" or can be recorded at leisure. Real time holography is a virtual necessity for some objects (e.g., swimming fish, flexing muscles). It is important to remember that the object must not only be photographically still (motion less than the desired resolution) but also holographically still (motion less than a quarter of a wavelength). Thus, although at-leisure acoustic holograms have been widely suggested for industrial inspection, biomedical acoustic holography is almost exclusively concerned with real time techniques. The second choice is object illumination method. Since the outsides of objects are readily recorded by optical holography, acoustic holography is seldom used to record surface scattered sound. Rather, it is used almost exclusively in seeing through optically opaque objects. Thus the object must be transilluminated or, better, insonified. To couple the ultrasound efficiently to the object and then to the recording plane, the whole apparatus and object are normally immersed in a liquid (usually water). Since low focal number, fair quality acoustic lenses are not hard to make, such lenses are often used to bring an image of the object close to the hologram plane thus allowing a low focal number hologram to be recorded with relatively distant objects. The next step is to introduce the reference beam. The transducers and driving electronics are so good and the frequencies are so low (compared with optical frequencies) that it is possible to generate the reference and object beams from separate transducers. We choose the geometry to be such that it produces the finest fringes resolvable by the recording medium (thus recording the maximum amount of information).

The advantages of acoustic imaging over non-acoustic imaging for biomedical purposes are clear and straightforward. Ultrasound is much safer than X-rays for imaging internal organs, although safety requirements are still being debated vigorously. Even ultrasound is not harmless however, and allowable dosage estimates seem to be revised downward each year. Thus sensitivity of the various techniques is of great importance. Sensitivity limits may arise from ultrasonic effects or from recording or readout effects. Thus, for example, quantum noise may limit the sensitivity of those real time acoustic methods using laser beam readout. Ultrasound readily distinguishes among soft tissues which are almost identically transparent to X-rays.

On the other hand, the advantages of acoustic holography over the most advanced non-holographic acoustic imaging methods are not equally clear. Even depth resolution is achievable by non-holographic means [7.20]. High lateral resolution is easily achievable by scanning transducers.

Thus, we have a hierarchy of certainties. The most certain fact is the usefulness of ultrasonic imaging in the biomedical sciences. Less certain is whether that imaging will be holographic or non-holographic. Least certain is whether the visible image forming step in acoustic holography will continue to involve coherent light even if acoustic holography prevails. The coherent optical methods are most useful where computer processing is most difficult: real time imaging.

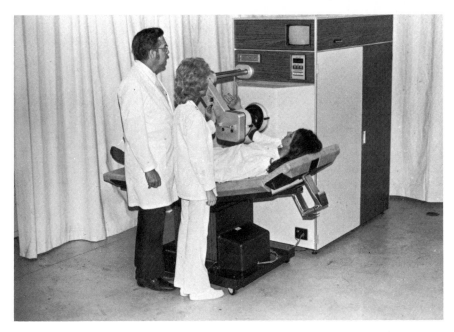

Fig. 7.10. A commercially available ultrasonic holography unit. By permission of Holosonics, Inc.

Acoustical three-dimensional imaging affords real time viewing of objects of biomedical interest in selectable depth planes. The dynamic images are always far superior (cosmetically) to the single still frames to be shown below, because the motion tends to blur out the "coherent artifacts". Figure 7.10 shows a commercial ultrasonic holography system based on standing surface ripples in a liquid surface resulting from the interference pattern between acoustic reference and object beams. Interrogation of that surface with a laser beam produces a faithful tomographic image of the object. Thus a vidicon can scan through the image to look at different depths in the object. One of the most useful applications is visualizing objects of changing and unknown depth. Figure 7.11 shows blood vessels in various limbs (deep lying abdominal structures of adults appear too difficult to image with present equipment). These pictures were taken from the TV display of the system just described as the limb was inserted into the insonified water tank. There are many potential applications of acoustic holography. The possibility of monitoring cholesterol build up in vessels is indicated by the opacity of cholesteric crystals.

Another real time coherent optical system is Bragg diffraction imaging. In that system the object is illuminated ("insonified") by a single frequency extended transducer at the bottom of a tank of liquid. The three-dimensional sound field formed in the liquid tank is characteristic of the three-dimensional structure of the object. Illumination of that three-dimensional sound pattern

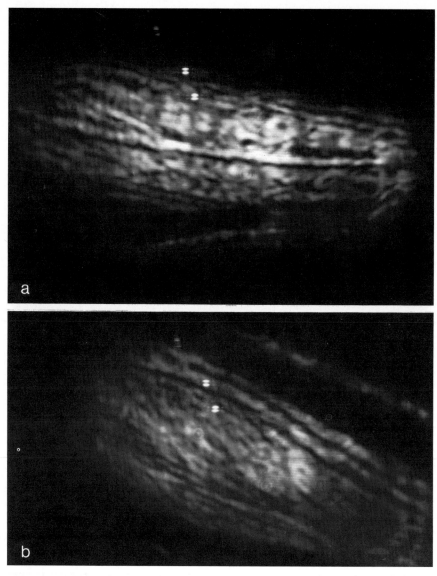

Fig. 7.11a and b. Images from the ultrasonic holography unit of Fig. 7.10 showing (a) a bifurcating blood vessel in the upper arm and (b) a deep blood vessel in the lower leg next to the tibia. By permission of Holosonics, Inc.

with a laser beam produces diffraction of the light. Diffraction from three-dimensional structures is called "Bragg diffraction". Analysis of the diffracted light with a lens produces a three-dimensional optical image of the object as "seen" at the acoustic wavelength chosen. Because the optical wavelength and

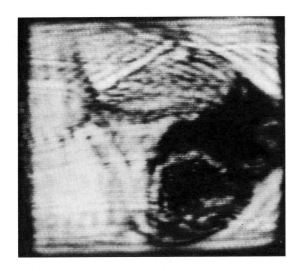

Fig. 7.12. Orthoscopic image in real time of a tropical fish taken at the University of California, Santa Barbara by *Wade* and *Landry* in 1968

the acoustic wavelength are not equal, the transverse and longitudinal magnifications are unequal, i.e., the optical image is somewhat distorted. Figure 7.12 shows one of the first Bragg diffraction images of a biological object. In the seven years since that image was taken, Bragg diffraction imaging has been improved considerably in resolution and quality, but no images of biological interest seem to have been taken.

7.3.2 Coded Aperture Imaging

"Coded aperture imaging" is a term adopted for a lensless, two-step image formation process in exact analogy with ordinary holography. In both cases the first step is to record an encoded image of the object. In holography the encoded image is called a "hologram". In coded aperture imaging no generally accepted name for the encoded image has arisen. In analogy with "hologram", let us call it a "codogram". The second step is to form a three-dimensional image by decoding the hologram or codogram. Holograms are formed by interference between a reference wavefront and an object wavefront. Codograms are formed by using self-radiant objects to cast shadows of specially designed masks onto the recording plane. If the mask happens to be a Fresnel zone plate as originally proposed by *Mertz* and *Young* [7.21, 22], the codogram of an object is identical to the hologram of a very similar object, so the decoding techniques are identical. If the encoding mask is very different from a Fresnel zone plate (which is just a binary hologram of a single point object), different decoding means will be needed.

The codogram can be shown to be a convolution of the object pattern with the aperture (the scaling of each depending on the recording geometry and the depth of the object feature). *Chang* et al. [7.23] distinguish three types of decoding operations-correlation, diffraction, and deconvolution. Correlation with the encoding mask pattern is a means for converting the mask pattern to a point (if the autocorrelation of the mask pattern is sharply peaked). Diffraction is useful if the encoding mask is self-imaging (e.g., if it is a Fresnel zone plate or a computer generated hologram of a point). Deconvolution involves complex filtering of the Fourier transform of the codogram. There are advantages to each decoding scheme as *Chang* et al. [7.23] and many others have shown.

Coded aperture imaging is complementary to ordinary holography in that it works best at very short wavelengths where recording an interference pattern is difficult. At short wavelengths even small mask features cast sharp shadows a long distance away. For a mask aperture of dimension 2a, radiation of wavelength λ will cast a sharp shadow out to distances as far away as a^2/λ. Thus, for γ-rays and X-rays the shadow casting distance for a given aperture may be 10^4 or more than that of the same aperture with visible light. The spatial resolution of the image is roughly 2a, so it is clear that for the same recording geometry we can use a much finer shadow casting aperture and hence achieve much higher resolution with γ-rays and X-rays than with visible light. On the other hand, we cannot achieve diffraction limited resolution with waves of any wavelength by coded aperture imaging. To prove this we note that the diffraction limit is about λ and the limit with coded aperture imaging is a which must be much larger than λ. In the current state of the art the resolution is seldom better than a few millimeters.

Let us see how shadow casting encodes three-dimensional object information. Because we assume each point in the object to be radiating independently, the shadow is just the sum (or integral for continuous objects) of the shadows from each individual point. The shadow due to a single object point is the same shape as the mask. If we move the point to the left, the shadow moves to the right. The mask plane offers a pivot point between the point and each feature of the mask. As the point moves toward the mask the shadow is enlarged and vice versa. Thus, if we know the mask size and its location with respect to the shadow plane, we can infer from the shadow where the object point must have been. Furthermore that inference can be done optically with coherent light.

If we choose the mask to be a Fresnel zone plate [7.21, 22], we can do this image extraction by coherent optics. Moving the zone plate laterally moves its focus laterally. Changing its magnification changes its focal length. Thus, a three-dimensional object leads to a three-dimensional image. If the mask is not suitable for such direct decoding, we can use coherent optical matched filtering to convert a mask-shaped input to a point output [7.24]. Different matched filters can be used to decode different object depths. Similarly, incoherent optical correlation can serve the same purpose [7.25].

Several hidden complications lurk about what has been said so far. These deal with codogram contrast (a problem with extended objects solved first by *Barrett* et al. [7.26, 27] and later by others). Each object point contributes a shadow of the encoding mask to the codogram as can be seen in Fig. 7.13. The magnification of the shadow is S_0/S_1 and its center is displaced in the opposite

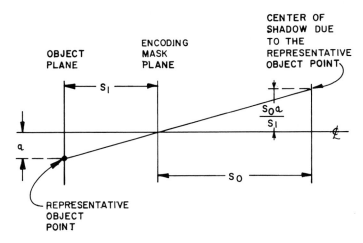

Fig. 7.13. Geometry of coded aperture imaging

direction from the origin. Thus a point a distance "a" off center (the central axis is that normal to the encoding mask which passes through the center of the encoding mask) leads to a shadow centered at $S_0 a/S_1$ on the other side of the center on the codogram plane. For a few single points as an object, any kind of encoding mask suffices. For extended objects, bright parts of the shadows from some points may fill in the dark parts due to other points and thus obliterate all pattern from the shadowgram. The solution of *Barrett* et al. [7.26, 27] was to use an encoding mask of fairly restricted spatial frequency (an off-axis Fresnel zone plate) and then restrict the object spatial frequency (by insertion of an appropriately spaced and aligned ruling of equal opaque and clear lines near the object) in such a way that the shadow cancellation could not occur. In time it came to be recognized that, with careful attention to object dimensions, recording geometry, and encoding mask scale, a very wide variety of encoding masks could be used. The signal-to-noise ratio in the image is never better than that for a pinhole camera, so the dosage for a single image is not improved. Object features go out of focus as the depth plane is changed in such a way that they can lead to artifacts. These subjects are dealt with in a recent review [7.28] and in papers referred to therein.

The depth resolution achievable by coded aperture imaging is illustrated in Fig. 7.14 showing different depth planes 1 cm apart of a gamma ray image of a Picker thyroid phantom. The hot and cold lobes in different planes are clearly visible. Also illustrated are difficulties associated with the way points go out of focus slowly. The top and bottom pictures were focused on planes above and below the actual object.

The aperture need not be a Fresnel zone plate. It need merely have a well-defined center and (if three-dimensional imaging is desired) a well-defined scale. Figure 7.15 shows coded aperture imaging with a simple annular aperture with radii of 1.1 and 1.2 inches. The image is derived by correlation. The "rho filter"

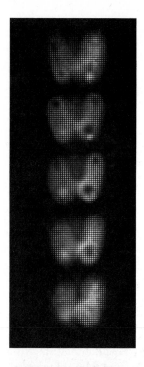

Fig. 7.14. Digital reconstruction from an on-axis Fresnel zone gamma-ray image of Picker thyroid phantom at focal planes separated by 1 cm. dc bias is removed by subtracting encoded images of two zone plates with a 180° phase difference. By permission of G.D. Searle and Co.

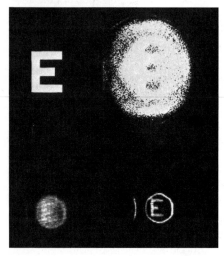

Fig. 7.15. The radioactive object (an "*E*") on the upper left and the encoded image produced by an annular aperture (upper right). The image produced by correlation with the encoding aperture (lower left) is unsatisfactory, but a simple filtering operation improves the situation greatly (lower right). Courtesy *R. Simpson* and *H. H. Barrett* of the University of Arizona

used to obtain the improved image has a linear spatial frequency weighting. The ring around the *E* is an unimportant and easily eliminated artifact of the shielding. Although the processing was digital, it could have been done optically.

A recent variation of this approach uses multiple masks in rapid succession to accomplish some results not achievable by a single mask. In particular, points go out of focus quicker with depth in this technique [7.29]. In an image formed by light rays coming from a codogram (or, for that matter, by back-projected mathematical "rays" in a computer reconstruction) the rays must pass through some planes enroute to the image plane and pass through all others in exiting the image plane. Thus a point in a single object plane causes traces in all planes of the image. This guarantees spurious information. The task is to minimize the effect of "out-of-focus" images. There are two basic complementary ways to do this. First, use as high a numerical aperture as possible (large codogram and close object). From simple geometry we see that point images formed with higher numerical apertures lead to a more spread out artifact in any adjacent plane than images formed with lower numerical apertures. Second, we can seek to "cancel out" the residual out-of-focus image with other out-of-focus images. This requires two or more reconstructions which give the same in-focus image but different and some cancelling of out-of-focus images. *Chang* et al. [7.23] have used 50% transmissive coding masks and their complements for this purpose. *Akcasu* et al. [7.29] have extended this concept to a large number of masks. This approach has been quite successful.

Where, then, does coded aperture imaging stand in the scheme of things for biomedical usage? Potentially it offers several unique advantages. The image quality appears to be slightly better than that produced by present methods, e.g., the Anger camera[1]. The improvement in image quality is both cosmetic (smooth, more pleasing because the image is formed by an analog technique as opposed to being formed as an arrangement of discrete points as with the Anger camera) and substantive (depth resolution of features offers information often useful and never previously available). The required exposure times are only marginally worse for coded aperture imaging. It is hard to be quantitative. We would like to record a conventional image (say with an Anger camera and a pinhole aperture) and a codogram using the same object activity for different lengths of time until they produce equivalent and acceptable images. Unfortunately, for the reasons just explained, equivalence of images is not easy to define. Equivalent usefulness to a medical doctor is even ill defined. Some doctors prefer the grainy Anger camera pictures they are used to. In signal-to-noise terms, the quantum noise in the background in coded aperture imaging will always make it less sensitive than direct imaging methods. With all of these caveats, we can estimate a 10–20% loss in sensitivity for any coded aperture system relative to the best direct imaging systems. The apparatus required is light, cheap, and easily portable. The three-dimensional nature of the image may be quite useful (it is limited to one-plane-at-a-time viewing for the reasons explained with regard to acoustic holography). Some would-be users object to the time delay involved in developing film and subjecting the resulting codogram to optical processing. It is possible to design devices which directly convert incident γ-ray and X-ray patterns into

---

[1] The Anger camera is a thick scintillation crystal with an array of photomultipliers attached to determine the position at which the incident γ-ray strikes the crystal. This is an image detector. The image itself can be formed on the crystal by any of several methods, e.g., by a pinhole imager.

modulation of coherent light. Unfortunately this would not help. The time-integrated codogram is what is required. On the other hand, the time-integrated codogram can be decoded almost instantly using real time coherent light spatial modulators [7.76]. A suitable detector array would allow digital (and hence almost instantaneous) image display and manipulation. Again, the idea inspired by the coherent optical analogy seems certain of eventual application, but the coherent optical processing part may be replaced by digital processing because of speed factors. This move toward digital processing is possible because the number of pixels (picture elements) in the codogram is relatively easy to handle digitally. Again biomedicine leads to rather small numbers of pixels, so the high data handling capacity of coherent optics is unnecessary.

7.3.3 Transaxial Tomography

Readers from the biomedical sciences need no introduction to transaxial tomography. Other readers may wish to refer to a recent introductory paper [7.30]. The basic idea is to display a transaxial slice through a solid object by properly combining X-ray images taken from many different angles around the object. Of course, the X-ray picture contains no depth information. Each X-ray is attenuated by the integral of all absorptions in its path. At the moment computers do all of the processing, but perhaps this is a case in which coherent optics may yet win out. There is evidence of some effort along that line. The most successful coherent optical processing method known to us for transaxial tomography is that due to *Peters* [7.31]. In optical computing for transaxial tomography, the data is normally recorded photographically on a moving sheet of film as the object (patient) is rotated between a source of a thin fan of X-rays and the film. Thus the exposure at any time is the projection of a narrow slice of the object onto the film with a particular object orientation. By "projection" we mean that the attenuation of the X-ray intensity along the line between source and any portion of the film is due to the integral of all absorptions along that line. The simplest way to envision what the object must look like in the plane of the X-ray fan is crude "back projection" and summation of all of the recorded projections. By "back projection" we mean acting on the assumption (easily implemented optically) that the absorption along each line occurred because of a uniform absorption in the object along that line. The image so produced is the actual object absorption pattern convolved with a $1/r$ pattern (where r is the polar coordinate of the cross-section). Deconvolution is a classical operation of coherent optics. *Peters* [7.31] sought to perform that operation coherently. Others since then have done it incoherently. Still others have done the inversion by computer. It is not clear as of this writing which way will ultimately prevail. Research in this area is in its infancy; all of the basic operations are compatible with coherent optics; and the data base is large enough to make coherent optics attractive.

7.3.4 Three-Dimensional X-Ray Imaging

We have just noted that X-ray images are collapsed in one dimension. The technique of coded aperture imaging may be extended to the retrieval of that information by parallax methods in full analogy with transaxial tomography. Thus, a shaped X-ray source [7.32] consisting of a carefully spaced array of point X-ray sources [7.33] can record a form of X-ray codogram which can be decoded one plane at a time.

7.3.5 Wavelength Encoding

A long-practiced application of coherent optics is grid decoding [7.34]. When a grid (e.g., a Ronchi ruling or a grating pattern) is illuminated by coherent light it produces a very distinct and predictable diffraction pattern or Fourier transform. By choosing the proper portion of that pattern with a spatial filter and then reimaging, the image is formed without the grid. If the grid covers only part of the original image, only that part of the image is produced. The product of a ruling, call it $r(x, y)$, and the object pattern $o(x, y)$ is the grid-encoded image

$$g(x, y) = o(x, y)r(x, y).$$

By Fourier transforming both sides of this equation we have

$$G(f_x, f_y) = O(f_x, f_y) * R(f_x, f_y)$$

where

$$G(f_x, f_y) = \mathscr{L}[g(x, y)]$$
$$O(f_x, f_y) = \mathscr{L}[o(x, y)]$$
$$R(f_x, f_y) = \mathscr{L}[r(x, y)]$$
$$\mathscr{L}[\cdot] \quad = \text{Fourier transform operator}$$
$$* \quad\quad = \text{convolution operator}.$$

Since $r(x, y)$ is periodic, so is $R(f_x, f_y)$. Thus there will be peaks in the Fourier transform plane corresponding to each peak of $R(f_x, f_y)$. Each of these peaks contains in its vicinity $O(f_x, f_y)$, from which $o(x, y)$ can be reconstructed. By filtering in the Fourier transform plane we obtain a reconstruction of $o(x, y)$. *Macovski* [7.35] has devised a large family of techniques whereby a physical grating made of alternate strips of two different materials is placed in the image plane of an X-ray imager or a standard passive radiological camera. By choosing materials with known sharp absorption edges, he forms a "contrasty" grating image only for radiation of energy falling between the two absorption edges. For those portions of the scene emitting radiation to which both grid components are transparent, the grid pattern is not visible. Likewise for those portions of the scene emitting radiation stopped by both materials, no grid pattern is visible.

Thus only radiation transmitted by one grid material and blocked by the other produces a grid pattern. Therefore only such portions of the image transform to the proper portion of the Fourier transform plane and hence contribute to the final image. This and similar techniques enable him to ignore certain ubiquitous features (water, bone, etc.) in some imaging situations. Clearly such gratings are also applicable for coded aperture imaging as well.

7.4 Signal Processing

In this section we deal with coherent optical processing of spatially displayed "signals". Those signals can represent images or other forms of data (e.g., EEG records).

7.4.1 Image Processing

Once an image is recorded, it may still need modification before it is in the form a human viewer needs or wants it. All of the image processing methods we will discuss are means of rearranging existing data according to known rules. Hence they add no information. Rather they weight information already present in such a way as to reflect the users' interests.

Image processing can be carried out by computer as well as by coherent optics. Computer processing is more versatile than coherent optical processing, so it is the method of choice when it is not excluded by cost, convenience, or calculation capacity. In all of those areas, optical processing has the advantage. In terms of cost, computer processing requires an image digitizer to enter the image, a computer to transform it, and a display module to present it to the viewer. All of these components tend to be more expensive than the full coherent optical processor (input film holder, lenses, laser, and output screen). In convenience, the optical computer has a profound advantage in speed. A fixed operation can be performed optically on scene after scene as fast as the film can be changed. The information handling capacity of the optical computer is, by digital computer standards, incredible. This brief discussion does not give adequate information for choosing between optical and digital processing but it suggests some of the primary considerations. The situation has been complicated by the advent of hybrid optical-digital computers as reviewed by *Casasent* [7.36]. Images of biomedical interest are not likely to contain enough information to strain digital computers, although issues of cost and convenience may call for optical processing provided it can do the desired job.

The types of image processing likely to be useful in biology and medicine include

1) *deblurring* (in which images blurred because of object-camera motion or poor focus can be sharpened up if sufficient signal-to-noise ratio is present in the original image),

2) *noise suppression* (in which statistically known noise factors are deemphasized),

3) *smoothing* (in which *a priori* desirable features are enhanced and *a priori* undesirable features are reduced) and

4) *feature enhancement* (in which all features with certain characteristics are enhanced).

These subjects are covered in Chapter 3 of this volume by *Considine* and *Gonsalves*, so they will not be reported here.

7.4.2 Biomedical Data Processing

Coherent optical processing of roughly periodic biomedical data (EEGs, EKGs, PCGs, etc.) is very attractive for a number of reasons. First, most of the operations one might wish to perform on such data (frequency analysis, cross-

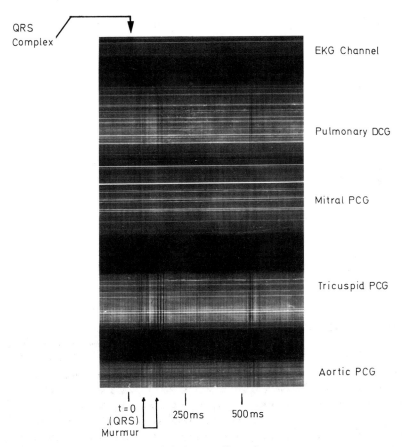

Fig. 7.16. Directly optically recorded phonocardiographs

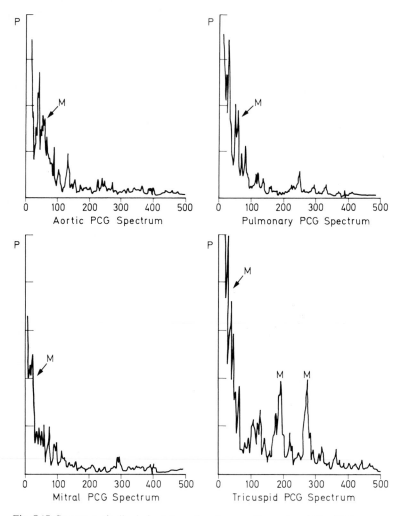

Fig. 7.17. Spectra optically derived from the phonocardiographs of Fig. 7.16

correlation, smoothing, band pass filtering, matched filtering, etc.) are readily performed optically. Second, the analysis is instantaneous and hence readily interactive. *Everett* et al. [7.37] have constructed recorders for direct recording of such data on film in a form compatible with multi-channel optical processing. Figure 7.16 shows directly recorded phonocardiograph (PCG) records and Fig. 7.17 shows their optically generated power spectra. Such systems could be automated for mass screening operations at relatively low costs.

Another approach to coherent optical signal processing is to process the signal not as it is recorded optimally for optical processing but as it might be recorded off an oscilloscope face or on a strip recorder. Under certain rather common conditions, one dimension of the Fourier transform pattern of this two-dimensional input is the required power spectrum [7.38].

The ultimate usefulness of either of these signal processing techniques relative to the now-straightforward technique of digitization and computer fast Fourier transformation must rest on speed (the display can be real time if the data is read in continuously onto a suitable input device for coherent optics [7.36]).

The subject of coherent optical signal processing is treated by *Casasent* elsewhere in this volume (Chap. 8).

7.5 Image Display

The ultimate "consumer" of biomedical images is a human being: the biomedical scientist. Effective use of coherent optical display methods can make the images much more readily understandable to people. No new information is produced but information may be presented in a new way.

7.5.1 Pseudo-Parallax

We have noted that coded aperture imaging and acoustic holography both allow us to focus on various depth planes in succession. If we record those images, adjust them all to the same lateral magnification, and stack up transparent images at the proper depths, we can simulate the actual three-dimensional object. Physical transparencies suffer from some major drawbacks for these purposes though. First, nearer transparencies obscure our view of farther ones. Second, it is not convenient to stick rulers through the transparencies to measure distances between parts of the object. Third, a stack of transparencies is a clumsy object, not convenient for storage, transportation, or reproduction. Multiplexing the images of diffusely lit transparencies at proper distances from the hologram provides a simultaneous solution to all three problems just outlined. Let us examine them in order.

First, because each plane is recorded in the absence of the others and with equal diffraction efficiency as the others, each plane is independently viewable at its proper depth. That is, the far planes are clearly viewable "through" the near ones in the perceived image. Second, because the image is formed in the air and not on a physical transparency or screen, we can insert rulers in it to measure distances. Third, since the hologram is an easily copied planar object, storage, transportation, and reproduction are all convenient.

Conceptually slightly different is the display in three dimensions of a series of truly two-dimensional "slices" (instead of different focal planes which, in general, contain artifacts due to out-of-focus images from other planes). Ultrasonic B scans provide such two-dimensional images. So does transaxial tomography. Thus the goal of pseudo-parallax is to allow the human viewer to obtain a concept of the true three-dimensional relationships among a series of two-

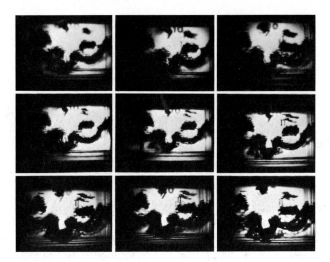

Fig. 7.18. Many views of holographically synthesized 3D image made from 2D ultrasonic B scans at different depths

dimensional images. This concept was introduced by *Redman* [7.39] and advanced by others [7.40, 41]. Figure 7.18 shows numerous views taken from a single hologram. The individual planes are evenly spaced "slices" (ultrasonic B scans) parallel to one another across both eyes. The dark spot above one eye indicates a cancer. From the pseudo-parallax hologram the three-dimensional size, shape, and location of the cancer could be seen.

Several multiplexing schemes are available to accomplish this pseudo-parallax. The three which deserve most attention are simple multiple exposure, space division multiplexing [7.42] and holographic movies [7.43]. Simple multiple exposure (changing only the object transparency and its locations between exposures) is the simplest multiplexing technique as well as the best when only a few depth planes are to be used. The problem with multiple exposure multiplexing is that the diffraction efficiency of any one of the N images is about $1/N^2$ the diffraction efficiency obtainable with $N = 1$. Diffraction efficiency in itself is of little concern. We can always use a more powerful laser for reconstruction. Unfortunately, the background optical noise is also directly proportional to the laser power and is essentially independent of N. Thus, the signal-to-background ratio varies as $1/N^2$. The best we can do in principle is a $1/N$ dependence. That is, the best we can do is divide the brightness evenly. There are two ways of doing this. Both involve making N separate holograms. One means (space division multiplexing) shows them all simultaneously. The other means (holographic motion pictures) shows them sequentially. Both means endeavor to trick the viewer into believing he is looking at one stationary image of many depth planes. Space division multiplexing does this by distributing each individual hologram across the face of the photographic plate in many small regions (see Figs. 7.19 and 7.20). The patchiness of the hologram plane is invisible

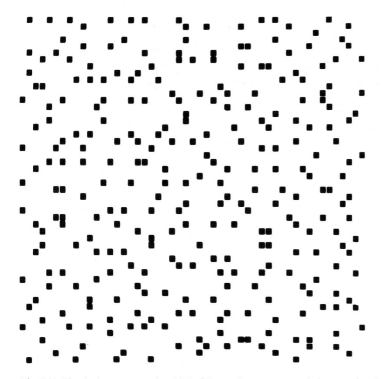

Fig. 7.19. The dark areas, covering 1/16 of the total area, were made by exposing through one of 16 spatially complementary masks

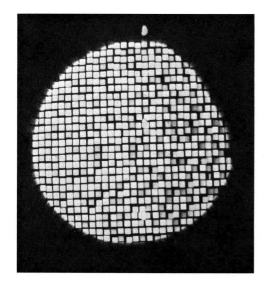

Fig. 7.20. The superposition of exposures through all 16 masks is shown here

and undistracting on a bleached hologram. By inserting the mask used in recording a particular depth slice over the hologram, we can view the corresponding image separately.

Holographic movies can be used not only to simulate motion but also to paint a still picture of many depth planes. The idea is to display each two-dimensional image at its proper depth, not simultaneously as in the methods just discussed but in sequence. If all N images are shown at least once during the eye's integration time, the human viewer will perceive them as being simultaneously (and hence continuously) present. Ordinary holographic motion picture techniques fail for an obvious reason: the hologram motion would have to be too fast. To move ten 10 cm holograms past the viewer in the period of 1/20 of a second requires a film speed of 2000 cm s^{-1}. Fortunately, however, a solution can be devised. Continuing the same example, we might record ten 1 mm strip holograms (one for each two-dimensional image) and arrange them into one 1 cm strip. Thereafter we would repeat that composite strip enough times to make a continuous loop of holographic film. When moved continuously, that loop produces a very satisfactory three-dimensional image except that vertical parallax is lost [7.43]. The required film speed is now 20 cm s^{-1} a high but perfectly manageable speed.

7.5.2 Other Three-Dimensional Displays

Holography is widely used for the three-dimensional display of a series of two-dimensional images taken by conventional means. The subject requires a full review of its own, and several short reviews are available [7.44, 45]. Again *Redman* has been among the pioneers both with electron microscope images [7.46] and X-ray images [7.47]. Rather than repeat the reviews referred to, we will look at one display method in some detail. The antecedent developments are given explicitly in those reviews.

The method of display we want to examine is particularly suited to whole body display and hence is of interest to biologists, human factors researchers, orthopedic workers, neurologists, etc.

The technique we refer to is cylindrical multiplexed holograms. The hologram is recorded in two fully automated steps in the scheme as it is practiced by *Cross* [7.48]. In the first step, a series of photographs are taken of the object from positions on an imaginary circle centered (more or less) on the object. Either the object is placed on a turntable or piano stool and rotated past a stationary observer or the camera is moved to fixed positions around the object. The angular step between photographs should be small for reasons which will become apparent. For many purposes one per degree is a good choice. It will turn out that the image quality requirement may be quite modest for many biological purposes, so a fixed circle of, say, 360 evenly spaced inexpensive cameras could be used to give an instant capability. The second step is to multiplex these views onto a cylindrical hologram. Normally long vertical strip holograms 1° wide (if a

1° photographic separation is used) are illuminated through a diffuser with laser light. Some distance away is the hologram plane. The hologram plane is blocked by a vertical slit of width $2\pi r/N$, where r is the radius of the cylindrical hologram to be used (25 cm would be a convenient value) and N is the number of multiplexed images (360 in the example we used). The reference beam is derived from a point source above the object transparency. The N holograms are recorded sequentially on a strip of film $2\pi r$ long. The developed (and usually bleached) hologram is rolled into a cylinder to provide the final cylindrical hologram. To view the image we illuminate the hologram from above with a point source and either move around the hologram or rotate the hologram to see different views. The object appears to be perfectly real and three dimensional, floating in the center of the cylinder. *Cross* [7.48] has also pioneered an interesting and useful variation of this scheme. In addition to changing the direction of viewing between photographs, he changes the object as well. Thus human subjects smile, wave, throw kisses, etc., as they are being photographed. The motion shows up in the image as the cylinder is rotated or the observer rotates around it. The film may be moved continuously so events of arbitrary duration can be recorded and played back as a three-dimensional image.

7.6 Extraction of Object Data

Coherent optics can be used to extract data about biological objects or to make certain features of the object easy to perceive. In this it performs tasks which are not simply image formation and indeed may not involve image formation at all.

7.6.1 Mensuration

The measurement of biological objects in three dimensions has been avoided until recently for two major reasons. First, the data handling problem was beyond the capability of most computers and memory systems until recently. Second, measurement techniques were very crude. Tape measures do not provide adequate descriptions of complicated objects. Computer science is solving the former problem while coherent optics is solving the latter one.

For ultra precise mensuration of an object from one viewpoint, the technique of *Gara* et al. [7.11] previously described is as accurate an optical method as can be devised. For studying objects from many views, *Upatnieks* et al. [7.49] have developed a method which is the inverse of the *Cross* [7.48] cylindrical hologram synthesis method just described. *Upatnieks* uses a now-routine method [7.50, 51] to record cylindrical holograms directly with coherent light. Recording a hologram of a living object requires a pulse of laser light short enough to "freeze" object motion to within a fraction of a wavelength, coherent enough to record the full object depth, and intense enough to expose the low-sensitivity holographic emulsion. Such lasers are now commercially available [7.52].

Upatnieks then "unwraps" the cylinder and illuminates a section at a time to produce accurate two-dimensional images from any viewing direction he chooses.

The classical optical means for extracting three-dimensional object data is by stereo methods. Much effort has gone into the use of holography as an aid to the extraction of quantitative data from stereo pairs. This work has demonstrated improved ease and reliability over the classical methods as well as new possibilities such as superposition of three-dimensional grids on the stereo image. A review of this work has been published recently [7.12] and is discussed elsewhere in this volume by *Balasubramanian* (Chap. 5).

7.6.2 Depth Contours

For both microscopic and macroscopic objects it is convenient to be able to see depth contours. These contours accomplish several useful things. First, they present a useful and easily understood representation of the third dimension in a two-dimensional image. Second, they show where the depth is changing fastest. Third, they allow quantitative depth measurements.

Coherent optics can produce depth contours in a variety of ways but the two most important are holographic double exposure interferometry and projected fringes. Double exposure holographic contouring involves recording two holograms of the object on the same photographic plate with slightly different parameters (wavelength, index of refraction, intermediate material, etc.) and replaying the image at one wavelength. Projected fringes involve the illumination of the scene with a spatially nonuniform pattern. Being an illumination scheme, it is suitable for real time use. These subjects have been reviewed elsewhere in this volume by *Abramson* (Chap. 6).

7.6.3 Gross Motion Detection

Coherent optics provides several means for recording and studying gross object motions.

Holography provides an easy way to record the three-dimensional orbit of a microscopic particle or organism through a medium [7.55, 56]. The time-integrated hologram is simply a hologram of the path (orbit) of the source.

For extended objects, motion tends to reduce the contrast of the time-integrated fringes of a hologram, so stationary parts of a scene produce brighter images than moving parts. *Feleppa* [7.57] showed, using motion-induced contrast of a slime mold, that there is a continuous gradation of contrast between unit contrast (bright image) for stationary parts and zero contrast (black image) for large-motion portions.

Another approach to gross object motion is to subtract a scene (live or recorded) from an image of that scene recorded earlier. Of course, coherent light has built in subtraction (phase effects), so it is ideal for use in this enterprise. Fortunately an excellent comprehensive (54 references) review of these techniques has been given recently by *Ebersole* [7.58], so a lesser review here would be unwarranted.

Another form of gross motion detection using coherent light is the simple Schlieren system of *Rounds* et al. [7.59]. The beam is shaped by a slit mask, directed through a sample chamber, and then focused down to a thin image where it is blocked by a mask. As cells migrate into the previously cleared illuminated area of the sample chamber, they scatter the light away from the blocking mask and onto a detector. The scattered intensity is proportional to cell density in the illuminated area. Continuous monitoring of diploid fibroblast migration was used to measure the cell migration index. The variations on this simple technique are many and straightforward. Distance migrated can be measured by monitoring the cell density at various distances from the edge of the fully confluent culture. Another version uses the light scattered around the block to photograph particles traveling through a tube. From the length of the streak corresponding to a given short exposure, particle velocities can be determined. This technique can be used in studying flow anomalies (eddies, stagnation points, etc.) in blood vessels, etc.

7.6.4 Minute Motion Detection

Coherent optics provides the biomedical sciences with totally new and powerful ways to observe small changes. Note that these changes can occur slowly (the actual growth of mushrooms can be observed) or quickly (changes in the chest during respiration can be observed a few milliseconds apart). The motions of interest range from sub micrometer to a few millimeters.

The two broad categories of coherent optical motion detection are holographic interferometry and speckle interferometry. We will examine each briefly so we can arrive at a basis for comparing them. Holographic interferometry is based on the perfection of holography (that is its ability to record object detail to the accuracy of optics, usually wavelengths). Speckle interferometry is based on the chief imperfection of holography speckle.

Holographic interferometry is a rapidly developing field which has been summarized not only by *Abramson* (Chap. 6 of this volume), but also in a recent paper [7.60]. It suffices here to note some of the unique advantages of holographic interferometry over classical interferometry as applied to biomedical objects.

First, while classical interferometry can be applied only to certain thin, transparent objects, holographic interferometry can be applied further, e.g., to people.

Second, whereas classical interferometry requires high quality optics for success, holographic interferometry requires no such precautions.

What, then, can holographic interferometry do? Among the demonstrated capabilities are

1) observations of the strains in objects (e.g., bones, skulls, etc.) subjected to various kinds of stresses,

2) observation of certain motions (e.g., the motion of the chest during respiration), and

3) observation of subtle periodic motions such as those due to blood pressure.

Speckle interferometry [7.61] is a similar technique with three advantages and one disadvantage with respect to holographic interferometry. One advantage is that greater object motion during the observation is tolerable. Another advantage is that the motion detection sensitivity is relatively tailorable (rather than being restricted to the wavelength domain as in holographic interferometry). The third advantage is the possibility of instant direct observation without any photographic recording. The primary disadvantage is that the image quality and fringe contrast are usually less in speckle interferometry than in holographic interferometry.

Some uses in biology and medicine are already emerging, *Burian* et al. [7.62] used speckle interferometry to study eardrums. Others [7.63, 64] have used time-averaged holograms to determine tympanic membrane vibration modes. *Bally* [7.65] studied eardrums with double exposure holography. *Wedenall* studied tooth mobility by the same method [7.66]. Others [7.67–69] have used holographic interferometry to study orthopedics. *Greguss* [7.70] has recorded exhaled air patterns by a form of time-averaged holography.

7.7 Pattern Recognition

There are four quite distinct approaches to coherent optical recognition of biomedical objects. These can be classified in two ways. First, the recognition can occur either on light derived directly from the object (as derived from transmission, reflection, scattering, etc.) or on light passing through an image of the object. Obviously, the former is preferable when it is applicable. Second, the recognition can operate either on single objects or on an ensemble of objects. We will discuss these two sets of independent choices below.

The choice between the object and its image for recognition is not always easy. The object or image must have certain well-defined properties before it can be inserted into a coherent optical pattern recognition system. First, the object or image must not diffuse the light (this excludes many objects and people as directly usable). Second, the object or image must be accessible to the optical system (this excludes objects internal to other opaque or diffuse objects and objects not easily brought into laboratories). Third, the light must represent object features useful for recognition (for some objects the most useful features do not coincide with the wavelength domain of coherent optics, so X-ray or sonic images must be used rather than the object itself). On the other hand, direct use of the object itself is sometimes advantageous. It makes recognition faster (essentially instantaneous). The real object(s) can be probed simultaneously or successively with different wavelengths, different polarizations, etc.

The choice between single objects (or images) and an ensemble of objects (or images) is also difficult and important. We will list some advantages of each and follow that by a more general discussion. A single object or image has a unique orientation (the three angular degrees of freedom are fixed). Thus it is possible to use many different optical filters and image rotators to cause one filter to be more or less aligned with the object orientation. Consider an opaque cylindrical object for instance. Viewed from either of two directions (along its axis) it looks like a circle. Viewed in any direction normal to the axis it is a rectangle. Viewed from other directions it has other shapes. With a circle mask, a rectangle mask, and many other masks, we can be relatively certain that we can identify the object and its orientation. Viewing the three orientation angles θ_1, θ_2, and θ_3 as independent random variables we can write a distribution function $P(\theta_1, \theta_2, \theta_3)$ to describe the probability of any particular orientation. Let the image corresponding to $\theta_1, \theta_2, \theta_3$ be $I(x, y, \theta_1, \theta_2, \theta_3)$. One thing we can do with a single mask is to recognize the average or expected image

$$\bar{I}(x, y) = \iiint I(x, y, \theta_1, \theta_2, \theta_3) d\theta_1 d\theta_2 d\theta_3 .$$

For many objects $\bar{I}(x, y)$ is rather featureless. A second approach is to recognize the $I(x, y, \theta_1, \theta_2, \theta_3)$ for a particular range

$$\theta_1 \text{ to } \theta_1 + \Delta\theta_1, \quad \theta_2 \text{ to } \theta_2 + \Delta\theta_2, \quad \text{and} \quad \theta_3 \text{ to } \theta_3 + \Delta\theta_3,$$

where $\Delta\theta_1$, $\Delta\theta_2$, and $\Delta\theta_3$ are the maximum values which still give "good" correlation with $I(x, y, \theta_1 + \Delta\theta_1, \theta_2 + \Delta\theta_2, \theta_3 + \Delta\theta_3)$. Then by sampling many objects we can assume that the total number of the type we are seeking is equal to the number correlating well with $I(x, y, \theta_1, \theta_2, \theta_3)$ divided by the quantity $P(\theta_1, \theta_2, \theta_3)\Delta\theta_1 \Delta\theta_2 \Delta\theta_3$. We can now choose the $\theta_1, \theta_2, \theta_3$ set which gives the most distinctive features. Accuracy requires that we count a statistically significant number of good correlations. Of course by examining multiple objects in parallel (a powerful and almost unique ability of optical processing), we can accomplish the statistical averagings simultaneously. Both one-object-at-a-time flow systems and parallel systems are being used at present.

How, then, does coherent optical pattern recognition proceed? The answer, well documented elsewhere [7.71] is to operate on the optical Fourier transform of the input distribution (formed at plane P_2 by passing coherent light through a lens L_1 as shown in Fig. 7.21). The Fourier transform pattern so formed has several unique properties. A partial list follows.

1) Its amplitude characteristics are independent of the transverse object or mask location.

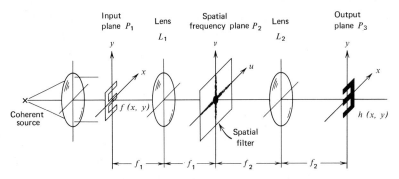

Fig. 7.21. Optical Fourier transformation and image modification. The lens L performs an optical Fourier transform of the amplitude $f(x, y)$ in plane P_1. Lens L_2 Fourier transforms the amplitude in plane P_2 [itself the Fourier transform of $f(x, y)$]. In the absence of a spatial filter in P_2, the output in plane P_3 is simply an image of the input reversed ($x \rightarrow -x$, $y \rightarrow -y$) and magnified by f_2/f_1

2) Its amplitude characteristics are unchanged by the transformation $(x, y) \rightarrow (-x, -y)$. Thus, for example, 6 and 9 have Fourier transforms with identical amplitude distribution.

3) When coherently recorded (i.e., interference with a reference beam), phase information is preserved and a 6 and a 9, etc., can be distinguished. Such a complex filter is commonly referred to as a matched spatial filter.

4) Its spatial pattern rotates as the object rotates.

5) Its spatial pattern is magnified proportionately to the demagnification of the object or image, and conversely.

6) Its brightest part is in the center of the pattern.

7) Its complex amplitude is the coherent sum of the individual complex amplitudes of the component parts of the object or image.

From Properties 1 and 7 we see that a field consisting of many objects can be treated in parallel. All objects contribute independent and perfectly aligned Fourier transforms independent of their transverse locations in the input plane.

7.7.1 Operational Methods

There are two separate ways of operating on the Fourier transform to achieve pattern recognition. First (appropriate to the one-object-at-a-time cases and some parallel processing cases), we can measure the amplitude (and sometimes phase) information about the Fourier transform and compare it optically or digitally with the patterns for various previously encountered objects. Optically this is done by placing a mask (positive or complex) in the Fourier transform plane and measuring the transmitted light. Digitally this is done by inserting special radial and ring detectors in the transform plane [7.72]. Second (appropriate to some parallel processing cases), we can allow the light passing through the filter to pass on to form an image of the input scene. The image is brightest for those parts of the input scene passing the most light through the mask. For a uniformly illuminated scene, this means that the objects most closely matching the test object used to make the mask show up as the bright spots. By thresholding the response, we can locate and count objects of the prechosen shape.

Variations in object size and angular orientation (about the optical axis) are important to different degrees with different object shapes, e.g., rotation is unimportant in recognizing donuts. In any case, rotation and magnification can be accomplished either physically or optically (e.g., by a rotating dove prism) to bring the object into correspondence with the test object. By suitable operation on the scene before processing, one can convert the Fourier transform to a Mellin transform (object scale invariant) as well as achieve a rotation invariant transform [7.73].

7.7.2 Applications

The obvious application areas for coherent optical pattern recognition are of two types. First, the scene, object, or pattern may be too complex to permit convenient digitization. Second, the rate of object measurement may preclude digitization. In both cases optical recognition is the needed solution. Optical pattern recognition is also the obvious approach when the measurements to be made are inherently optical.

A representative application is the automatic counting of reticulocytes by computer-generated matched filters. Skilled technicians can count as many as 500/min. By coherent optics we can process a million (roughly the number in a 1.5 cm diameter area on real blood slides) almost instantaneously [7.74]. This particular application used parallel processing of all of the illuminated cells. Thus it worked because for large numbers of cells certain average properties are predictable. For example, in a large field of match sticks, the fraction oriented vertically $\pm 5°$ is predictable with great accuracy. Conversely if we measure the number so aligned we can calculate the total number. The spatial filters employed looked for certain generalized reticulocyte patterns probably not embodied perfectly in any cell but embodied well enough by many cells to provide a basis for counting. The actual filter, being idealized, was generated by computer.

Another application which has been demonstrated is the screening of chest X-ray images for pneumoconiosis (black-lung disease) [7.75]. In this case the criterion is an increase in high spatial frequency components in the shadow-grams of subjects with pneumoconiosis. Similar measurements have been made on several other images of medical interest.

Perhaps the most interesting application to data has been the identification of cells (e.g., types of leucocytes) in a flowing system [7.76]. In this case, no image is formed. Light of various wavelengths is used to illuminate individual cells as they pass a fixed illumination point. The fraction of light diffracted at each of various angles is a measure of the size and shape of the cells. Since a great many cells are interrogated, statistical analysis can be quite accurate. Of course object motion (always present by definition in a flowing system) does not cause motion of the Fourier transform pattern.

7.8 Conclusions

Biomedical applications of coherent optics have been numerous, effective, but sporadic. With the few notable exceptions mentioned earlier, commercial exploitations have not been attempted. Only with more such efforts will these techniques find widespread application.

7.9 Appendix: The Varieties of Three-Dimensional Images

So much has been said of three-dimensional imaging that some confusion is possible. This appendix is an attempt to organize the various terms and concepts so they can be understood and compared easily.

Given a three-dimensional object which may contain internal structure, how can we record it on a two-dimensional medium? There are four basic solutions. First, we can record its hologram. The hologram records the full three-dimensional information (except for shadowing effects in planar holograms which vanish in a cylindrical hologram). Second, we can collapse one dimension to provide an image accurate in two dimensions and ambiguous in the third. X-ray projections provide good examples. With a point source we can project the shadow of an object onto the screen (as in Fig. 7.22a). Note that we can construct for each point in the shadow a line between that point and the source. The location of absorbers along that line is undetermined (from the total absorption along that line anyway). Normal X-ray images are of this nature. Let us call such projections (for the purposes of this section) two-dimensional projections. A single slice from a two-dimensional projection (as could be obtained from a fan beam as shown in Fig. 7.22b) will be called a one-dimensional projection. By taking projections (one- or two-dimensional) from many viewing angles and back projecting we can synthesize an image of the three-dimensional object (from two-dimensional projections) or the two-dimensional cross-section of the object in the fan beam (from one-dimensional projections). Examples of three-dimensional image synthesis from two-dimensional projections are pseudo-parallax images (Sect. 7.4.1) and cylindrical multiplexed holograms (Sect. 7.4.2). An example of two-dimensional image synthesis from one-dimensional projections is transaxial tomography (Sect. 7.2.3). In all of those cases the additional dimension is synthesized from multiple projections taken from many directions. Third, we can ignore one of the three coordinates altogether. The profiling techniques described in Section 7.1.2 are examples of this approach. Calling the

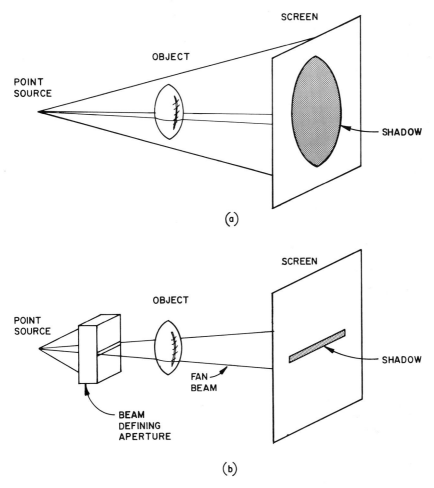

Fig. 7.22a and b. A point source produces a cone of rays directed toward the object. That cone casts a shadow of the object on a screen as in (a). If a beam defining aperture is inserted, only a fan of rays is emitted. We then have a transaxial illumination as in (b)

transverse coordinates x and y and the depth coordinate z, the profiles are $x - z$ images at fixed y or $y - z$ images at fixed x. Fourth, we can record the $x - y$ image accurately and encode the z (depth dimension) in some way (e.g., depth, contours as described in Sect. 7.5.2).

We must now pay more attention to low numerical aperture holography (which includes acoustic holography and coded aperture imaging). Let us suppose we reconstruct an image from that hologram at an optical wavelength λ. If the hologram aperture is A and the image distance (from the hologram) is D, the lateral resolution is about $\lambda D/A$. The depth of focus is roughly $\lambda D^2/A^2$. Thus portions of the three-dimensional image separated by more than $\lambda D^2/A^2$ can be viewed successively. The easiest way to do this is to move a viewing screen toward or away from the hologram through the real image.

Now we can comment on the term "tomography". Tomography has come to mean two-dimensional imaging of a cross-section of an object. Clearly transaxial tomography is well named. The image is tomographic and the illumination was in the plane of the cross-section. Let us call a central normal to the cross section its "axis". We see then the reason for the word "transaxial" as a description for the illumination. Successive depth planes from codograms or acoustic holograms are tomographic images along the axis. Unfortunately the words "axial" is sometimes used when "transaxial" should be used (as in CAT or "computerized axial tomography"), so we are left with no good word for this other kind of tomography. Workers in acoustic holography and coded aperture imaging simply refer to their "tomographic" images.

The tomographic images can be synthesized holographically in such a way that the viewer sees each tomographic image at its proper three-dimensional relationship to each other tomographic image (Sect. 7.4.1). This supplies no new information, but it helps the human viewer to more easily assimilate the information already there.

References

7.1 E. Abbe: Arch. Mikrosk. Anat. **9**, 413 (1873)

7.2 D. Gabor: Nature **161**, 777 (1948)

7.3 E. N. Leith, J. Upatnieks: J. Opt. Soc. Am. **52**, 1123 (1962)

7.4 L. Toth, S. A. Collins, Jr.: Appl. Phys. Letters **13**, 7 (1968)

7.5 M. E. Cox, R. G. Buckles, D. Whitlow: Appl. Opt. **12**, 128 (1971)

7.6 D. H. McMahon, H. J. Caulfield: Appl. Opt. **9**, 91 (1970)

7.7 B. J. Thompson: J. Opt. Soc. Am. **53** (1963);
     B. A. Silverman, B. J. Thompson, J. H. Ward: J. Appl. Met. **3**, 792 (1964)

7.8 E. A. Boettner, B. J. Thompson: Opt. Eng. **12**, 56 (1973)

7.9 For a comprehensive bibliography on speckle see K. Singh: Atti. Fond. **27**, 197 (1972)

7.10 Volume II of J. Opt. Soc. Am. **66** (1976) is dedicated to speckle

7.11 A. D. Gara, R. F. Majkowski, T. T. Stapleton: Appl. Opt. **12**, 2172 (1973)

7.12 N. Balasubramanian: Opt. Eng. **14**, 448 (1975)

7.13 H. J. Caulfield, T. Hirschfeld, J. M. Weinberg, R. E. Herron: Proc. IEEE **65**, 84 (1977)

7.14 A. N. Rosen: Opt. Laser Tech. **7**, 127 (1975) and references therein

7.15 D. H. McMahon: Laser Focus **6**, 34 (1970); Appl. Opt. **11**, 798 (1972)

7.16 R. K. Mueller: Acoustical Holography Survey. In *Advances in Holography*, ed. by N. H. Farhat, Vol. 1 (Dekker, New York 1975)

7.17 R. K. Mueller, N. K. Sheridon: Appl. Phys. Letters **9**, 328 (1966)

7.18 P. Greguss: Acoustica **29**, 52 (1973)

7.19 J. Landry, H. Keyani, G. Wade: Bragg Diffraction Imaging. In *Acoustical Holography*, ed. by G. Wade, Vol. 4 (Plenum Press, New York 1972)

7.20 R. L. Whitman, M. Ahmed, A. Korpel: A Progress Report on the Laser Scanned Acoustic Camera. In *Acoustical Holography* (Plenum Press, New York 1974)

7.21 L. Mertz: J. Opt. Soc. Am. **50**, 505 (1960)

7.22 N. O. Young: Sky and Telescope **25**, 8 (1963)

7.23 L. T. Chang, B. Macdonald, V. Perez-Mendez: Proc. SPIE **89**, 9 (1977)

7.24 J.D.Gaskill, F.R.Whitehead, J.E.Gray, R.E.O'Mara: Matched Filter Restoration of Coded Gamma and X-Ray Imaging. In *Applications of Optical Instrumentation in Medicine* (SPIE, Vol. 35, 1973)

7.25 L.T.Chang, S.N.Kaplan, B.Macdonald, V.Perez-Mendez, L.Shiraishi: J. Nucl. Med. **15**, 1063 (1974)

7.26 H.H.Barrett: J. Nucl. Med. **13**, 382 (1972)

7.27 H.H.Barrett, F.A.Horrigan: Appl. Opt. **12**, 2686 (1973)

7.28 W.L.Rogers: Coded Aperture Imaging in Nuclear Medicine, Review and Update. In *ERDA Conf. on Applications of X- and γ-Rays* (Ann Arbor, May 1976)

7.29 A.Z.Akcasu, R.S.May, G.F.Knoll, W.L.Rogers, K.F.Koral, L.W.Jones: Opt. Eng. **13**, 117 (1974)

7.30 H.Zaklad: Electronics **14**, 89 (1976)

7.31 T.M.Peters: IEEE Trans. BME-**21**, 214 (1974)

7.32 H.H.Barrett: Radiology **104**, 429 (1972)

7.33 H.Weiss: Three-Dimensional X-Ray Information Retrieving by Optical Filtering. In *Proceeding of the 1974 International Optical Computing Conference* IEEE (1974)

7.34 K.Biedermann: J. Opt. Soc. Am. **61**, 1439 (1971) and references therein

7.35 A.Macovski: Phys. Med. Biol. **19**, 523 (1974)

7.36 D.Casasent: Hybrid Processors. In *Optical Data Processing*, ed. by S.Lee; Topics in Applied Physics (Springer, Berlin, Heidelberg, New York) in preparation; also D.Casasent, W.Sterling: IEEE Trans. Comput. C-**24**, 318 (1975)

7.37 R.L.Everett, G.Lopez, W.L.Anderson, J.W.Simpson: A Fourier Optical Phonocardiogram Record-Analyze System. In *Proceedings of the San Diego Biomedical Symposium* (SPIE, Vol. 1, 1972)

7.38 J.Shamir, G.Winzer: Opt. Acta **19**, 795 (1972)

7.39 J.D.Redman: J. Sci. Instr. **2**, 651 (1969)

7.40 P.Greguss, H.J.Caulfield: Science **177**, 422 (1972)

7.41 M.Falus, H.J.Caulfield, P.Greguss: Laser and Unconventional Optics **51**, 3 (1974)

7.42 H.J.Caulfield: Appl. Opt. **9**, 1218 (1970)

7.43 D.J.DeBitetto: Appl. Phys. Letters **12**, 176 (1968)

7.44 H.J.Caulfield, S.Lu: *The Applications of Holography* (Wiley-Interscience, New York 1970) Chapt. VIII

7.45 S.A.Benton: Opt. Eng. **14**, 402 (1975)

7.46 J.A.Chapman, S.M.W.Grundy, W.P.Wolton, J.D.Redman: Three Dimensional Reconstructions From Electron Micrographs by Holography. In *Proc. 5th Eur. Congr. on Electron Microscopy* (1972)

7.47 J.D.Redman, W.P.Wolton, E.Shuttleworth: Nature **220**, 58 (1968)

7.48 L.Cross: School of Holography, San Francisco, unpublished

7.49 J.Upatnieks, C.D.Leonard, E.S.Mattila: Archival Storage of Three Dimensional Images. In *International Opt. Comp. Conf. 1975* (IEEE No. CH0941-5c)

7.50 T.H.Jeong, R.Rudolph, P.Lockett: J. Opt. Soc. Am. **56**, 1203 (1966)

7.51 Sh.D.Kakichashvili, A.I.Kovaleua, V.A.Rukhadze: Sov. J. Opt. Spect. **24**, 333 (1968)

7.52 In the USA Apollo Lasers, Hadron, and International Laser Systems market such lasers

7.53 H.J.Caulfield, T.Hirschfeld, J.M.Weinberg, R.Herron: Proc. IEEE **65**, 84 (1977)

7.54 J.R.Varner: Holographic Contouring, Alternatives and Applications. In *Developments in Holography* (SPIE, Vol. 25, 1971)

7.55 S.Lu, H.W.Hemstreet,Jr., H.J.Caulfield: Phys. Lett. **2514**, 294 (1967)

7.56 R.E.Brooks, L.O.Heflinger, R.F.Wuerker, R.H.Briones: Appl. Phys. Letters **7**, 92 (1965)

7.57 E.J.Feleppa: IEEE BME-**19**, 194 (1972)

7.58 J.F.Ebersole: Opt. Eng. **14**, 436 (1975)

7.59 D.E.Rounds, R.S.Olson, J.Booher: Measurement of Cell Migration Index With a He-Ne Laser. In *Third Conference on the Laser* (Anals of the N.Y. Acad. Sci., Vol. 267, 1976)

7.60 J.E.Sollid: Opt. Eng. **14**, 460 (1975)

7.61 K.A.Stetson: Opt. Eng. **14**, 482 (1975)

7.62 K. Burian, W. Firtze, W. Schwomma: Holographic Study of the Ear Drum. In *Symposium 1976 on Electro-cochleography and Holography in Medicine* (Münster, March 1976) A29

7.63 J. Tonndorff, S. H. Khanm: J. Acoust. Soc. Am. **49**, 120 (1971)

7.64 K. Hogmoen, T. Gundersen: Holographic Vibration Analysis of the Osskular Chain. In *Symposium 1976 on Electro-cochleography and Holography in Medicine* (Münster, March 1976) A30

7.65 G. van Bally: Trommelfell als Mittel zur Differentialdiagnose von Schalleitungsstörungen MEDEX 76 (3rd International Exhibition and Congress on Medical Electrics and Bioengineering) (Basle, June 1976)

7.66 P. R. Wedenall; cited in P. Gieguss: Opt. Laser Technol. **8**, 153 (1976)

7.67 G. Häusler, T. Schuenk, K. Seidel: Holographic Deformation Measurement for Optimizing Hip-Joint Prosthesis. In *Symposium 1976 on Electro-cochleography and Holography in Medicine* (Münster, March 1976) p. 7

7.68 D. Vukicevic, J. Hancevic, V. Nikolic, S. Vukiceric: Application of Holographic Interferometry in the Biomechanics of the Locomotor System. In *Symposium 1976 on Electro-cochleography and Holography in Medicine* (Münster, March 1976) p. 7

7.69 G. R. Bremble, M. J. Laker, K. Hardinge: A Preliminary Study of Fracture Fixation Using Holographic Interferometry. In *Holography in Medicine* (P. Greguss, IPC Science and Tech. Press. Richmond, England, 1975) pp. 65—68

7.70 P. Greguss: Opt. Laser Technol. **8**, 153 (1976). This is the only published review of holographic interferometry in biology and medicine known to this author

7.71 The classical paper is A. Vander Lugt: IEEE Trans. IT-**10**, 139 (1964). For later developments see H. J. Caulfield: "Holographic Pattern Recognition—New Thoughts on Old Problems," in *Holography and Optical Filtering*, NASA SP-299 (1973)

7.72 S. T. Thomasson, T. J. Middleton, N. Jensen: *Coherent Optics in Mapping* (SPIE, Vol. 45, 1974), also N. George, T. Thomasson, A. Spindel, U.S. Pat. 3, 689, 772 (1972)

7.73 D. Casasent, D. Psaltis: Appl. Opt. **15**, 1795 (1976)

7.74 N. K. Shi, F. P. Carlson: IEEE Trans. BME-**23**, 84 (1976)

7.75 R. P. Kruger, W. B. Thompson, A. F. Turner: IEEE Trans. SMC **4**, 40 (1974)

7.76 G. C. Salzman, J. M. Crowell, C. A. Goad, K. M. Hansen, R. D. Hiebert, P. M. LaBaure, J. C. Martin, M. L. Ingram, P. F. Mullaney: Clinical Medicine **21** (1975)

8. Optical Signal Processing

D. Casasent

With 23 Figures

Because of their two-dimensional nature, real-time and parallel processing features, optical systems have received considerable attention in various data and information processing applications. Most optical data processing research has concentrated on image processing applications of these systems. However, much of the data that is presently analyzed and processed consists of single- or multichannel electronic signals. In this chapter, we will thus consider the major recent optical signal processing systems and applications.

8.1 Overview

The simplest and most basic coherent optical processor is shown in Fig. 8.1. If the amplitude transmittance of the input plane P_0 is $f(x_0, y_0)$, the light distribution in the back focal plane of spherical lens L_1 of focal length f_1 is the two-dimensional Fourier transform of f or

$$F(x_1, y_1) \propto \int\int f(x_0, y_0) \exp[-j2\pi(x_0 x_1 + y_0 y_1)/\lambda f_1] dx_0 dy_0.$$

This Fourier transform property of a lens [8.5] is the hallmark of a coherent optical processor. From Fig. 8.1, it is also clear that a transparent z-axis modulated version of the input data must be prepared and placed at P_0 before it can be operated on by coherent light. The coordinates (x_1, y_1) of the transform plane are related to the spatial frequency coordinates (u, v) or (f_x, f_y) of the transform plane by $u = x_1/\lambda f_1$, $v = y_1/\lambda f_1$ where λ is the wavelength of the light used and f_1 is the focal length of the transform lens chosen.

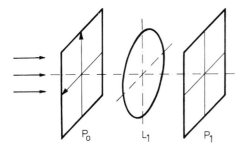

Fig. 8.1. Basic 2-D optical Fourier transform system

This need for a transparent representation of the input data is one reason for the increased attention given to image processing rather than signal processing. Slides of imagery are readily available as inputs to a optical processor. However, such transparent replicas of signals are not readily available. If any of the advantages of optical data processing are to be realized at the throughput possible, real-time and reusable spatial light modulators (SLMs) at P_0 are essential. Such devices are more crucial in optical signal processing systems than in image processing systems, since no convenient method for producing input transparencies of signals exists. Real-time and reusable SLMs thus deserve major attention in any discussion of optical signal processing. Brief remarks on the most promising SLMs and those that have been used in optical signal processors are thus included in Section 8.2.

Since the two-dimensional nature of an optical system is one of the major features of such processors, only 2-D SLM devices and optical signal processing systems will be considered. Although acousto-optic and similar devices have seen considerable use in signal processing, these 1-D transducers are discussed elsewhere and are thus only briefly mentioned in Section 8.2.

Another unique feature of an optical signal processor is the ability to format the input signals to facilitate processing, data extraction, and the output display. Such flexibility is not readily available in image processing simply because there is only one conventional coordinate representation of an image. (Space variant processing is one approach to more flexible image processing.) Real-time and reusable input SLMs greatly facilitate signal processors.

One optical signal processor that demonstrates this input signal format control and fully utilizes the large space bandwidth (SBW) of an optical processor is the folded spectrum analyzer. Most data are long 1-D signals, whereas an optical system is inherently a 2-D processor. However, the 2-D nature and large SBW of an optical processor can be utilized in 1-D signal processing if the input signal is recorded in a raster scan format. The resultant folded spectrum output format that results has many advantage and uses which will be discussed in Section 8.3.

A major application area for optical systems, radar signal processing, is discussed in Section 8.4. This application area is most appropriate for optical processing techniques because of the high input data rate and bandwidth, the need for real-time processing, and the similarity between the basic-optical processing operations (Fourier transformation and correlation) and those conventionally performed on this data.

The optical correlator is the most powerful type of optical data processor. The two most used optical correlators (that do not require mechanical motion of one pattern) are shown schematically in Figs. 8.2 and 8.3. In the frequency plane correlator of Fig. 8.2, $f(x_0, y_0)$ is placed at P_0 and the conjugate transform $G^*(x_1, y_1)$ of a second function $f(x_0, y_0)$ is placed at P_1. L_1 forms $F(x_1, y_1)$ at P_1; the light distribution transmitted by P_1 is $F(x_1, y_1) G^*(x_1, y_1)$. Lens L_2 forms the Fourier transform of FG^* and thus the correlation $f \circledast g$ of the input and reference function at P_2. $G^*(x_1, y_1)$ is formed at P_1 by holographic techniques by

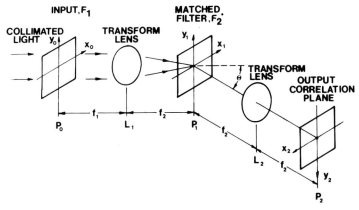

Fig. 8.2. Frequency plane optical correlator

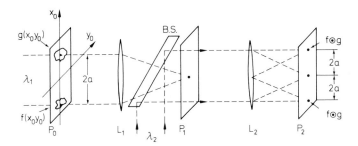

Fig. 8.3. Joint transform optical correlator

placing $g(x_0, y_0)$ at P_0 and interferring its transform $G(x_1, y_1)$ at P_1 with a plane wave at an angle θ. The term of interest in the pattern recorded at P_1 is proportional to G^* and the term FG^* emerges from P_1 at an angle θ, hence the arrangement shown in Fig. 8.2 in which L_2 and P_2 lie at an angle θ to the optical axis.

In the joint transform correlator of Fig. 8.3, the two functions to be correlated $f(x_0, y_0)$ and $g(x_0, y_0)$ are placed side by side at P_0 and separated by 2a. The transmittance of P_0 can then be described (in 1-D for simplicity) by $f(x_0 + a)$ $+ g(x_0 + a)$. Lens L_1 forms the transform of this distribution $|F \exp(-jua) + G \exp(+jua)|^2$ at P_1. The term of interest in the pattern at P_1 is $FG^* \exp(-ju2a)$. When P_1 is now illuminated by a plane wave (λ_2 beam in Fig. 8.3), lens L_2 forms the transform of $FG^* \exp(-ju2a)$ or $f \circledast g$ at $x = 2a$ in P_2.

Lens L_1 in any of these systems can be replaced by a cylindrical/spherical lens combination to produce a multichannel 1-D Fourier transform. This operation is extremely useful in many optical signal processing applications. These and other optical processors are discussed at length elsewhere. While the majority of the optical signal processing applications to be discussed here involves the use of coherent light, several non-coherent optical signal processors of importance are discussed in Section 8.5.

8.2 Electronic-to-Optical Transducers

Because of the importance of these devices in optical signal processing (and in all of optical computing), a brief summary of the most promising input transducers and those used in the various applications to be discussed is included. More extensive surveys on devices and materials for displays [8.1], coherent optical processing [8.2–5] and mass storage [8.6] as well as specifically electronically addressed [8.7] and optically addressed [8.8] devices exist. The following device descriptions will thus be brief and only the major references on each device will be included.

While real-time and reusable spatial light modulators are of primary concern, film or similar materials are used in many initial feasibility demonstrations of optical signal processing. The input for much of the folded spectrum signal processing data (Sect. 8.3) that can be presented at this time has been produced on film using a laser beam recorder (LBR), electron beam recorder (EBR) or by imaging a raster scanned z-axis modulated CRT image onto film. These systems can produce high-resolution transparencies of the input signal pattern with delays of only several minutes by the use of film transports and Bimat or similar developer sections. Current LBR systems allow 6 μm spots to be recorded with positioning accuracies of 0.6 μm over a full 10 mm aperture. A space or time bandwidth product of $3 \cdot 10^5$ points can be recorded on 16 mm film at a resolution of 38 cycle/mm. This allows 20 Hz frequency resolution of a 6 MHz bandwidth input signal [8.9].

8.2.1 Fixed Window Transducers

Two major classes of real-time and reusable input spatial light modulators are those in which data is recorded by a scanning and modulated laser beam, or by an electron beam. One promising optically addressed device is the PROM [8.10]. It consists of a thin transparent photoconductive and electro-optic $Bi_{12}SiO_{20}$ crystal with parylene insulating layers and transparent uniform electrodes on both large faces. The crystal is voltage biased by applying 2 kV between electrodes, and the input data is then recorded by a scanning and modulated focused laser beam. The electric field across the crystal is spatially reduced by photocarriers in proportion to the intensity of the incident light. A different wavelength of light is needed to nondestructively read this stored data.

The phase of the reading light is spatially modulated in proportion to the varying electric field across the crystal by the linear, longitudinal electro-optic or Pockels effect [8.11]. When used between crossed polarizers, amplitude modulation results. Device specifications include: 15 line/mm resolution at 50% modulation (a limiting resolution of 150–500 lines/mm and a peak contrast of 5000:1), a sensitivity of 5 K erg s cm^{-2}, and device dimensions of 2.5·2.5 cm^2. Erasure is rapid and is achieved by flooding the crystal with light from a xenon flashlamp, while peak recording sensitivity occurs at 440 nm and reading is usually at 633 nm.

In two of the most promising real-time and reusable spatial light modulators for optical signal processing, the input data is used to modulate the beam current of a scanning electron gun, and a charge pattern corresponding to the input signal is deposited on the target. In one of the most promising devices, the target is a $5 \cdot 5 \, cm^2$ thin (0.025 mm) electro-optic potassium dideuterium phosphate (DKDP) crystal with a transparent conducting rear electrode. The electric field pattern produced across the crystal by the deposited charge pattern causes a spatial variation in the target's index of refraction and amplitude or phase modulation of a collimated input light beam by the Pockels effect. With the polarization of the collimated input laser beam at $45°$ to the induced crystallographic axes of the DKDP and a crossed output analyzer, the device spatially modulates the amplitude of the input laser beam. With no output analyzer and the polarization of the input light along one of the induced crystallographic axes, spatial phase modulation of the input laser beam results.

The resolution of the DKDP light valve is $1000 \cdot 1000$ points at 50% modulation (maximum contrast is 150:1) and sealed systems have operated for over three years. All electron beam addressed devices generally operate at television rates of 30 frames/s and a 5–10 MHz bandwidth, although higher bandwidths are possible. The DKDP device has a useful storage of over an hour, but erasure has been demonstrated by secondary emission using a flood gun so that a complete write/read and erase cycle in 16–33 ms has been achieved. The coherent optical quality of the PROM ($\lambda/4$ flatness) and DKDP ($\lambda/5$ at present) are excellent. Many optical signal processing examples using the DKDP light valve will be discussed in Section 8.4.

One of the most developed electron-beam addressed spatial light modulators uses a thin dielectric oil film target which deforms in proportion to the deposited charge, thus producing a surface relief pattern and phase modulating a collimated input light beam [8.13]. Present oil film target devices have excellent lifetimes of over 3000 h, a large 40 dB dynamic range, and $500 \cdot 500$ point resolution. The lack of storage (since erasure is by charge decay in 3–300 ms) and the presently poor optical quality of this device are its major limitations.

Another electronically addressed spatial light modulator used in signal processing until 1972 was the membrane light modulator (MLM) [8.14]. This device consists of a thin membrane stretched across an array of regular perforations. It is addressed by stripe electrodes and thus allows only one-dimensional addressing and provides limited 100 line resolution. Several examples of its use in radar signal processing are included in Section 8.4.

8.2.2 Moving Window Acousto-Optic Transducers

Acousto-optic devices [8.15] are basically one-dimensional transducers and present a moving input data window rather than a fixed data window as in other transducers. Their major attraction is their ability to accommodate high carrier frequencies (1 GHz) and signal bandwidths (300 MHz). The basic transducer types are bulk and surface-wave devices with both Raman-Nath and Bragg effects used in the bulk devices.

The interaction of light and sound waves is well known. If an electrical signal at frequency f_0 is applied to an acoustic propagating medium, a grating of acoustic wavelength $\lambda_a = V_s/f_0$ is produced where V_s is the acoustic propagation velocity. When light of wavelength λ_1 is incident on the transducer at the Bragg angle, it is diffracted into symmetrical orders separated in angle by λ_1/λ_a. Since the diffraction angle changes with f_0, while the diffraction efficiency (and hence the intensity of each diffracted spot) varies with the amplitude of the input electrical signal, these Bragg processors are useful in wideband spectrum analysis above 100 MHz.

In the Raman-Nath bulk wave devices, the phase of the input light (which is now incident perpendicular to the ultrasonic delay line) is spatially advanced or retarded by the acoustic grating, and phase modulation of the input light (similar to that obtained in the oil film light valve) results. These devices are useful with lower bandwidth (below 100 MHz) signals.

Various one-dimensional acousto-optic filtering and signal correlation schemes have been proposed and demonstrated [8.16], but most research has concentrated on radar pulse compression applications of these devices. In one of several pulse compression schemes [8.17], an input light beam from a point source is incident on the acoustic medium and will diffract through a slit onto a photodetector only if the Bragg condition is simultaneously met throughout the acoustic medium. This occurs only when the entire input signal fills the delay line at which time all diffracted beams focus on the detector.

Severe problems exist in the fabrication of multichannel ultrasonic transducers, although a device with 24 parallel channels in a 75 mm aperture with 5 MHz channel bandwidth was fabricated and used in phased array radar signal processing [8.18]. Low signal integration time has been another limitation of these transducers, since the signal duration that just fills the transducer's aperture L is L/V_s. A 340 μs delay in a 15 cm aperture with 35 MHz signal bandwidth (limited by attenuation) has been achieved by acoustically folding the path [8.19].

No discussion of signal processing would be complete without a brief mention of the rapidly growing area of surface acoustic wave (SAW) devices [8.20]. SAWs are characteristically Rayleigh waves that propagate in a surface layer whose thickness is the acoustic wavelength. These waves are produced and controlled by interdigital transducers on the surface. Ripples and periodic variations in the material's index of refraction result and modulate the input light. Integrated SAW devices have also been demonstrated [8.21]. They are only one dimensional, but offer great promise and represent a new and emerging technology, with 300–500 MHz signal bandwidths and 20–40 μs delays possible.

8.3 Folded Spectrum Techniques

In optical signal processing, the time coordinate of the input data is converted to a spatial coordinate (and thus signal frequency to spatial frequency) when the signal is recorded on the input transducer. The resolution and linear dimension of the input transducer thus limit the input signal duration that can be recorded on one line and hence the output frequency resolution obtainable.

However, if the input signal is recorded in a raster scan format, its *two-dimensional* Fourier transform contains coarse frequency loci along one axis and fine frequency resolution along the other. This input and *folded spectrum* format fully utilize the two-dimensional nature of the optical system, its parallel processing features, and the large time and space bandwidth products possible in optical processing.

8.3.1 Theoretical Considerations

The details of such a wideband optical signal processor were originally described by *Thomas* [8.22] and later implemented and demonstrated by *Markevitch* [8.23] and others. An explanation for and description of the resultant folded spectrum can be seen by considering a long one-dimensional signal $s(t)$ recorded on n raster lines (vertical raster lines assumed) spaced d units apart with p points per line in an aperture of width b and height a (the length of the raster lines). The amplitude transmittance of a transparent version of this input distribution (see Fig. 8.4a) is

$$t_p(x, y) = A_0 + B_0 \sum_n [1 + ms(y + an)] \, \delta(x - nd), \qquad (8.1)$$

where A_0 represents the average transmittance of the plane, B_0 is a bias term, and m is the modulation constant.

With the transmittance of P_0 in Fig. 8.1 given by (8.1), its 2-D Fourier transform formed by lens L_1 at plane P_1 including the effects of the input aperture $w(x, y)$ is

$$U(f_x, f_y) = A_0 W(f_x, f_y) + B_0 W(f_x, f_y)$$
$$+ [\delta(f_y) C_\infty(f_x) + m S(f_y) C_\infty(f_x - f_y a/d)]. \qquad (8.2)$$

Capital letters in (8.2) represent the transform of the corresponding small letter functions and

$$C_\infty(f_x) = \frac{1}{d} \sum_{k=-\infty}^{+\infty} \delta(f_x - k/d) \qquad (8.3)$$

corresponds to a series of delta functions at $f_x = k/d$ and simply reproduces the spectrum of the window function at horizontal spatial frequency increments of $1/d$. The term $C_\infty(f_x - f_y a/d)$ in (8.2) produces the coarse frequency loci at vertical spacing $\lambda f/a$ (λ is the wavelength of the laser light and f is the focal length of the transform lens). This output format is shown in Fig. 8.4b.

To better visualize the locations of various frequencies in this folded spectrum, consider the following input function and its transform

$$s(y) = \exp(j2\pi f_0 y) \qquad (8.4a)$$

$$S(f_y) = \delta(f_y - f_0), \qquad (8.4b)$$

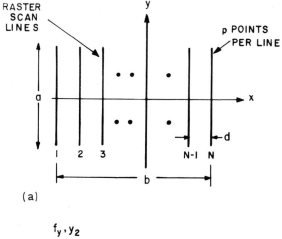

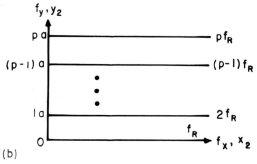

Fig. 8.4a and b. Input (a) and output (b) format for a folded spectrum

which corresponds to a sinusoid at a spatial frequency f_0. Substitution into (8.2) shows that the position in the transform plane corresponding to any input frequency f_0 will always lie on one of the loci lines. Furthermore, as f_0 is slowly increased, one sees that the corresponding point in the frequency plane will move linearly along the loci line. Finally, if f_0 is increased by exactly the line scan rate f_R, the point is found to move vertically by $1/a$ in spatial frequency (or $\lambda f/a$ in distance) to the next frequency loci.

Frequencies that are integer multiples of f_R will appear both at the far left ($f_x = 0$) and far right ($f_x = 1/d$) of each loci line. Frequencies from 0 to f_R appear on the first frequency loci, frequencies from f_R to $2f_R$ along the second loci, etc. For these reasons, the vertical axis f_y in the frequency plane is referred to as the coarse frequency axis, the horizontal frequency plane axis f_x as the fine frequency axis and thus a vertical input raster was assumed.

The shape of the spot in the f_y dimension in the transform plane corresponding to an input frequency f_0 is sinc $a(f_y - f_0)$. Since the first zeroes of this function lie on the loci above and below the one on which f_0 occurs, spots on adjacent loci can be resolved. It follows from (8.2) and (8.4) and the system's maximum spatial frequency that there are p loci lines (p is the number of spots per input raster line). *Thomas* [8.22] has also shown that n spots can be resolved

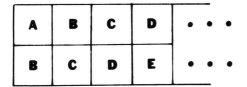

Fig. 8.5. Input format for double recording

on each frequency loci (n is the number of raster scan lines in the input aperture of width b). The space bandwidth product of an input raster of n lines and p points per line is $N = np$. If T seconds of data are recorded in a line scan time T_R (a line scan rate $f_R = 1/T_R$), the maximum frequency recorded will be

$$f_m = p/T_R = pf_R \tag{8.5}$$

and the fine frequency resolution f_F along any loci is

$$f_F = f_R/n = f_m/N = 1/T. \tag{8.6}$$

If a larger separation between frequency loci is desired to facilitate detection of frequencies on adjacent loci, multiple raster recording can be used. The input format for double recording is shown in Fig. 8.5. Successive $T_R/2$ segments of the input signal are denoted by A, B, C, etc. The same line scan time T_R is used but the second portion of the signal recorded on the bottom raster line is repeated at the top of the second raster line, etc. The line separation in the resultant folded spectrum is then twice what it would be for conventional raster recording thus easing the detection problem. However, the space or time bandwidth product of the system is reduced by two as either f_R is increased by two or f_m is reduced by two. Extensions to triple or quadruple recording as well as other extensions are also possible.

The power of such a folded spectrum can best be seen by numerical example. Consider 30 ms of a 100 MHz bandwidth signal recorded on 1200 raster lines with 2500 cycles/line. A transparency with spatial transmittance proportional to this signal format is placed in front of a spherical lens, illuminated with collimated laser light, and the folded spectrum formed in the back focal plane of the lens. The raster line scan rate is 100 MHz/2500 = 40 kHz and thus the coarse frequency resolution in the transform plane is 40 kHz. The fine frequency resolution is 40 kHz/1200 = 33.3 Hz which agrees with $1/T = 1/30$ ms = 33.3 Hz.

Real-time systems with such performance are within the framework of present technology. Several examples of high resolution and bandwidth signal processors and signal analysis using the optical folded spectrum are contained in the following subsections. Although all examples included were obtained by imaging a raster scanned CRT onto film or by LBR on film systems, they are representative of many diverse and typical signal processing applications.

8.3.2 Wideband RF Signal Analysis

One of the more remarkable demonstrations of a folded spectrum output is shown in Fig. 8.6. A recording of the wideband broadcast spectrum in the San Francisco Bay Area was made on film with a 12 MHz EBR with 400 cycle resolution per raster line [8.23]. The optical transform of a 50 ms segment of this recording (750 raster lines) is shown. The time-bandwidth product of the input recording was $3 \cdot 10^5$ and a frequency resolution of 40 Hz in a 12 MHz signal bandwidth is visible upon close examination of the spectrum. Several specific stations and their harmonics are noted in the orthographic display. A 7.02 MHz recorded pilot signal is visible on the 234th locus line. Station WWV is visible at 2.5 MHz as well as its first harmonic at 5 MHz and the separation of its 500 Hz sidebands. While such a display of the entire broadcast spectrum is impressive, operator analysis and recognition of the various signals is enhanced by the three-dimensional isometric display of this spectrum shown in Fig. 8.6b.

8.3.3 Fetal Electroencephalogram Analysis

The optical analysis of the RF broadcast signals represents a high bandwidth signal processing application and shows the powerful display potential of a folded spectrum. A lower bandwidth signal processing application of the folded spectrum arises in the analysis of fetal EEG data [8.24]. Most of the practical clinical value of EEG data arises when visual graphical EEG records are correlated with clinical observations. However, this visual interpretation requires carefully distinguishing EEG patterns in background activity. The specific fetal EEG tests to be analyzed were associated with the use of drugs during labor. Ninety minutes of fetal EEG data were recorded prior to and following application of a paracervical block. A digital computer analysis of the mean zero-line-cross count and integrated mean amplitude values were plotted. No discernable differences were found in the mean number of zero-line crosses, but the integrated amplitude data showed a precipitous drop 15 min after the paracervical block was administered [8.25].

The optical analysis of this same data was performed to confirm its usefulness and accuracy. Optical transparencies of the EEG data were prepared from magnetic tape recording data using a CRT raster film recorder and Bimat film developer. The low 30 Hz bandwidth of the EEG data allows 30 min of data to be recorded on 1 cm^2 of film; however, for this case frames containing about 2.75 min records were used to allow analysis of the EEG spectrum at precise moments before and after application of the paracervical block. The input data was recorded at 2.5 s per line (0.4 Hz). The resultant folded spectra (Fig. 8.7) have coarse frequency loci of 0.4 Hz, whereas the entire spectrum displays the

---

Fig. 8.6a and b. Orthographic (a) and isometric (b) display of the folded spectrum output for a 50 ms ▶ recording of the RF signals in the San Francisco Bay area [8.23]. Courtesy Ampex Corp.

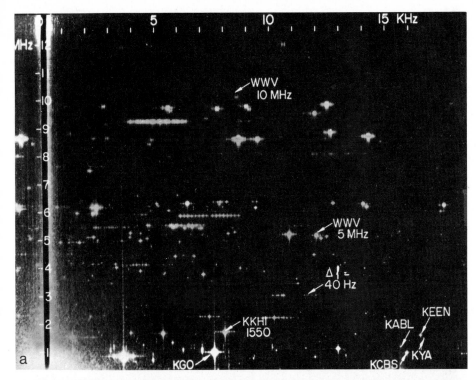

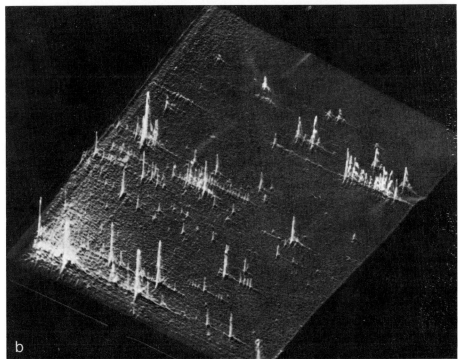

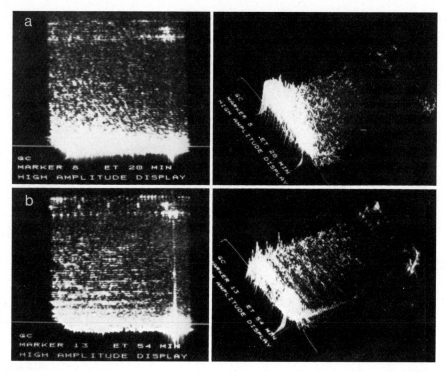

Fig. 8.7a and b. Orthographic (left) and isometric (right) display of the folded spectrum for a 2.75 min fetal EEG record before (a) and 15 minutes after (b) application of a paracervical block [8.24]. Courtesy Ampex Corp.

bandwidth from 0 to 27 Hz at a remarkable fine frequency resolution of 0.0083 Hz.

Two output displays (the conventional orthographic display and an isometric display) of the EEG spectrum prior to (Fig. 8.7a) and 15 min after (Fig. 8.7b) application of the paracervical block are shown [8.24]. A marked decrease in the brightness of the spots and an overall reduction in the amplitude of the isometric display are apparent in Fig. 8.7b and in agreement with the results of the digital analysis of this same data. The corresponding optical displays for other 2 min data intervals show the return of the fetal EEG amplitude to its baseline level 50 min after application of the block.

Whether EEG data reflects fetal central processing is not of concern in this present discussion. Both the digital and optical analysis of data from several patients showed similar results. The fine resolution of the optical spectrum analyzer can be in excess of 10^{-6} of the signal bandwidth whereas conventional electronic signal analyzers have time bandwidths of 10^3. The results presented were obtained with a simple screw electrode and, as the data suggests, only minimal artifact effects arise and no higher harmonics beyond the fundamental of the fetal heart rate appear. Optical folded spectrum signal analysis clearly appears to be a useful adjunct in identifying the presence and shifting of discrete frequencies as well as a powerful display tool. A detailed analysis of the fetal EEG data for the presence of characteristic frequencies, the ratio of the amplitudes of various harmonics, and frequency shifts that occur remains to be pursued.

8.3.4 Engine Vibration Analysis [8.26]

A preliminary folded spectrum analysis of aircraft engine vibration signals as a means of failure prediction has been performed [8.26]. Such methods involving the analysis of signals from an accelerometer mounted on the engine would be superior to present methods involving the disassembly, inspection, and re-assembly of equipment. A considerable number of folded spectrum outputs were obtained from accelerometers mounted at various locations on a jet engine. Various scan rates were used for the CRT raster scanned film recorder used.

The spectra for a new and badly worn bearing from the starter assembly of a JT8D jet engine are shown in Fig. 8.8. Test jigs were constructed for the bearings to restrain the outer race and permit the inner race to accept a radial, or axial load or both. An accelerometer was mounted on the outer race retainer, a spot painted on the drive shaft and a photodetector placed at this point to provide an electrical signal corresponding to the shaft's revolution. This signal was used to phase lock the CRT recorder scan rate to the rpm of the bearing.

The bearings were run at 3000 rpm and the shaft frequency R in Fig. 8.8 was 50 Hz. In both displays, the input consisted of 512 scan lines with input line scan rates of about 50 Hz and about a 12 kHz frequency bandwidth. Although the origin of all of the frequency bands and signals noted in Fig. 8.8 has not been completely explained, many coherent signals from 2–5 kHz appear in the spectrum of the worn bearing (Fig. 8.8a) whereas the 60 Hz signal and its harmonics are the only coherent signals present in the spectrum of the new bearing (Fig. 8.8b). Worn bearings were also characterized by a strong frequency band at low frequencies and new bearings by wide noise bands at 52 and 102–114 times the shaft frequency $R = 50$ Hz. Extensive analysis on much more data and use of a hybrid optical/digital processor [8.12, 27] are required to complete such detailed spectral analysis. However, the optical folded spectrum system makes such an analysis possible.

8.3.5 Signal Buried in Noise

Before discussing various spatial filtering operations possible in a folded spectrum, the ability to extract signals buried in 40 dB of noise in real-time using a folded spectrum analyzer will be shown. A 20 Hz signal mixed with 40 dB of noise was recorded in raster format on the DKDP light valve. The entire folded spectrum plane is shown in Fig. 8.9. The locations of the bright spots in the first four quadrants correspond to the 20 Hz input frequency. Higher harmonics of

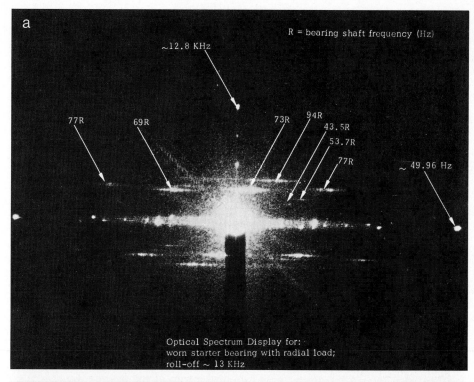

a

R = bearing shaft frequency (Hz)

~12.8 KHz

77R   69R   73R 94R
              43.5R
              53.7R
                77R   ~ 49.96 Hz

Optical Spectrum Display for:
worn starter bearing with radial load;
roll-off ~ 13 KHz

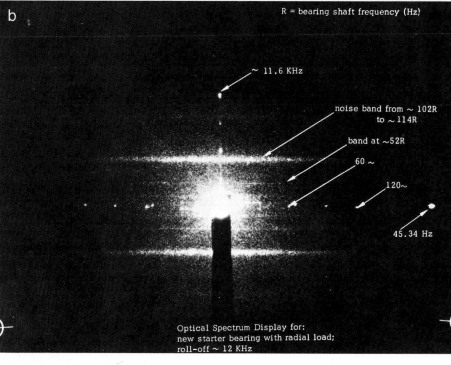

b

R = bearing shaft frequency (Hz)

~ 11.6 KHz

noise band from ~ 102R
to ~ 114R

band at ~52R

60 ~

120 ~

45.34 Hz

Optical Spectrum Display for:
new starter bearing with radial load;
roll-off ~ 12 KHz

Fig. 8.9. Detection of 20 Hz signal buried in 40 dB of noise

this signal are also visible. Extracting signals in the presence of considerably more noise (e.g., 60 dB) is possibly by properly choosing the input scan rate, number of input lines, and hence the input time bandwidth product.

8.3.6 Spatial Filtering

The compact folded spectrum display provides the operator with a powerful analysis tool. However, in automated and real-time signal processing applications, the extensive operator interaction and digital computer analysis of the output data can be reduced if the specific frequency components or signals for which one is searching are known. Often a specific time signal present in the data is desired. These operations can be realized by placing spatial filters in the transform plane and a second lens behind the transform plane.

The light distribution in the output plane of this second lens is the original input signal or a filtered version of it. By passing only certain spatial frequencies (by appropriately placed slits or apertures in the transform plane), the time signatures of the data in the pass band of the filter appear in the output plane. This technique can greatly reduce the quantity of output data to be analyzed while enhancing the signal-to-noise ratio of the signals of interest. Pulse repetition frequencies present in the input and pulse width data can be obtained by measurements at certain frequencies in the folded spectrum or by direct time domain measurements on the filtered output.

In the frequency analysis of the RF data in Fig. 8.6, the data of interest may include spread spectra and frequency hopping (e.g., frequency shift keyed, FSK) signals plus AM and FM signals. As a simple example of such a filtering

---

◀ Fig. 8.8a and b. Optical folded spectrum of accelerometer data from a worn (a) and new (b) ball bearing with radial force. The shaft frequency R was about 50 Hz [8.26]. Courtesy Ampex Corp.

Fig. 8.10. Filtered reconstruction of one/zero code
for FSK station from fol-
ded spectrum RF data
[8.50]

technique a slit was placed in the transform plane of the RF signal spectrum to pass only an FSK station. The transmitted code sequence of ones and zeroes for the FSK station shown in Fig. 8.10 was reconstructed in the output plane of the second transform lens [8.50].

Similar techniques can be used to reconstruct and select various AM stations for display and analysis and more complex methods for the reconstruction of FM signals [8.23]. Holographic matched filter techniques (to be described in Sect. 8.4) have thus far seen limited use in folded spectrum systems although matched spatial filter correlations of the spectra of new and worn ball bearings (Fig. 8.8) have been obtained and found to be helpful in analysis [8.23]. These folded spectrum signal processing techniques appear to represent a major future application of optical processing. The brief explanations of the spectrum format and applications included should vividly demonstrate the potential of such a system.

8.4 Radar Signal Processing

As noted in Section 8.1, one of the most promising applications of optical processing techniques is radar signal processing. A brief review of phased array and pulsed radar systems and selected examples of optically processed radar data are included.

8.4.1 Phased Array Antennas—Theoretical Considerations

The advantages and theory of phased array antennas are well known and documented [8.28]. Their widespread use has been limited by the complexity of the required processing. For this reason, considerable attention has been given to the use of optical techniques in processing the received signals from such arrays. Many of the techniques developed for radar signal processing are also appropriate for radio astronomy, sonar, and other applications, and thus this application area will be given considerable attention. The relationship between the electronic signals applied to the elements of the phased array and the resultant radiation pattern is the dual of that between the signals received at a detector array and the target's location. Since this relationship is a two-dimensional Fourier transform that is easily implemented in a coherent optical processor, the use of optical processing techniques is apparent. To provide adequate background and a unified presentation, the beam forming theory of phased array antennas [8.28] will be briefly reviewed.

For a linear array of N elements equispaced at distances d, the far field [distances greater than $2(Nd)^2/\lambda_c$] radiation pattern $E(\theta)$ for equal amplitude and phase signals applied to all elements is

$$E(\theta) = E_e(\theta)E_a(\theta) = E_e(\theta)\frac{\sin[(Nd/\lambda_c)\sin\theta]}{N\sin[(\pi d/\lambda_c)\sin\theta]}, \tag{8.7}$$

where λ_c is the RF wavelength, E_e is the element pattern (about 1 for isotropic radiators and about $\cos\theta$ for well-designed arrays), and θ is the angle in space with respect to the boresight direction. The $1/N$ factor in (8.7) is used to normalize $E_a(\theta)$ to unity gain at boresight. For a continuous aperture antenna of isotropic radiators,

$$E(\theta) = E'(\theta) = \frac{\sin[(\pi D/\lambda_c)\sin\theta]}{(\pi D/\lambda_c)\sin\theta}, \tag{8.8}$$

where D is the antenna's aperture.

To steer the beam from such an antenna, a nonuniform excitation

$$J(n) = I(n)\exp[j2\pi\phi(n)] \tag{8.9}$$

is applied across the array elements and the resultant array factor becomes

$$E_a(\theta) = \frac{1}{N}\sum_{-\frac{N-1}{2}}^{\frac{N-1}{2}} I(n)\exp[j2\pi\phi(n)]\exp[(j2\pi nd/\lambda_c)\sin\theta]. \tag{8.10}$$

With $I(n) = 1$ and a linear phase increment $\phi(n)$ per element,

$$\phi(n) = -(nd/\lambda_c)\sin\theta_0. \tag{8.11}$$

Equation (8.10) has a closed form solution only for particular J_n values and the resultant array factor for the discrete $E_a(\theta)$ and continuous $E'_a(\theta)$ case becomes:

$$E_a(\theta) = \frac{\sin[(N\pi d/\lambda_c)(\sin\theta - \sin\theta_0)]}{N\sin[(\pi d/\lambda_c)(\sin\theta - \sin\theta_0)]} \tag{8.12a}$$

$$E'_a(\theta) = \frac{\sin[(\pi D/\lambda_c)(\sin\theta - \sin\theta_0)]}{(\pi D/\lambda_c)(\sin\theta - \sin\theta_0)}, \tag{8.12b}$$

from which we see that the antenna pattern can be steered to specific angles θ_0 by varying the applied phase slope $\phi(n)$.

The antenna pattern is repetitive with main grating lobes at θ values for which

$$(nd/\lambda_c)(\sin\theta - \sin\theta_0) \leq n\pi \tag{8.13}$$

for $n = 0, \pm 1, \pm 2, \ldots$ For array geometries satisfying

$$(nd/\lambda_c)(\sin\theta - \sin\theta_0) \leq \pi, \tag{8.14}$$

the array factor has a single major lobe at $\theta = \theta_0$ for θ values from $-90°$ to $+90°$ if $d/\lambda_c < 0.5$. With smaller scanning angles θ, larger d/λ_c element spacings can be used. As $\phi(n)$ is varied, the antenna pattern can be steered to different θ_0 directions. Applying the Rayleigh resolution criteria to this case, N unambiguous resolvable beam positions exist in the cone defined by (8.14).

The analogous optical processing required [8.18, 29, 30] to extract the target angle θ_0 from the signals received at an array of N detectors will now be considered. The heterodyned signal received at the n-th detector array element is

$$V_{in}(x) = P_{Tp}(xT_i/D)\cos[2\pi(f_{if} + f_d)xT_i/D - 2\pi n\alpha], \tag{8.15}$$

where:

$P_{Tp}(x) = 1$ if $|x| \leq T_p/2$, 0 if $|x| > T_p/2$

$T_p =$ transmitted pulse width

$\tau_R = 2R/c =$ range delay

$\tau = (d/c)\sin\theta_0 =$ differential time delay between consecutive array elements

$f_{if} =$ IF frequency

$f_d =$ Doppler frequency

$T_i =$ integration time

$\alpha = \tau(f_c + f_d) = (d/\lambda_c)\sin\theta_0.$

The distance x across the aperture D of the input transducer is related to time t by $x = Dt/T_i$, where $n\tau \ll T_p$ and $f_d \ll f_c$ are assumed. If the N signals received at N antenna elements given by (8.15) are recorded on N lines of an input transducer, the transmittance of the input is given by

$$t(x, y) = \sum_{-\frac{N-1}{2}}^{\frac{N-1}{2}} \delta(y - nl)[1 + \mu v_{in}(x)]P_{X_p}(x), \tag{8.16}$$

where l is the spacing between scan lines. The two-dimensional transform of this distribution produced in the back focal plane of a lens is:

$$T(u,v) = E \frac{\sin \pi X_p u}{\pi X_p u} \frac{\sin N\pi v l}{\sin \pi v l} + \frac{E}{2} \frac{\sin \pi X_p (u - 1/\lambda_x)}{\pi X_p (u - 1/\lambda_x)} \frac{\sin N\pi(\alpha + vl)}{\sin \pi(\alpha + vl)}$$

$$+ \frac{E}{2} \frac{\sin \pi X_p (u + 1/\lambda_x)}{\pi X_p (u + 1/\lambda_x)} \frac{\sin N\pi(\alpha - vl)}{\sin \pi(\alpha - vl)}, \tag{8.17}$$

where $X_p = T_p D/T_i$ and $\lambda_x = D/T_i(f_{if} + f_d)$, and where $T_i > T_p$ and $D > X_p$ have been assumed.

The coordinates of the first-order diffraction terms in (8.17) occur at

$$v_1 = -\alpha/l = -(d \sin \theta_0)/l\lambda_c$$

$$u_1 = 1/\lambda_x = T_i(f_{if} + f_d)/D. \tag{8.18}$$

The optical processor thus forms the correlation of the received signals from all N antenna elements, and the target's azimuth angle can be determined from the vertical coordinate of the first-order diffraction term. The first term in (8.17) is the cross-section of the ambiguity function of the transmitted waveform across the Doppler axis. With $vl = -(d \sin \theta)/\lambda_c$, the second term becomes the array factor. The output of such an optical processor thus has the angular resolution N of the transmitting antenna and the Doppler resolution of an ideal processor. To realize such operations, the resolution of the input transducer on which the distribution described by (8.16) is recorded must be sufficient to resolve $T_i(f_{if} + f_d)$ cycles of the signal per line with N line resolution in y.

These techniques can also be extended to a planar array of $M \cdot N$ elements equispaced at distances X^g and Y^g. The received signal $v_{mn}(t)$ at array element (m, n) is given by

$$v_{mn}(t) = P_{T_p}(t) \cos[2\pi(f_{if} + f_d)t - 2\pi(m\alpha_x + n\alpha_y)], \tag{8.19}$$

where $\alpha_x = (X^g \sin \theta_X)/\lambda_c$, $\alpha_y = (Y^g \sin \theta_Y)/\lambda_c$, and θ_X and θ_Y are the target's azimuth and elevation angles. In practice, only a thinned array is processed. This is accomplished by selecting one detector element per row and per column so that only the returns from N elements need be processed. When these time histories are recorded on an input transducer for optical processing, the starting location of the signal on each line is shifted by a distance proportional to that element's horizontal displacement from the center of the array. The coordinates (x_i^g, y_i^g) of the array elements in the input plane are related to the geometrical displacements (X_i^g, Y_i^g) of the sensors from the center of the array by $k_x = X_i^g/x_i^g$ and $k_y = Y_i^g/y_i^g$.

The signal recorded on line i of the input transducer is

$$v_i(x) = s_{X_p}(x - x_i^g) \exp[2\pi j f_{if}'(x - x_i^g) - 2\pi j(\alpha_x x_i^g + \alpha_y y_i^g)], \tag{8.20}$$

where now $\alpha_x = (k_x \sin \theta_X)/\lambda_c$, $\alpha_y = (k_y \sin \theta_Y)/\lambda_c$, $X_p = DT_p/T_i$, and $f'_{if} = f_{if}T_i/D$. The transmittance of the input with N such signals recorded on N lines is

$$t(x, y) = E \sum_{-\frac{N-1}{2}}^{\frac{N-1}{2}} [1 + \mu v_i(x)]\delta(y - y_i^g)P_{X_p}(x - x_i^g). \tag{8.21}$$

The two-dimensional Fourier transform of this distribution contains first-order maxima at

$$v_1 = -\alpha_y = -(k_y \sin \theta_Y)/\lambda_c \tag{8.22a}$$

$$w_1 = -\alpha_x = -(k_x \sin \theta_X)/\lambda_c. \tag{8.22b}$$

From (8.22), we see that the target angles can be determined from the coordinates of the first-order maxima, where to effect this result $f'_{if}x_i^g$ is chosen to be an integer for all i.

8.4.2 Optical Processing of Phased Array Data

In one of the first published demonstrations of electro-optical processing of phased array data, a multiplexed, 24 channel, solid type, Debye-Sears input transducer was used and beam forming and aperture weighing demonstrated [8.18] using the methods described above.

Similar results were also obtained on a 100×100 element membrane light modulator (MLM) [8.29]. Because of the parabolic shape of the deflected elements in this modulator, it is necessary to image its surface onto an array of circular apertures on the same centers as the membrane's modulator elements but with smaller diameters. The image of this masked MLM is formed in the front focal plane of a Fourier transform lens and the transform of the light transmitted through the mask in the back focal plane. The light intensity in this transform plane is read by a scanning mirror system in which an image of the transform plane is scanned across a slit in front of a photomultiplier by a rotating mirror. The output current from the photomultiplier versus time thus corresponds to the intensity of the transform pattern versus position.

All elements along each row of the MLM are controlled by a single electrode. In addition, the phase of the light reflected from the MLM elements is proportional to the square of the applied voltages. Thus, to produce one-dimensional phased array beam steering, a voltage slope normal to the electrode directions must be applied to the MLM electrodes, with the voltages proportional to the square-root of the phase of the signal at each element in the linear phased array. As the linear phase slope perpendicular to the electrode directions is varied, the location of the main lobe in the transform pattern moves and its position is proportional to the target's azimuth angle.

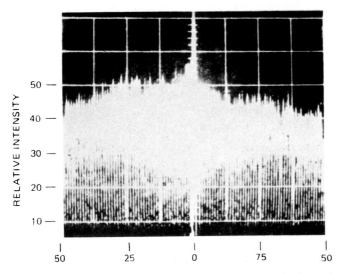

Fig. 8.11. Output oscilloscope display of 100 beam positions for linear phased array beam steering using the membrane light modulator [8.31]. Courtesy Applied Physics Laboratory, the John Hopkins University

A photograph of the oscilloscope output for all 100 beam positions is shown in Fig. 8.11. As the phase slope (and hence the target's azimuth angle) changes, the location of the peak on the oscilloscope trace shifts as shown. The large variations in peak intensity from one beam position to the next are due to the variation in the element pattern with applied voltage. With no voltage applied to the MLM, the wavefront incident on the mask is flat. However, with an applied voltage the wavefront becomes parabolic, the main lobe widens and the intensity on boresight drops. The theoretical and experimental values of intensity at boresight agree fairly well up to a peak phase of $3\pi/4$. Beyond this value, lens aberrations seem to dominate results.

Two-dimensional beam steering has also been demonstrated using the MLM. To produce the required phase slope parallel to the MLMs electrodes, reflected light from only one MLM element per row is used (recall the phase of all elements on one row is the same). The mask onto which the MLM element pattern is imaged now contains only one transparent area per row and thus effects the thinned array processing format previously discussed. Because of the previously noted problems due to the parabolic wavefronts and the low light levels resulting from the thinned transmit mask, the output pattern in the transform plane was of low contrast and low intensity. Detection of the first-order peaks with a thresholded interface device [8.12, 27] and use of a more powerful laser would enhance the output data.

Similar linear and thinned planar phased array beam steering have also been demonstrated on a multichannel lithium tantalate crystal phase modulator [8.31]. The transducer structure consisted of an 0.1 mm thick crystal 15 mm wide and 23 mm long. The large ($15 \cdot 23$ mm^2) bottom surface (normal to the crystal's c-axis) was coated with a thin chromium-gold grounded electrode and the crystal bonded to a brass block on this surface. Forty-six parallel electrodes (0.2 mm wide on 0.5 mm centers) were formed on the large top face, with the electrodes parallel to the crystal's b axis. Input laser light propagating in the b direction and polarized along the crystal's a or c axes can be phase modulated (varying the voltage applied to the stripe electrodes. Since the field under the electrodes is uniform only near the center of each electrode, the modulating crystal elements must again be imaged onto a mask and only the light in the central area (100 μm) of each mask element transmitted. Crystal fabrication difficulties limit the length of this device to 25 mm, while cross-talk between electrodes prohibits smaller element spacings.

The electron-beam addressed DKDP light valve is a more promising electro-optic crystal transducer. To demonstrate its use, we recorded on the light valve the returned signals for a 100 element linear phased array (8.15) in the format described by (8.16) for various target azimuth angles [8.30]. A similar input format is also used in pulsed radar signal processing (Sects. 8.4.3 and 8.4.4). The general optical output transform plane pattern given by (8.17) is shown in Fig. 8.12a. The output pattern for all radar data processed on the DKDP light valve is similar to this, with different interpretations for the coordinates of the first-order diffraction peaks for different radar systems.

The characteristics of the phased array used are listed in Table 8.1. The output pattern for a target at 11° is shown in Fig. 8.12b. The horizontal coordinate of the first-order diffraction term $u_1 = 1050$ m^{-1} is determined by f_{if}. With an effective focal length of 45.2 m for the transform lens, the vertical displacement of all first-order diffraction terms for this linear phased array case lie at $x_1 = u_1 \lambda f = 30$ mm. The vertical displacements of each first-order term are $y_1 = v_1 \lambda f$, where v_1 is given by (8.18), and they determine the target's azimuth angle. These coordinates can be determined by an optical/digital interface device [8.12, 27] that analyzes these optical output patterns. The binary/digitized version of Fig. 8.12b, obtained in real time in our interface, is shown in Fig. 8.12c. By repeating this procedure for targets at various azimuth angles, the vertical coordinate of the first-order diffraction term will vary, its value can be determined, and the corresponding target angle calculated. The results of such an experiment are shown in Fig. 8.13 from which the accuracy of this system is apparent [8.32].

Linear phased array radar data has also been processed on this transducer with the DKDP light valve operated in a phase modulation mode [8.30]. Planar

Table 8.1. Parameters for linear phased array radar processing on the DKDP light valve

$\lambda = 633$ nm	$N = 100$
$f = 45.2$ m effective	$d/\lambda_c = 0.5$
$l = 0.19$ mm	$T_p = 20$ μs
$D = 5$ cm	$f_{if} = 1$ MHz
$T_i = 52.5$ μs	

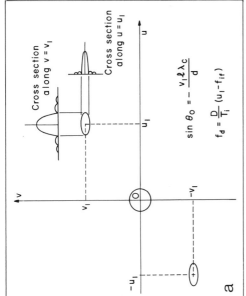

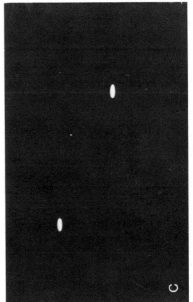

Fig. 8.12a–c. Real-time optical processing of linear phased array radar [8.30] using the DKDP light valve. (a) Output format. (b) Optical output pattern using amplitude modulation for target at 11°. (c) Binary/digitized version of (b). The target's azimuth angle is proportional to the vertical displacement of the first-order diffraction peaks

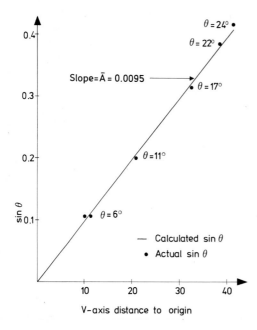

Fig. 8.13. Graph of theoretical and experimental values of target azimuth angle from linear phased array data, optically processed in real-time using the DKDP light valve [8.32]

phased array radar data has also been processed in real time on the DKDP light valve [8.30]. The thinned array format described by (8.20–22) was used and a 70·70 element planar array with a transmitted 13-bit Barker code employed.

8.4.3 Pulsed Doppler and FM Radar Systems—Theoretical Considerations

In a typical pulsed Doppler system [8.33], the transmitted frequency f_0 is derived from the sum of STALO and COHO reference oscillator frequencies f_s and f_c. Prior to transmission, the signal is modulated with a pulsewidth T_p at a $\mathrm{prf}=f_r=1/T_r$. The heterodyned n-th returned pulse from a target of velocity v_r can be described by

$$v_n(t) = P_{T_p}(t) \cos 2\pi(f_{if} - n\alpha),\tag{8.23}$$

where normal approximations similar to those used in (8.15) have been made and where $\alpha = 2v_r T_r/\lambda_0$ and $f_c T_r$ has been chosen to be an integer.

To optically process this data [8.34], the pulsed returns for N such signals are recorded on N lines of spacing l on an input transducer; the input transmission function is

$$t(x, y) = \sum_1^N \delta(y - nl)[1 + \mu v_n(x T_i/D)] P_{Xp}(x).\tag{8.24}$$

From (8.23) and (8.24), the similarity between the pulsed Doppler signal format and that used in the linear phased array radar formulation (Sect. 8.4.1) should be apparent. A linear phase slope that is proportional to the target's fine velocity exists across the input signal data. This slope and hence the target's fine velocity can easily be determined from the v_1 coordinate of the first-order diffraction term in the two-dimensional optical Fourier transform of (8.24),

$$u_1 = 1/\lambda_x = T_i f_{if}/D \tag{8.25a}$$

$$v_1 = -\alpha/\lambda = 2v_r T_r/l\lambda_0 . \tag{8.25b}$$

The transform is obviously quite similar to (8.17) with the distribution in u and v being the power spectrum of the transmitted signal and the cross-section of the ambiguity function of the transmitted waveform along the Doppler axis. The unambiguous velocity bin is $\Delta v = \lambda_0/2T_r$ in which N values of Doppler shift are resolvable from N pulsed returns, just as N target positions were resolvable from the returns from an N element linear phased array.

The Doppler system described differs from the classical one in which frequency discrimination is performed by a band of contiguous filters and in which velocity determination involves correlations of rotated vectors of the returned pulses by assumed phases and a vector addition over all pulses with the process repeated for all velocity bins. By optically processing this data, the search is automatic. Because of the linearity of the system, targets at different velocities will produce diffraction peaks at different locations. Similar remarks apply to multiple targets in the case of optically processed phased array antenna data and in the FM step system to be discussed.

A linear FM stepped waveform results if the frequency f_0 of a series of N pulses is stepped in increments Δf from pulse to pulse. This produces a broad frequency band coverage and a fine range resolution R_F in the unambiguous range bin $\Delta R = T_p c/2$ with N resolvable fine range positions in the spacing $\tau_i = 1/\Delta f$ between ambiguities. The n-th received pulse after heterodyning can be expressed as

$$v_n(t) = P_{T_p}(t) \cos 2\pi(f_{if} - \beta_0 - n\beta) , \tag{8.26}$$

where $\beta_0 = t_0 t_F = t_0 2R_F/c$ is the final phase term for a given target while $\beta = \Delta f t_F$ is the number of cycles of phase shift per pulse or the linear phase slope across consecutive i.f. returns. When the returns for N such signals are recorded in the format described by (8.24), the slope β and hence R_F can be found from the coordinates of the first-order diffraction term in the Fourier transform of (8.24) with v_n given by (8.26). By analogy with the cases of linear phased array and pulsed Doppler processing, the vertical coordinate is

$$v_1 = -\beta/l = 2R_F \Delta f/lc . \tag{8.27}$$

To ensure no ambiguities in fine range within ΔR, $\beta_{max} = \Delta f 2 R_{Fmax}/c$ is kept at unity. With $R_{Fmax} = cT_p/2$, we find $\beta_{max} = \Delta f T_p$ and thus select Δf and T_p such that $\Delta f T_p = 1$ so that $\beta_{max} = 1$.

8.4.4 Optical Processing of Pulsed Radar Signals

The MLM has been used to process pulsed Doppler and FM stepped radar data [8.14]. The optical configuration is the same as that used in Section 8.4.2 for linear phased array processing. With voltages proportional to the square root of the phase of 100 echo pulses applied to the MLMs 100 electrodes, the location of the diffracted light peak will be proportional to the target's fine velocity or fine range because the phase slope across the MLMs electrodes is proportional to α or β. The oscilloscope outputs for six successive sets of 100 pulsed Doppler echoes are shown in Fig. 8.14a. The location of the pulse on each trace is proportional to the target's Doppler frequency and hence to its fine velocity. A fine target velocity of $0.62\,\mathrm{m\,s^{-1}}$ in a $62\,\mathrm{m\,s^{-1}}$ unambiguous velocity interval was demonstrated.

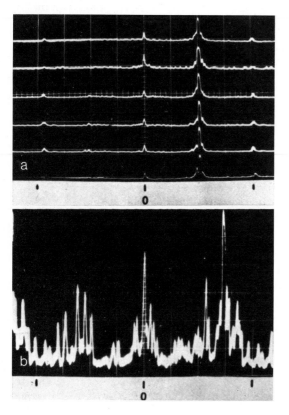

Fig. 8.14a and b. Real-time optically processed pulsed Doppler (a) and FM stepped (b) radar data on the MLM [8.14]. The location of the peak pulses is proportional to the target's fine velocity (a) and fine range (b). In all cases 100 pulsed echoes were processed

The results of the optical processing of 100 returns from an FM stepped radar are shown in Fig. 8.14b. The transmitted frequency was increased by 5 MHz for each pulse and a 500 MHz bandwidth was covered. The location of the pulse in the oscilloscope output is now proportional to the target's fine range. A 1 foot range resolution in a 100 foot unambiguous range interval was demonstrated. For a complex stationary target, the resultant signature provided by data like that in Fig. 8.11 can be used for target identification.

Real pulsed Doppler radar signals have also been optically processed on the DKDP light valve [8.34]. With $D = 5$ cm, $l = 0.19$ mm, $T_p = 20$ μs and $T_i = 52.5$ μs, $N = 100$ Doppler echos heterodyned to an $f_{if} = 1$ MHz and described by (8.23) were recorded on 100 successive lines of the DKDP light valve in the format of (8.24). The optical output transform plane pattern for a single aircraft target with a pulsed radar prf $= 2.5$ kHz is shown in Fig. 8.15a. From (8.25a), the horizontal displacement of the first-order off-axis term is $u_1 = f_{if} T_i / D = 1050$ m^{-1}. An eyepiece and objective were used to project the output patterns to the reasonable sizes shown in Fig. 8.15. The effective focal length of the transform lens was $f = 44$ m giving a horizontal displacement $x_1 = u_1 f = 29$ mm (where $\lambda = 633$ nm for all experiments). The vertical coordinate of this term $y_1 = 37.5$ mm or $v_1 = 1328$ m^{-1} is proportional to the target's fine velocity. From (8.25b), $v_1 = 1328$ m^{-1} corresponds to a fine velocity of $v_r = -17$ m s^{-1} within an unambiguous velocity interval $\Delta v_r = (c/2f_0)(1/T_r) = 62$ m s^{-1}.

The output pattern in Fig. 8.15b was obtained from the same pulsed radar system with a lower prf $= 1.25$ kHz and a shorter effective focal length lens $f = 33$ m. The horizontal coordinate of the first-order term is $u_1 f \lambda = 22$ mm. Two pairs of first-order diffraction terms in different quadrants appear in Fig. 8.15b. The measured displacements $y_1 = 19.5$ mm and $y_2 = 41.5$ mm of these terms correspond to spatial frequencies $v_1 = 930$ m^{-1} and $v_2 = 1980$ m^{-1} where $y = v \lambda f$. From (8.35b), the corresponding target velocities are -5.8 m s^{-1} and 12.5 m s^{-1}, where the two pairs of peak are due to two aircraft crossing in the same velocity bin (31 m s^{-1}) for the lower radar prf used in this case. These values agree with digitally calculated velocities from the same data.

Real linear FM stepped radar data has also been optically processed on the DKDP device [8.34]. The target crystal parameters ($D = 5$ cm, $l = 0.19$ mm, and $T_i = 52.5$ μs) were the same as before. The transmitted frequency $f_0 = 5.650$ GHz was stepped in increments $\Delta f = 5$ MHz between pulses and the returned signals were heterodyned to the system's COHO frequency $f_{if} = 2$ MHz. The pulsed echos $T_p = 0.2$ μs from $N = 100$ pulsed returns were recorded on successive lines on the DKDP device in the conventional format [(8.26) and (8.24)]. The output optical Fourier transforms for two sets of FM stepped radar data are shown in Fig. 8.16. The horizontal spatial frequency of the first-order terms are $u_1 = f_{if} T_i / D = 2100$ m^{-1}. A 2.5 X objective, 15 X eyepiece and 495 mm focal length transform lens provided an effective $f = 17$ m and a displacement $x_1 = u_1 \lambda f = 22.5$ mm for these terms. The fine target range data is obtained from the measured vertical displacement 24 mm in Fig. 8.16a, corresponding to $v_1 = 2340$ m^{-1} and from (8.27) to a fine range of 128 m in the 300 m range bin

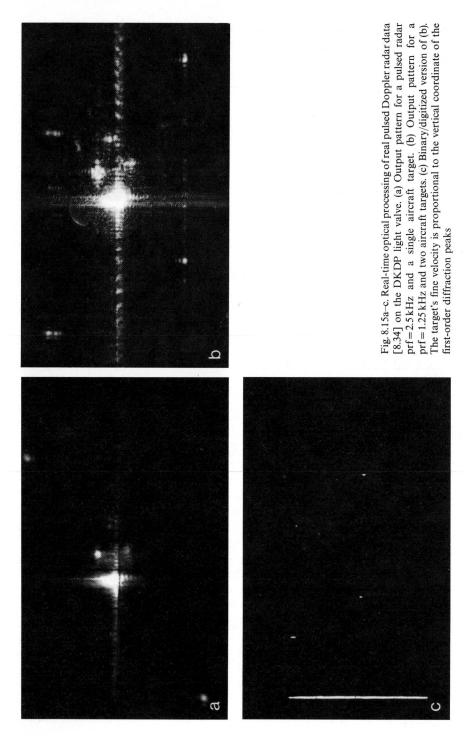

Fig. 8.15a–c. Real-time optical processing of real pulsed Doppler radar data [8.34] on the DKDP light valve. (a) Output pattern for a pulsed radar prf = 2.5 kHz and a single aircraft target. (b) Output pattern for a prf = 1.25 kHz and two aircraft targets. (c) Binary/digitized version of (b). The target's fine velocity is proportional to the vertical coordinate of the first-order diffraction peaks

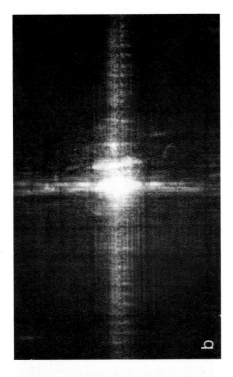

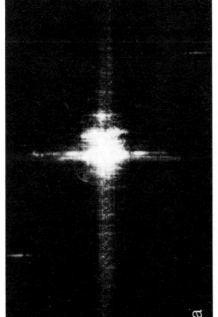

Fig. 8.16a–c. Real-time optical processing of real linear FM stepped radar data [8.34] on the DKDP light valve. (a) Output pattern for a static target (a pair of towers). (b) Output pattern for a moving aircraft target. (c) Binary/digitized version of (b). The target's fine range in the range bin chosen is proportional to the vertical coordinate of the first-order diffraction peaks

chosen. The target in Fig. 8.16a was a static pair of towers, while in Fig. 8.16b the target was a moving aircraft whose fine range was determined (from the $y_1 = 36.5$ mm displacement of the first-order term, corresponding to $v_1 = 3500$ m^{-1}) to be 20 m in the range bin used.

8.4.5 Other Considerations

Thus far, the ability of two devices (the MLM and DKDP light valve) to optically process various radar system data has been demonstrated. The MLM is a one-dimensional row-addressed device in which all electrodes are addressed in parallel. In phased array processing, this device is useful since delay lines are not required as in the DKDP device. However, in pulsed radar systems, the window mode MLM modulator requires the phase of all echo signals to be stored and applied to the MLM electrodes in parallel. The MLM device has a more limited resolution (100) and requires *a priori* knowledge of the phase of the radar signals.

A hybrid optical/digital system [8.27] is necessary to utilize the output pattern data from one radar system in processing data from secondary radars for the full embodiment of these optical radar signal processors. Another feature of the optical radar signal processors presented thus far is that the two-dimensional optical Fourier transform of the input data format is produced in all cases and in general only one coordinate or dimension of the output pattern contains useful target information. Other optical configurations, input formats, the use of optical matched filtering techniques, and other factors in the data previously presented will be considered in this and future sections.

In Fig. 8.16b the target was a moving aircraft rather than a static target. The phase of the returned echo will then be a function of target velocity and range and a linear phase slope will not result. This distortion can be compensated by adjusting the transmission time of the n-th pulse to

$$t_n = \frac{f_0 n \Delta t}{f_0 + (n-1)\Delta f} \simeq \left[1 - \frac{(n-1)\Delta f}{f_0}\right] n \Delta t, \tag{8.28}$$

where Δt is the pulse spacing at f_0 and the frequency of the n-th pulse is $f_n = f_0 + (n-1)\Delta f$.

In a frequency diverse pulsed Doppler radar in which the frequency ordering is not linear, the frequency of the m-th pulse is $f_m = f_0 + n(m)\Delta f$. If these returned echos are arranged in the input plane in the format of (8.34), a linear phase slope with respect to frequency exists across the echoes that is a function of the target's fine range. Thus a two-dimensional phase slope, similar to that obtained in optically processed planar phased array radar data, exists across the input pattern and the coordinates of the first-order diffraction peak in the output pattern are proportional to the target's fine range and fine velocity. Thus, both dimensions in the optical output plane are utilized. The advantages of such optical signal processing is again that the correlation of all target velocities and ranges are performed simultaneously for multiple targets.

An input format somewhat similar to that used in obtaining Fig. 8.15 has also been suggested [8.35]. In this alternate format, film was suggested as the recording medium with the recording sweep proceeding across the film in a zig-zag pattern for a period of time equal to one range element (T_p) and then retracing to record the next range element alongside the prior one. The range elements thus lie in the transverse direction with each element recorded longitudinally for several IF cycles.

Extensions of many of these optical processing systems have been suggested. A system analogous to the thinned phased array correlator has been suggested for sonar processing [8.36] and simultaneous beam-forming and cross-correlation [8.37] in multidimensional arrays. Pulse compression [8.16] has been another major application area, in which optical systems for simultaneous pulse compression and beam forming [8.38] have been suggested.

8.4.6 Multichannel 1-D Optical Correlator [8.51]

In the prior phased array and pulsed radar optical signal processors, only the Fourier transform property of a coherent optical processor was utilized. The full potential of an optical signal processor is realized when the correlation property of such systems is used. If the optical Fourier transform correlator of Fig. 8.2 is modified as shown in Fig. 8.17 (by replacing L_1 in Fig. 8.2 with a cylindrical L_1 spherical L_2 lens combination), a multichannel 1-D optical correlator results.

The use of this system is described for the case of a linear phased array radar. The input signal recorded on line n is now

$$v_n(x_0) = p(x_0') \cos 2\pi(f_{if}' x_0' + n\alpha + \beta) \qquad (8.29)$$

where $x_0' = x_0 T_i/D$, p denotes the transmitted coded waveform,

$$f_{if}' = f_{if} + f_d, \qquad \alpha = f_{if}' \tau_1 = (s \sin\theta)/\lambda_c,$$

and

$$\beta = f_{if}' \tau_2 = R_F \tau_2/T_i,$$

where τ_1 and τ_2 denote the time delays of the received signal corresponding to the target's azimuth angle θ and fine range R_F. For simplicity the θ zero reference is taken at boresight and the range bin R_B has a reference at $\tau_2 = 0$. For future use, the distances across the aperture corresponding to the time delays τ_1 and τ_2 and phase delays α and β are defined by $\alpha' = \alpha D/f_{if}' T_i$ and $\beta' = \beta D/f_{if}' T_i$.

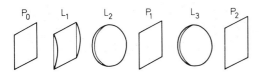

Fig. 8.17. Multichannel 1-D optical correlator [8.51]

N signals in the form of (8.29) are recorded on N lines at P_0 of Fig. 8.17 and its transmittance is then

$$t(x_0, y_0) = \sum_n \delta(y_0 - nl_0)[1 + v_n(x_0)].\qquad(8.30)$$

The 1-D horizontal transform of $t(x_0, y_0)$ formed at P_1 is

$$T(u_1, y_1) = \sum_n \delta(y_1 - nl_1)\delta(u_1 \pm f''_{if}) * P(u_1)$$
$$\cdot \exp[-j2\pi u_1(n\alpha' + \beta')]\qquad(8.31)$$

where f''_{if} is the spatial frequency corresponding to f_{if} and P is the Fourier transform of p at P_1, the conjugate transform of a reference function [identical to $t(x_0, y_0)$ with new α_0 and β_0 references] is stored. The term of interest in the transmittance of P_1 is

$$\sum_n \delta(y_1 - nl_1)\delta(u_1 \pm f''_{if}) * P^*(u_1)$$
$$\cdot \exp\{-j2\pi x_1[\gamma + (n\alpha'_0 + \beta'_0)/\lambda f_2]\}\qquad(8.32)$$

where $\gamma = (\sin\theta)/\lambda$. To form (8.32), conventional holographic methods are used. The same reference function is recorded on N lines at P_0 of Fig. 8.17 and its 1-D transform interferred with a plane wave reference beam at an angle θ to P_1.

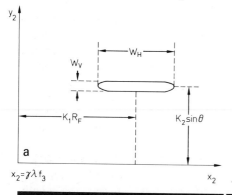

Fig. 8.18a–c. Real-time phased array correlation using the system of Fig. 8.17. (a) Schematic representation of output plane, (b) output plane for target at $\theta = 5°$, $R_F = 0.45 R_B$, (c) output plane for target at $\theta = 30°$ and $R_F = 0.55 R_B$ [8.51]

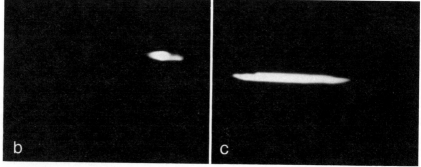

The transmittance of P_1 is then given by the product of (8.31) and (8.32). The 2-D Fourier transform of this product formed at P_2 of Fig. 8.17 by lens L_3 has a first-order term given by

$$\delta(y_2 - \lambda f_1 f_3 \Delta\alpha/l_0 f_2)\delta[x_2 - \gamma\lambda f_3 - f_3(N\Delta\alpha' + \Delta\beta')/f_1]*(p\circledast p) \qquad (8.33)$$

where $\Delta\alpha' = \alpha'_0 - \alpha'$ and $\Delta\beta' = \beta'_0 - \beta'$. From (8.33), the contents of P_2 contain the autocorrelation of the transmitted coded waveform. The coordinates of the correlation peak are proportional to $\Delta\beta$ and $\Delta\alpha$ and hence the target's azimuth angle and fine range as shown in Fig. 8.18a. The output plane for a transmitted Barker coded waveform and a 100 element array are shown in Fig. 8.18b and c for a target at $\theta = 5°$ and $30°$ and a fine range R_F equal to 0.45 and 0.55 of the range bin R_B.

A more extensive analysis of this processor is found in [8.51]. The same processor (Fig. 8.17) is applicable for use with LFM and pulsed Doppler radar waveforms (in which case the coordinates of the autocorrelation at P_2 are proportional to the target's fine range and Doppler). All of these systems can of course accommodate multiple targets, by virtue of the linearity of an optical system.

8.4.7 Correlation with Long Coded Waveforms

In the optical processing of planar phased array radar data on the DKDP light valve [8.30], a 13-bit Barker code was transmitted. This coded waveform is widely used because of its excellent correlation properties. In many radar and other signal transmission systems, long coded waveforms are used. For an enhanced output signal-to-noise ratio (SNR), the input data can be correlated with a matched spatial filter of the transmitted coded waveform [8.39]. When the input code is so long that it occupies more than one line of the input transducer and when the starting location of this code is not known, advanced signal correlation techniques are needed.

One approach of relevance to this problem was reported by *Stann* [8.40]. It involved the use of a pseudo-random coded sequence which, when properly arranged in a rectangular format, always produced a correlation. As originally described the correlation was intended to be implemented by digital or non-coherent optical image correlation and required a format determined by the prime factors of the length of the sequence. These basic ideas have now been extended [8.41] to include any coded sequence and holographic matched spatial filtering methods.

To demonstrate this scheme, consider the 63-bit coded sequence

101110011000010101010001111101010010101101000011101101001010101000,

where the technique is also useful for longer coded waveform sequences. The problem is the detection of this coded sequence and the starting location of the

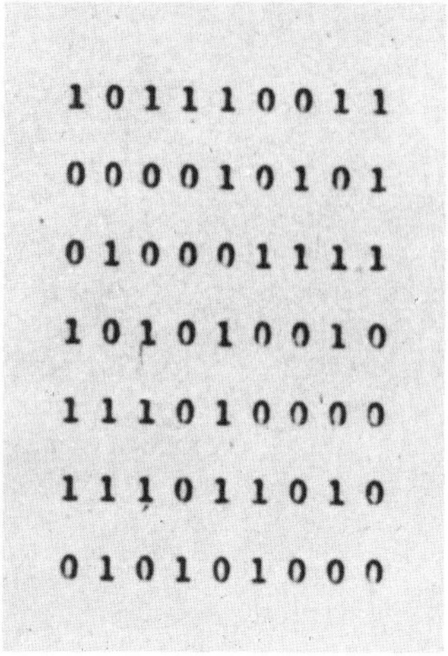

1 0 1 1 1 0 0 1 1

0 0 0 0 1 0 1 0 1

0 1 0 0 0 1 1 1 1

1 0 1 0 1 0 0 1 0

1 1 1 0 1 0 0 0 0

1 1 1 0 1 1 0 1 0

0 1 0 1 0 1 0 0 0

Fig. 8.19. Input $9 \cdot 7$ bit format [8.41] for a pseudo-random 63-bit binary code starting at bit-1

code. If we consider a $9 \cdot 7$ element spatial light modulator on which the received signal is recorded in raster form, the received pattern for the code starting at location 1 would appear as shown in Fig. 8.19. A holographic matched spatial filter of this $9 \cdot 7$ bit pattern would successfully correlate with a received pattern that originated at bit location 1. However, a severe decrease in SNR would result if the received coded sequence began at bit location 42 (see Fig. 8.20a).

To achieve conventional matched spatial filter correlation of an MN bit code, the reference mask would have to contain $(MN)^2$ bits. The mask used in the present scheme for the above 63-bit coded sequence is arranged in the $M \cdot N = 9 \cdot 7$ bit format of Fig. 8.19 as shown in Fig. 8.20a. This mask pattern is generated by selecting any starting bit location in the code (in this case bit-33) and recording the next 2M bits of the code on the first line of the mask. The 2M bits of the code recorded on line two begin $M = 9$ bits (at bit-42) after the starting bit location (bit-33) chosen for line one. This pattern is continued for $2N$ lines until the pattern in Fig. 8.20a is completed.

As shown in this figure, the $9 \cdot 7$ bit input pattern for all starting bit locations of the 63-bit code under consideration are present at a unique location in this reference pattern. The $9 \cdot 7$ bit blocks for starting bit locations 1, 42, and 52 are shown in Fig. 8.20a. To avoid ambiguities, the first row and column of this pattern are deleted. If a holographic matched spatial filter of this reference mask is formed and placed in the transform plane of an optical frequency plane correlator with various $9 \cdot 7$ bit patterns in the input plane, the output plane will contain a correlation peak whenever the input sequences matches the 63-bit reference code. The location of the correlation peak denotes the starting bit in the coded sequence, since the region of the mask in which the $9 \cdot 7$ bit block occurs moves as shown in Fig. 8.20a. The output optical correlation plane for coded sequences starting at bit locations 42 and 52 is shown in Fig. 8.20b and c. The location of the correlation peaks agrees with the position of the indicated

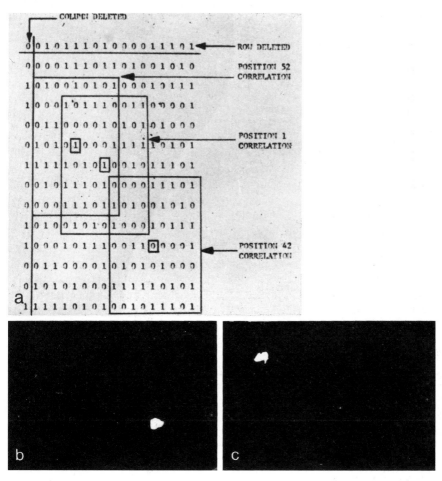

Fig. 8.20a–c. Matched spatial filter correlation [8.41] for the 9·7 bit input format in Fig. 8.19. (a) Reference mask pattern, (b) correlation plane pattern for the code starting at bit position 42, and (c) starting at bit position 52

9·7 bit data blocks in Fig. 8.20a. For this simple example, only a $(2M-1)(2N-1)$ $= 17(13) = 221$ bit mask is needed for a $63 = M \cdot N = 9 \cdot 7$ bit code rather than $63(63) = 3069$ bits. The savings in storage space is even more dramatic for longer bit sequences.

8.4.8 Doppler Signal Processing [8.52, 53]

A novel approach to optical processing that has greatly increased the flexibility of a coherent optical processor involves the optical implementation of operations other than the conventional Fourier transform. One of these new operations is the optical implementation [8.52, 53] of the Mellin transform $M(\omega)$ of $f(x)$, where in one dimension

$$M(\omega) = \int_0^\infty f(x)x^{-j\omega-1}dx. \tag{8.34}$$

This operation can be realized in a coherent optical system by logarithmically scaling the input signal to form $f(\exp\xi)$ on an input transducer. The Fourier transform of this logarithmically scaled function is equivalent to the Mellin transform of $f(x)$,

$$M(\omega) = \int_0^\infty f(\exp\xi)\exp(-j\omega\xi)d\xi. \tag{8.35}$$

The property of this transform of major interest is its scale invariance. If M_1 and M_2 are the Mellin transforms of two scaled signals $f_1(t)$ and $f_2(t) = f_1(at)$, then it has been shown [8.52] that $|M_1| = |M_2|$. This property of a Mellin transform can be utilized to perform correlations on input signals that differ in scale [8.52], such as Doppler signals [8.53]. Of major importance in Doppler signal processing are the facts that: there is no loss in the SNR of the correlation peak even though the two signals differ in size, and that the location of the correlation peak is proportional to the scale factor "a" between the two input signals [8.52].

Since the frequency ω_d detected by a stationary receiver is related to the radiated frequency ω_0 by

$$\omega_d = \omega_0/(1-v_s/v_0), \tag{8.36a}$$

or

$$\omega_d = \omega_0(1+v_r/v_0), \tag{8.36b}$$

or

$$\omega_d = \omega_0(1+2\dot{R}_0/c), \tag{8.36c}$$

or

$$\omega_d = \omega_0[(1+v_s/c)/(1-v_s/c)]^{1/2}, \tag{8.36d}$$

where v_s and v_r are the radial velocity of the source object and receiver respectively, v_0 is the velocity of propagation in the medium in which the signal is transmitted, and c is the speed of light. Equations (8.36a and b) apply to the case of the source object moving toward a stationary receiver and the receiver moving toward a stationary source, respectively. Only when $|v_s - v_r| \ll v_0$ do these two effects approach one another. For the case of electromagnetic waves in space (8.36d) applies, while (8.36c) describes the case of backscattered radiation in radar ($\dot{R}_0$ is the rate of change of range R_0).

All of these effects are equivalent to a scaling of the frequency of the received signal from ω to $a\omega$, where for the case of backscattered radiation in radar,

$$a = [1/(1 + 2v_s/c)] \simeq 1 - 2v_s/v_c. \tag{8.37}$$

This follows from the equivalence of a scaling in frequency (from ω to $a\omega$) to a scaling in time, i.e.,

$$f(t/a) \leftrightarrow |a| F(a\omega), \tag{8.38}$$

where F is the Fourier transform of f and $\leftrightarrow$ denotes the Fourier transform operation.

To see the scale invariance of the Mellin transform, consider two signals $f_1(t)$ and $f_2(t) = f_1(at)$ which differ in Doppler and hence in scale by a factor "a". Logarithmically scaled versions $f_1(\exp \xi)$ and $f_2(\exp \xi)$ of these signals are produced by log amps in the deflection system of an input transducer. Refer to Fig. 8.2. If $f_2(\exp \xi)$ is placed in the input plane P_0 and its Fourier transform M_2 is interferred at plane P_1 with a reference beam at an angle θ as in conventional Fourier transform holography, the pattern recorded at P_1 will contain a term proportional to M_2^*. If $f_1(\exp \xi)$ is then placed in P_0, the reference beam blocked, and the filter at P_1 kept in position, the light distribution emerging from P_1 contains a term proportional to

$$M_1 M_2^* = M_1(\omega) M_2(\omega) \exp(-j\omega \ln a). \tag{8.39}$$

Lens L_2 forms the Fourier transform of this distribution at plane P_2. The pattern at $y_2 = -f \sin \theta$ in plane P_2 (where f is the focal length of lens L_2) is the correlation of f_1 and f_2

$$f_1(\exp \xi) \circledast f_2(\exp \xi) * \delta(x - \ln a). \tag{8.40}$$

From (8.40), the correlation is seen to be the same as the auto-correlation and thus there is no loss in SNR. But more important is the fact that the scale difference "a" which is proportional to the Doppler of the signals is contained in the location of the correlation peak (at $x = \ln a$).

To demonstrate the use of the Mellin transform and correlation in Doppler signal processing [8.53], the modified joint transform correlator of Fig. 8.3 was used. A logarithmically scaled input signal f_1 was recorded on nine lines in the left half of the input plane and nine logarithmically scaled Doppler-shifted versions of it were recorded on the same nine lines but in the right half of the input plane. With $n = 9$ lines, a separation y_0 between lines, and a spacing $2x_0$ between signals on a given line, the transmittance of the input plane can be described by:

$$\sum_n f_{n1}(x + x_0, y - ny_0) + f_{n2}(x - x_0 + x_n, y - ny_0). \tag{8.41}$$

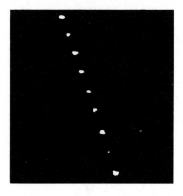

Fig. 8.21. Output correlation plane for the Mellin transform of 9 signals differing in Doppler. The horizontal coordinate of each correlation peak is proportional to the Doppler shift of that signal with respect to the reference signal [8.53]

A one-dimensional Fourier transform of this input pattern was recorded on film. This film was then reinserted in the input plane, illuminated with parallel light, and a second one-dimensional Fourier transform produced. This output distribution contains the correlation of f_1 with all of the Doppler shifted signals $f_{n1} f_{n2}$ at $x'_n = 2x_0 - x_n$.

A photograph of this output pattern (displayed on a thresholded monitor) in the region of the output plane around $x' = 2x_0$ and $y' = 0$ is shown [8.53] in Fig. 8.21. The location of the correlation peak x'_n on each line "n" is proportional to the $\log_e$ of the scale change "a" between the signals on line n and thus to the Doppler shift between these signals. All correlation peaks are of the same intensity and only their location contains information. For convenience, a constant Doppler increment was applied to each of the signals in this experiment. This technique appears to have far-reaching implications in sonar and radar processing as well as in radio astronomy and synthetic aperture radar signal processing.

8.5 Non-Coherent Optical Signal Processing

The systems and examples presented in Sections 8.3 and 8.4 are some of the more promising and extensively documented signal processing applications of coherent optical processing. In this final section, two rather interesting but different optical signal processors using non-coherent optical processing methods are discussed.

8.5.1 Optical Correlator for Speech Recognition

Yu [8.42] has described several uses of optical processing for speech recognition in which the folded spectrum (Sec. 8.2) and other optical signal processing configurations can be used. The system described here makes use of a multichannel version of the non-coherent matched filter system described by

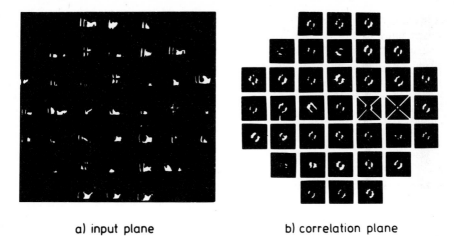

a) input plane   b) correlation plane

Fig. 8.22a and b. Multichannel non-coherent correlation of speech spectrograms [8.44]: (a) Reference filter bank. (b) Optical output pattern showing the correlation of the sixth word of the fourth line of the filter bank with the input word

Armitage and *Lohmann* [8.43]. In this multichannel system [8.44], a bank of spatially separated filters of speech spectrograms s_i are illuminated with monochromatic light and their spatially separated intensity Fourier transforms $|S_i|^2$ produced on a diffuser. This $|S_i|^2$ intensity Fourier transform pattern is then reflected from a reflex mode DKDP light valve [8.45] and imaged onto an output plane. If an unknown speech spectrogram is recorded on the DKDP light valve, the output plane pattern is the non-coherent correlation of the input spectrogram S with the spectrograms s_i in the reference filter bank.

A filter bank of 37 speech spectrograms (Fig. 8.22a) was stored. The correlation plane pattern is shown in Fig. 8.22b. The origin of each of the 37 correlation images is given by

$$k_{s_{is}} = \int |S_i|^2 |S|^2 \, du dv, \qquad (8.42)$$

where the integral is over all space frequencies. These central correlation regions are dark for cross-correlations and bright only for auto-correlations. As shown in the output correlation plane pattern in Fig. 8.22b, only the center of the correlation pattern for the sixth word of the fourth row is dark (indicative of an autocorrelation), whereas the center of all other correlations is dark. For a review of non-coherent optical processing techniques, see [8.46].

8.5.2 Non-Coherent Optical Correlator

The need for a real-time input spatial light modulator can be avoided if the one-dimensional input signal is used to modulate the output of a light emitting diode (LED). In this non-coherent correlator [8.47], the light source is imaged by a condensor lens onto the entrance aperture of an imaging lens. A photographic transparency of a reference library of N one-dimensional signals is placed immediately behind the condensing lens and focused onto the output plane by the imaging lens. The input signal is

$$v(t) = B + Ks(t/a) + n(t),\tag{8.43}$$

where B is the bias level, s the signal, n the background noise, and where K and a allow scale and frequency changes to be made in the signal. If the transmission function of the i-th channel of the reference mask is

$$f_i(x) = B_i + K_i r_i(x/a_i),\tag{8.44}$$

the light leaving the mask is $v(t)f_i(x)$.

A rocking mirror placed between the mask and imaging lens causes this image to repetitively scan the output plane at velocity v. The light intensity incident on a vidicon placed in the output plane is

$$g_i(x, t) = v(t)f_i(x - vt - \phi),\tag{8.45}$$

where ϕ is the phase of the mirror's scan. The vidicon integrates this light intensity over a single scan T. One term in the integral of (8.45) is the correlation of s with r_i. The entire output plane contains the correlation of the input signal s with all reference signals r_i. A scale search of the signals is possible by varying v until $v = a_i/a$.

As a demonstration of the use of this correlator in signal processing, a mask transparency (Fig. 8.23a) containing twenty-five 90-bit binary codes was used and a waveform generator repetitively producing the code on the mask's fifth line was applied to the LED. The integrated output image (with a 100 scan/s scanning rate) is shown in Fig. 8.23b. The bright autocorrelation peak on line five indicates the correlation of the input signal with the proper channel of the mask. By the use of special binary masks, discrete cosine and Walsh transforms of the input signal are possible [8.48]. The output vidicon detector has recently been replaced by a linear and planar CCD array and the use of this system in non-coherent matrix multiplication discussed [8.49].

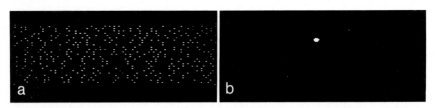

Fig. 8.23a and b. Multichannel non-coherent correlation of binary coded sequences [8.47]. (a) Reference bank of twenty-five 90-bit binary codes. (b) Optical output plane showing correlation of the input signal with the coded sequence on channel five of the mask

8.6 Summary and Conclusions

Several optical configurations for signal processing have been discussed. The ability to format the input signals to enhance the processing ability of the optical system has been emphasized together with the importance of the input transducer. Specific attention has been given to the use of the folded spectrum for high time-bandwidth signal processing and to the use of coherent optical techniques in radar signal processing.

From a simple description of the relation between the input raster format and output folded spectrum and selected examples of the use of this system, the potential of this powerful technique should be apparent. The extensive use of the DKDP light valve in radar signal processing has also been summarized in such a manner that the basic input format was identical in all instances. Extensions of these techniques in radar and other signal processing applications to include matched filter correlation are the subject of current research.

In several years these two systems promise to have major impact on signal processing since they utilize the real-time, parallel processing, high time-bandwidth, and correlation properties of a coherent optical processor.

Acknowledgments. The support of the Office of Naval Research on contracts NR048-600 and NR350-011 and the National Aeronautics and Space Administration on contract NAS8-28737 is acknowledged for much of the author's work included here. The assistance of Dr. Francisco Casasayas in performing much of the radar processing on DKDP is also gratefully acknowledged as is the assistance of Robert Markevitch of Ampex Corporation and James Queen of the Applied Physics Laboratory of the Johns Hopkins University for many fruitful discussions and for much of the imagery included in this chapter.

References

8.1   IEEE Trans. ED-**20** (1973)
8.2   D. Casasent: Proc. IEEE **65**, 243 (1977)
8.3   D. Casasent: Light Valves. In *Applied Optics and Engineering*, ed. by R. Kingslake and B. Thompson, Vol. VI (Academic Press, New York 1978)
8.4   D. Casasent: Recyclable Input Devices and Spatial Filter Materials. In *Laser Applications*, ed. by M. Ross (Academic Press, New York 1977)
8.5   S. H. Lee (ed.): *Optical Data Processing*, Topics in Applied Physics (Springer, Berlin, Heidelberg, New York) to be published
8.6   D. Chen, Z. D. Zook: Proc. IEEE **63**, 1207 (1975)
8.7   D. Casasent: J. Soc. Info. Disp. **15**, 131 (1974)
8.8   J. Bordogna, S. Keneman, J. Amodei: RCA Rev. **33**, 227 (1972)
8.9   S. Bousky: Third Ann. Wideband Rec. Symp., RADC (Sept. 1969)
8.10   P. Nisenson, R. A. Sprague: Appl. Opt. **14**, 2602 (1975)
8.11   B. H. Billings: J. Opt. Soc. Amer. **39**, 797 (1949)
8.12   D. Casasent, W. Sterling: IEEE Trans. C-**24**, 318 (1975)
8.13   M. Noble, W. Penn: Proc. Elec. Opt. Sys. Des. Conf., Anaheim (Nov. 1975)
8.14   K. Preston: *Coherent Optical Computers* (McGraw-Hill, New York 1972)
8.15   A. Korpel: SPIE **38**, 3 (1973)
8.16   W. T. Maloney: IEEE Spectrum **40** (1969)

8.17 M.B.Schulz, M.G.Holland, L.Davis: Appl. Phys. Letters **11**, 237 (1967)
8.18 L.Lambert, M.Arm, A.Aimette: Electro-Optic Signal Processors for Phased Array Antennas. In *Optical and Electro-Optical Information Processing*, ed. by J.T.Tippet et al. (MIT Press, Cambridge 1965)
8.19 M.Gottlieb, J.J.Conroy: Appl. Opt. **12**, 1922 (1973)
8.20 E.Lean, C.Powell: Proc. IEEE **58**, 1939 (1970)
8.21 L.Kuhn, M.Dakss, P.Heinrich, B.Scott: Appl. Phys. Letters **17**, 265 (1970)
8.22 C.Thomas: Appl. Opt. **5**, 1782 (1966)
8.23 B.Markevitch: Third Ann. Wideband Recording Symp., RADC (Apr. 1969)
8.24 P.Peltzman, P.Goldstein, R.Battagin: Am. J. Obstet. and Gynecol. **115**, 1117 (1973)
8.25 P.Peltzman, P.Goldstein, R.Battagin: Am. J. Obstet. and Gynecol. **116**, 957 (1973)
8.26 Ampex Corp.: Tech. Rept. on N00014-67-C-0401 (July 1970)
8.27 D.Casasent: "Hybrid Processors", in *Optical Data Processing*, ed. by S.H.Lee, Topics in Applied Physics (Springer, Berlin, Heidelberg, New York) to be published
8.28 T.Cheston, J.Frank: Array Antennas. In *Radar Handbook*, ed. by M.Skolnik (McGraw-Hill, New York 1970) Chap. 11
8.29 D.Grant, R.Meyer, N.Qualkinbush: Elec. Opt. Sys. Des. Conf. 1972
8.30 D.Casasent, F.Casasayas: IEEE Trans. AES-**11**, 65 (1975)
8.31 R.A.Meyer, D.G.Grant, J.L.Queen: Appl. Phys. Lab., Johns Hopkins Univ. Tech., Memo TG1193 (Sept. 1972)
8.32 D.Casasent: Internat. Opt. Comput. Conf., Wash. D.C. (Apr. 1975) IEEE Cat. No. 75CH0941-5C
8.33 D.Barton: *Radar System Analysis* (Prentice-Hall, Englewood Cliffs, N.J. 1964)
8.34 D.Casasent, F.Casasayas: Appl. Opt. **14**, 1364 (1975)
8.35 W.Hoefer: IRE Trans. MIL-**6**, 174 (1962)
8.36 R.Williams, K. von Bieren: Appl. Opt. **10**, 1386 (1971)
8.37 D.Beste, E.Leith: IEEE Trans. AES-**2**, 376 (1966)
8.38 E.Leith: IEEE Trans. AES-**4**, 879 (1968)
8.39 A.Vander Lugt: IEEE Trans. IT-**10**, 139 (1964)
8.40 R.Spann: Proc. IEEE (Corresp.) **53**, 2137 (1965)
8.41 D.Casasent, D.Kessler: Opt. Commun. **17**, 242 (1976)
8.42 F.T.S.Yu: IEEE Spectrum **51** (1975)
8.43 J.Armitage, A.W.Lohmann: Appl. Opt. **4**, 464 (1965)
8.44 H.Weiss: First Internat. Conf. on Pattern Recog., Wash. D.C. (1973). IEEE Cat. No. 73CH0821-9C
8.45 G.Marie, J.Donjon: Proc. IEEE **61**, 942 (1973)
8.46 A.A.Sawchuk: "Coherent Optical Processing", in *Optical Data Processing*, ed. by S.H.Lee, Topics in Applied Physics (Springer, Berlin, Heidelberg, New York) to be published
8.47 K.Bromley: Opt. Acta **21**, 35 (1974)
8.48 R.Bocker: Appl. Opt. **13**, 1670 (1974)
8.49 M.Monahan, R.Bocker, K.Bromley, A.Louie: Internat. Opt. Comput. Conf., Wash. D.C. (April 1975). IEEE Cat. No. 75CH0941-5C
8.50 D.Casasent, D.Kessler: Opt. Eng. **16**, 402 (1977)
8.51 D.Casasent, E.Klimas: Appl. Opt. **17** (1978)
8.52 D.Casasent, D.Psaltis: Proc. IEEE **65**, 77 (1977)
8.53 D.Casasent, D.Psaltis: Appl. Opt. **15**, 2015 (1976)

Subject Index

A monthly journal

Applied Physics

Board of Editors	**S. Amelinckx,** Mol. · **V. P. Chebotayev,** Novosibirsk
	R. Gomer, Chicago, Ill. · **H. Ibach,** Jülich
	V. S. Letokhov, Moskau · **H. K. V. Lotsch,** Heidelberg
	H. J. Queisser, Stuttgart · **F. P. Schäfer,** Göttingen
	A. Seeger, Stuttgart · **K. Shimoda,** Tokyo
	T. Tamir, Brooklyn, N.Y. · **W. T. Welford,** London
	H. P. J. Wijn, Eindhoven

Coverage   application-oriented experimental and theoretical physics:

Solid-State Physics   *Quantum Electronics*
Surface Physics   *Laser Spectroscopy*
Chemisorption   *Photophysical Chemistry*
Microwave Acoustics   *Optical Physics*
Electrophysics   *Integrated Optics*

Special Features   **rapid** publication (3–4 months)
no page charge for **concise** reports
prepublication of titles and abstracts
microfiche edition available as well

Languages   Mostly English

Articles   original reports, and short communications
review and/or tutorial papers

Manuscripts   to Springer-Verlag (Attn. H. Lotsch), P.O. Box 105 280
D-69 Heidelberg 1, F.R. Germany

Place North-American orders with:
Springer-Verlag New York Inc., 175 Fifth Avenue, New York. N.Y. 10010, USA

Springer-Verlag
Berlin Heidelberg New York

Springer Series in Optical Sciences

Editor: D.L. MacAdam

Springer-Verlag
Berlin
Heidelberg
New York